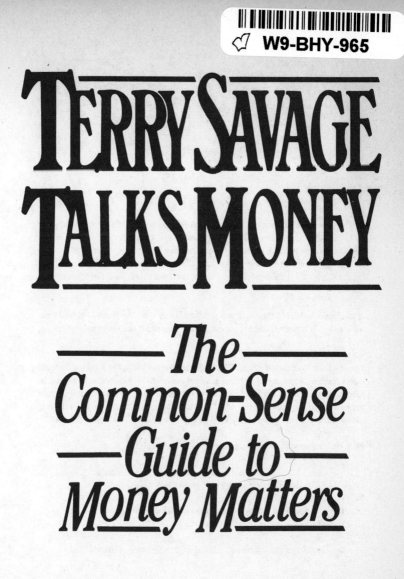

TERRY SAVAGE TALKS MONEY

The Common-Sense Guide to Money Matters

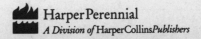
HarperPerennial
A Division of HarperCollins*Publishers*

W9-BHY-965

To RoRo

While a great deal of care has been taken to provide accurate and current information, the ideas, suggestions, general principles and conclusions presented in this book are subject to local, state and federal laws and regulations, court cases and any revisions of same. The reader is thus urged to consult legal counsel regarding any points of law—this publication should not be used as a substitute for competent legal advice.

A hardcover edition of this book was published in 1990 by Dearborn Financial Publishing, Inc. It is here reprinted by arrangement with Dearborn Financial Publishing, Inc.

First HarperPerennial edition published 1991.

Library of Congress Cataloging-in-Publication Data
Savage, Terry.
    Terry Savage talks money : the common-sense guide to money matters /
    Terry Savage — 1st HarperPerennial ed.
      p. cm.
    Reprint. Originally published: Chicago, Ill. : Dearborn Financial
Pub., ©1990.
    Includes index.
    ISBN 0-06-097418-4 (pbk.)
    1. Finance, Personal—United States. 2. Investments—United
States. 3. Estate planning—United States. 4. Tax planning—United
States. I. Title.
[HG179.S24 1991]
332.024—dc20   91-55109

---

91 92 93 94 95 PW/RRD 10 9 8 7 6 5 4 3

CONTENTS

PREFACE

In my ten years as a television financial reporter—and before that as a stockbroker and floor trader—I have often been asked to recommend *one* book on personal finance that would be easily understandable, practical, and not biased toward a particular type of investment. In spite of many excellent books on personal finance, I never felt I had found one that could meet *all* those criteria. And so *Terry Savage Talks Money* is my effort to share years of experience in communicating practical advice about money matters.

This book is directed to people with all levels of financial experience and of all ages. No question is too basic when it comes to money. And no strategy is too sophisticated once the basic facts are understood. As my mother always reminds me: "It's easy if you know it!"

There's a lot more to read and understand about money management these days. In the late 1970's it became obvious that the world of investments had changed. You couldn't just leave money sitting around in a passbook savings account—or buy stocks and lock them away in a safe deposit box. But the financial revolution of the last two decades has left many people even more overwhelmed. Now there are new products to understand. And there's a new industry of financial institutions and salespeople and planners trying to convince you it pays to use their services.

In 1991 the rules for financial success have changed—but very few people recognize we're in a different ball game. It's as if you were watching a football game on TV and left the room to get a soft drink at the end of the first quarter. If you didn't understand the rules of the game, you'd be plenty surprised to find that your team was heading to the *opposite* end of the field to score in the second quarter!

Well, in 1990 the referee "blew the whistle" on the economic ball game—ending a period in which the way to get ahead was to go into debt, borrow money, use other people's money, and leverage to the hilt. For the 1990's, the way to score is at the opposite end of the field—by being *out* of debt and *in* cash. By having "liquidity" you can buy—at bargain prices—assets that other debtors are forced to sell.

In a world where you can earn only single-digit interest rates on your deposits, it is the height of financial folly to pay 18 or 20 percent non-deductible interest on your credit cards. That's only digging yourself a deeper hole. Yet millions of Americans find themselves caught in this situation. There is currently a total of $146 *billion* dollars outstanding on bankcards—much of it subject to those high finance charges.

If you ever want to get ahead in the money game, now is the time—a time when you can take advantage of the new directions that others will only learn the hard way.

This book is designed to take the mystery out of money and give you the information you need to make important financial decisions with confidence. Why follow advice blindly—and pay for it too? After all, it's *your* hard-earned money. The challenge is to make your money work as hard for you as you worked for *it*. I know you can do it. Let's get started.

ACKNOWLEDGMENTS

It would be impossible to thank all the people who have contributed to the writing of this book and to my understanding of the financial markets. So much credit goes to my mother who not only motivated me but continues to provide the standard by which I judge the effectiveness of my communications.

This book and my entire career have been shaped from inception by my attorney, agent and friend Jeffrey Jacobs.

I owe uncounted special thanks to Sally Ann Gonzalez, my tireless producer and right hand, without whose assistance this book could never have been completed. My research assistants Christy Heady and Robin Allen never balked at the most tedious chores and were an invaluable help. It was my editor, Kathy Welton, who encouraged me and believed in me from the very first word, and I am especially grateful for the patience of copy editor Pat Stahl.

Numerous people were kind enough to read drafts of this work at various stages, and I benefited from their comments and suggestions along the way. Jim Schembari, my editor at the *Chicago Sun-Times,* was most generous with his time. I am also indebted to other experts in their respective fields: Robert Armstrong, Ben Baldwin, Jean Campbell, Michael Hartz, Lynne Hickey, Larry Hovde, Larry Keillor, Matt Kessler, Mike McGrail, Jerry Perritt, Steven Persky, David T. Phillips, William Sirola, Gerhard Stadler, Art Tepfer, Fred Uhde, Andrew Yemma and Doug Youngren.

Finally, this is a rare opportunity for me to acknowledge some people who have had a significant impact on my life and deserve much credit for any success I have achieved. My longtime friend and business partner Clyde Harrison was always convinced I had the ability to do more than I dreamed. His encouragement and friendship over the years are among my most valued assets. Warren Shore is my true confidant and an inspiration to creativity. Others gave me my start early on. Dr. Angus J. Johnston was my high school history teacher who introduced me to the study of economics and its impact on our world. Paul Mohling and the late John B. Elliott opened the doors to my career as a stockbroker when the business was an all-male club. My special thanks to my long-time CBS cameraman, Bob Hammond, and video editor, Carlos Monge, whose personal interest in our stories has helped make my television reports so successful.

It is impossible to thank those closest to the writer—who are for so many hours excluded from the process, but continue to provide support and encouragement. To my son, Rex Savage, I hope this work will provide inspiration in your life, as you have always inspired me to do my best. And to my husband, Edward Harshfield, my eternal gratitude for your confidence in me and for helping to make this the best part of my life.

PART 1

Understanding Your Money

CHAPTER 1

The Language of Money

Money talks. It speaks the language of financial success. And it's an easy language to learn. Knowledge is power. Nowhere is that more true than in money management. This book is designed to give you the knowledge and power to make your money work for *you*—as hard as you worked for *it!*

Like any other skill—playing tennis, learning French, or changing a tire—handling money becomes easy if you know what you're doing. And like any other learning process, you're bound to make some mistakes along the way. The secret is to minimize the mistakes and profit from your successes.

The president of Cartier Jewelers tells the story of how Cartier was able to acquire its incredible seven-story neo-Renaissance mansion on the corner of Fifth Avenue and 52nd Street in Manhattan. Back in 1916 a wealthy society matron, Mrs. Morton "Maisie" Plant, attended a jewelry exhibition at the small Cartier salon on 56th Street. A collection of fabulous jewels had been brought to New York from Paris as a safety precaution because World War I was approaching. Among the jewels on display was a magnificent double strand of oriental pearls. A matched double strand of large, perfect pearls was quite a rarity in those days, and the necklace carried a price tag of $1.2 million—*1916 dollars!*

Unable to persuade her husband to buy the pearls for her, Maisie proposed a deal. She would swap her mansion on Fifth Avenue for the pearl necklace. And that is how Cartier acquired its famed Fifth Avenue landmark building now worth at least $20 million: It was a swap; not a dime changed hands. As for Maisie—well, at the same time, a Mr. Mikimoto in Japan was developing the process for creating cultured pearls, and by the late 1920s her necklace had plunged in value as man-made pearls flooded the market. In 1957 Mrs. Plant's heirs sold the pearls for $385,000.

Bad luck for Maisie—or perhaps it was simply because she hadn't done her homework and didn't understand the risks involved in the trade. She wanted the pearls to wear immediately, so she was willing to trade her home.

The lessons of this book are designed to keep you from making the same mistake Maisie did—letting emotion overcome reason. When it comes to handling money, you'll come face to face with two very strong emotions: *fear* and *greed*. Fear keeps you from taking the very first step—getting started on a money-building program. Greed destroys all your previous planning work—urging you to take the big risk for big money and leaving you open to the loss of it all.

The fear is obvious: What happens to me if I lose money in this investment? The greed is more subtle. It often takes the form of a daydream: If I double my money I could...pay off the mortgage, buy a new car, take a trip. With such pleasant daydreams it's easy to be carried away into an investment that involves more downside risk than you're really able to accept.

Self-discipline is the essential ingredient of financial success. It lets you conquer financial fear and suppress dangerous greed. The need for self-discipline applies whether you're trying to save for a down payment on a house or finance a child's education—or whether you're speculating in the options or commodities markets. Exercising that kind of discipline is a lot easier if you have the basic knowledge to understand exactly what you're doing and why, instead of blindly following the advice sold by "experts."

BULLS, BEARS, AND CHICKENS

The world of investing is generally divided into the *bulls* and the *bears*. The *bulls* are optimists who believe prices are headed higher.

The *bears* are pessimists who are betting that values will go lower. The terms bull and bear can be applied to all sorts of investing—stocks, bonds, commodities—even the entire investment outlook. You may hear someone say, "I'm bullish on the economy."

I prefer to add a third category: the "chickens." The chickens don't want to risk losing *any* of their assets by betting that things will either get better or get worse. Nothing to be ashamed of there. "Chicken money" is money you simply cannot afford to lose. That means it does not belong in risk investments like the stock market where you must make a forecast about the future. Chicken money belongs in insured CDs, money market accounts, and Treasury bills. You won't get rich in those safe investments; you may just barely beat inflation. And income taxes may cut into your earnings. But at least you won't lose any of your principal.

There is a little bit of chicken in all of us. Clearly, if you are living off a pension and Social Security, your risk-taking ability is limited. You can't afford to lose any of your income because you won't be able to replenish your capital if you've stopped working. If you're widowed and living off the proceeds of a life insurance policy, you're in the same situation.

The ability to accept risk is not necessarily based on age. You may have saved money for a child's education or for the care of an aging parent. Even though statistically you still have plenty of years to make up for investment mistakes, you may be handling chicken money that you have set aside for a special purpose. That is money you cannot afford to lose. Yet certainly age is no barrier to successful speculation in risky markets. Legendary speculator Bernard Baruch was an active trader until he died at the age of 95 in 1965. He continued to trade because he had risk capital at his disposal.

Sometimes it's the *money* that's chicken, as in the case of funds set aside for a specific purpose. Sometimes it's the *personality* that's chicken. And that's nothing to be ashamed of either. Some people are better equipped psychologically to accept risk. You can see it in the personalities of traders on the commodities floors. Success there has as much to do with the ability to deal with risk unemotionally as it does with intelligence or financial knowledge. The key to investment success is understanding yourself and your own financial situation—and then making appropriate decisions.

There is one simple way to figure out which portion of your money is really chicken money and should be kept only in no-risk investments. Just ask yourself, "What would happen to my life if I lost this money?" If you would be devastated by the loss of even a little bit, read Chapter 4, "The Chicken or the (Nest) Egg—Safe Investments," and don't get tempted by stories of stock profits, high interest rates, or midnight calls from con artists promising to double your money in soybeans or sugar.

There's an old saying: "Desperate money never makes money." Forget the idea of parlaying your small savings into a fortune with one lucky roll of the dice. That's how race tracks and casinos make money—taking the sucker bets. Once in a while luck may smile on you, but don't count on luck to make the mortgage payments or send your child to college.

With a careful savings and investment plan, you will eventually build up "extra" money that can be invested with reasonable risk to bring you higher returns. But before you even think of investing, you need to carefully sort out the money you can afford to put at risk.

RISK AND REWARD

Risk is not necessarily something to be avoided. In fact, if you can assess risk properly, you can make it work for you in building your fortune. It's often said that risk and reward are opposite sides of the coin. And it's true that there are no really big rewards without substantial risk. The key is to balance the risk and reward in any investment you make. That's difficult because the risks are not always obvious.

The stock market is a good example. When the Dow Jones Industrial Average was trading at the 770 level in 1982 and the economy was in the midst of a recession, people avoided the stock market, calling it too risky. Yet, in hindsight, that was really a very low-risk opportunity. All the bad news was apparent, and stock prices had fallen to new lows. Clearly the risk was minimal. (Hindsight *is* wonderful!)

Then, in the summer of 1987, with the Dow at 2700, people rushed into the market. It was obvious that the economy was in good shape and stocks were going higher; they saw minimal risk in buying after stocks had already doubled and tripled. But events just two months later proved that the summer of 1987 was a high-risk entry point. Clearly, the common wisdom is not a good measure of risk.

The key to maximizing returns on your investments is to balance out the potential risk and reward—and act when that balance is most favorable. As that great speculator Jesse Livermore used to say, "There is only one side of the market, and it is not the bull side or the bear side, but the *right* side!"

One of the most dangerous traps for investors is the expectation of unattainable returns. If you think you can double your money every year, you should consider that, beginning with $100,000, just 25 years of doubling would yield all the wealth of the earth!

It is indeed possible to double your money over a period of years—and there is a simple formula to help you understand what kind of returns that would take. It's called "The Rule of 72," and it says that if you take any fixed annual rate of return and divide that number into 72, the result will be the number of years it will take your money to double.

If you are getting a return of 7 percent compounded, you will double your money in about ten years (divide 7 into 72). If you could get a 10 percent annual return you would double your money in 7.2 years. A 12 percent return would double your money in 6 years.

While that formula makes it seem easy to double your money with very conservative investments, you must take inflation into account. If inflation is running at 6 percent a year, it will take only 12 years for the value of your dollar to be cut in half. That's the reverse side of The Rule of 72. Divide the inflation rate into 72 and you'll see how many years it will take for the purchasing power of your savings to be cut in half!

When you have compound interest working *for* you and inflation working *against* you, it is tough to get ahead in the investment game. The spending power of one 1967 dollar is now worth only 26 cents. One 1980 dollar bought only 63 cents worth of goods and services in 1990. It's not surprising that people consider taking risks to make their savings grow. But risk is not for everybody, certainly not for those who cannot afford to accept any losses. Not for those with chicken money.

The glamor of any risk investment is the potential profit: How much can I make? But the smart investor looks at the downside first: How much can I lose? It's not just stocks that involve risk of loss. You can lose money on perfectly safe government bonds if interest rates rise, making your old bonds less attractive. Guaranteed returns on investment annuities may be subject to the investments made by the insurance company. The ups and downs of the economy add to the unpredictability of investments.

Along with market risk, there are other ways you can lose money right from the start. A broker's commission may take from 4 percent to 8 percent right off the top of your investment even though it's built into the price of your investment product. That's money you won't get back until your investment grows. Understand those costs before you buy, and be sure to ask how much you would lose if you had to sell out next week or next month.

Many investments carry additional penalties if you get out early—ranging from loss of three months' interest on a long-term CD, to steep surrender charges on annuities, to a 10 percent government penalty for withdrawing funds early from a pension plan, IRA, or other retirement program.

Many investments are easy to buy, but very difficult to sell. There's almost always a liquid market for a stock listed on the New York Stock Exchange, but just try selling a unit of real estate limited partnership. Big blocks of government securities are easy to sell, but you may not get a fair price when you try to sell a small lot of zero coupon bonds. So there is a risk that you will lose money—or part of your profit—as a result of the difficulty of exiting from your investment.

Before you decide on any investment for your money, you must assess *all* the potential risks—those that involve market timing and value, along with those that are inherent in the rules of that particular investment. Remember the old adage: "Investigate *before* you invest!"

There may be a time when you find you have invested in something that doesn't seem quite right for you. It's not that the price has fallen; it's just an undeniable feeling that you have done something wrong. There's one more investment adage that applies in this situation: "Sell down to the sleeping point." If an investment is keeping you awake at night, worrying, then sell it. You may take a loss, but no investment is worth losing sleep over.

·IT'S EASY IF YOU KNOW IT

Taking the time to learn about your investment personality and learning the basics of money management can seem so intimidating that many people just throw up their hands in despair. In reality, money management is simply an acquired skill—much like cooking, playing tennis, or understanding computers. And, as with those skills, you don't have to become an expert to enjoy and benefit from your new knowledge.

As in all the skills you acquire as an adult, learning comes from doing as much as from studying. Once you are in the driver's seat and making the decisions, you learn lessons you will never forget. That's much like the difference between renting a car in an unfamiliar city or taking a cab. Once you're behind the wheel, you must remember the streets and the turns required to get to your destination. If you are sitting in the back seat all the way, you will never be able to retrace your route.

The minute you decide to own a stock, you will always know where to find the closing price in your daily paper, or you'll memorize your broker's phone number. If you must make a choice between a certificate of deposit at one bank or another, you will be able to quote short-term interest rates over dinner that night. And if you decide to buy a gold coin, you will suddenly become aware of the price of gold in New York and London! In short, the more you handle your money yourself, the better your investment skills will become. It's like practicing your serve when learning tennis. In the world of finance you may make mistakes along the way, and those mistakes may cost you money. But if you know yourself and have studied the investment, you can limit your mistakes—and your losses.

Don't let the fear of loss paralyze you into inaction. In these days of fast-changing economic conditions, doing *nothing* can be as expensive to your financial situation as doing the wrong thing. And, please, don't let the fear of loss goad you into simply turning your money over to an "expert." Good financial advice is well worth the expense, but how will you know it's good advice unless you have some basic understanding yourself?

FINANCIAL PLANNERS AND OTHER ADVISORS

Whether you are making a decision about where to put your chicken money or considering riskier investments, it's important to remember that this is *your* money and, ultimately, *your* responsibility. Providing financial services and advice has become a multi-billion dollar industry. Unfortunately, most financial advisors are not paid in proportion to the profits they make for you, nor do they share in your losses. Securities regulations don't allow that, for the most part. Instead, brokers, salespeople, and financial planners are paid either by a commission on the products they sell, or by a fee.

If a broker or salesperson is making money for you, then it's probably worth more than the cost of the service. But it's still your job to learn enough about the product to approve the investment and judge the results. Along the way, you may learn enough to manage your own money. Following investment advice blindly can be a recipe for disaster. Ultimately you must be your own financial planner.

While the basic idea is to gain enough knowledge to make the final decisions yourself, there is obviously no substitute for competent professional advice. The best idea is to organize a group of consultants who will act as a system of checks and balances. An accountant, attorney, insurance specialist, and a stockbroker or investment advisor each can contribute to the financial planning process.

The best way to find competent professional help is to ask someone for a recommendation. Successful people are usually flattered to recommend their attorneys, accountants, or stockbrokers. You may want to interview several professionals until you find one who seems to understand your personal goals and problems. There should be no cost for the original consultation, although ultimately professional services are not inexpensive.

Legal and accounting professionals are generally compensated by a set fee, and you should understand what's involved in that fee. For example, an accountant may charge you by the hour or charge a set fee for preparing your tax return. An attorney may charge hourly or set a specific fee for his or her work—an estate plan, for instance. You should not hesitate to ask the hourly charge or fee in advance.

The insurance specialist may spend hours explaining the product but will be compensated only by commission when you buy a policy. That fee will be a part of your cost of the policy and will not be computed separately. A stockbroker's commission may be stated separately on your confirmation statement or may be built into the price of the stock. An investment advisor will usually charge a set management fee—or perhaps a percentage of the profits. If you use an investment advisor you'll pay those amounts in addition to commissions when stocks are bought and sold for your account.

When you bring in your own group of specialists to advise you on your financial plan, you can arrange to pay only for the services you use and the products you buy. It's helpful if you can get several of your advisors in a room together or on a conference call at least once a year to go over your financial situation. That way you can get the benefit of updated information on changing tax laws and investment opportunities. You get different viewpoints—and *you* get to make the final decisions.

You might decide to take a different path—hiring a financial planner to coordinate all the information and streamline the decision-making process. There are some advantages in this arrangement—mainly that you are relieved of some of the work involved and you may feel you are relieved of some of the responsibility. But you still have the ultimate responsibility of choosing the planner.

Who Is a Financial Planner?

The International Association for Financial Planning based in Atlanta, Georgia, is the trade association for financial planners. While it has 19,000 members, only 1,000 are listed in its registry of financial planners. To qualify for the registry these planners must pass a series of tests, including the submission of plans for typical clientele. The IAFP will send you a list of planners in your area who qualify for the registry if you contact them at 2 Concourse Parkway, Suite 800, Atlanta, GA 30328, 404-395-1605. Although choosing from this list is no guarantee of performance, at least you will be dealing with planners considered qualified by their trade association.

You might also want to see if your planner has the initials CFP (certified financial planner) after his or her name. This degree is given by the International Board of Standards for Financial Planners after applicants pass a series of six tests and demonstrate three years' planning experience. The training program for this test is given by The College for Financial Planning in Denver, Colorado (303-220-1200) which specializes in training planners. About 23,000 planners have been issued the CFP designation.

You may find a planner with the designation ChFC—chartered financial consultant. This degree is given by the American College at 270 Bryn Mawr Ave., Bryn Mawr, PA 19010. This college also gives insurance designations and is slightly more insurance oriented.

The American Institute of Certified Public Accountants has also created a planner designation—the APFS (accredited personal financial specialist). To get this title, the individual must be a certified public accountant with three years of experience. It requires a daylong examination.

Finally, there are plenty of insurance, securities, and real estate salespeople who simply hang out a shingle and call themselves "financial planners." That's why it's important to check the credentials and references of the person you are depending on for professional help.

Financial Planners and Fees

Financial planners sometimes combine the way they charge you for their services. That is, they may charge a fee for an overall plan, plus commissions on the insurance or mutual funds or real estate investments they sell you. Before you start working with a planner it's important to understand exactly how the planner will be compensated. Obviously there can be conflicts of interest. For instance, your planner may decide you need to have some real estate investments, and then sell you a partnership investment on which he makes a commission.

Ask the planner if he or she is *fee-based* or *commission-based,* or exactly how the charges are determined. Some planners will simply charge by the hour. It should cost only about $250 to set up a simple financial plan. Many planners will meet with you for the first time at no charge in order to determine what kind of plan you need.

The National Association of Personal Financial Advisors (NAPFA) is an association of about 200 fee-for-service advisors who do not accept commissions for the products they sell to their clients. If you are concerned about potential conflicts of interest and want to use a fee-only advisor, you can contact the NAPFA, 1130 Lake Cook Road, Buffalo Grove, IL 60089 (708-537-7722).

Don't be afraid to ask a planner for client references. It is perfectly acceptable for you to ask for names of clients who have worked with the planner for a number of years. Be sure to actually speak with the references, who should be people with a similar financial situation to yours. If the planner advises a famous sports star or wealthy industrialist, not only will your goals be different, but you may take a back seat to those more impressive clients.

Don't expect your financial planner to know *everything*. While a competent planner will keep abreast of changing tax laws and investment products, there may always be a need to call in a specialist such as a lawyer or accountant to advise on specific legal or tax matters.

Finally, don't let the apparent expertise of professionals overwhelm your own good instincts and judgment. If you have done your basic homework—by reading this book, for example—you will know the right questions to ask. Trust your own intuition in relating to the person who will be advising you about your money. Take time in making your selection so you can build a long-term relationship that will last through your changing financial circumstances.

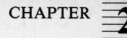

Getting Organized

Before you can take the first steps to your financial future, you have to organize the past and present. Getting your financial affairs in order will serve two purposes: It will let you know exactly what you have to work with, and it will help you set goals.

ORGANIZING YOUR FINANCIAL RECORDS

Let's start by sorting out all the information you will generally need for your income tax returns. This material should be kept for a number of years, so you'll want to set up an annual filing system. It doesn't have to be elaborate; depending on the complexity of your financial life, you might want to use a few large envelopes or buy one of those cardboard or plastic storage boxes available at stationery stores. Buy some manila folders to keep these larger boxes in sections. The important thing is that throughout the year you keep using the system to file away information that might be needed for your tax return. And while you're at it now, make *two* sets of files—one for this year's tax records and another that you will use to keep next year's paper trail.

In each year's box you should put the completed copy of your income tax return and all backup information that might be needed in case an audit requires you to justify your deductions. That means you should also include:

- checkbook register (start a new register every year)
- cancelled checks
- W-2 form (wage information)
- 1099 forms (dividends and interest income)
- receipts for deductible expenses (dues, subscriptions, business entertainment receipts, etc.)
- records of medical expenses (potentially deductible if totals are large enough)
- records of charitable contributions (including appraisals of property or expensive items)
- property tax receipts
- record of mortgage interest paid
- copies of brokerage confirms and statements

You might also want to store your daily appointment calendar in this year's tax box to help reconstruct records in case of an audit. The IRS generally has three years after a return is filed to call for an audit (or two years after the tax was paid, whichever is later). However, the IRS has a six-year period to start an audit if there has been at least a 25 percent understatement of income. And, of course, there is no time limit on IRS assessments if a taxpayer submits a fraudulent return or fails to file. So it's a good idea to keep your annual tax box in a safe place for at least six years.

But tax records aren't the only important financial documents that should be organized and stored safely. If you own a home, you should keep track of all expenditures to improve the property. Bills and receipts should be stored together. Later, if you sell the property, these expenses can be used to lower any taxable gains on the property.

If you are a regular investor in the markets, you should keep a notebook recording the date, price, and total amount spent or received on purchases and sales. That notebook is also a good place to keep track of stock splits and dividends. You might want to keep this notebook in a fireproof metal file box with your stock certificates. (If you are a frequent trader, leaving the certificates with your broker makes a lot of sense.)

There are other personal financial records that should also be stored together to save time and emotion in a financial emergency. Buy a separate file box for the following items:

* listing of bank account numbers
* brokerage accounts (include name and phone of broker)
* list of charge accounts and numbers
* credit cards and numbers
* insurance policy numbers and beneficiaries
* record of advisors and phone numbers (lawyer, accountant, stockbroker)
* doctor and hospital information
* family records (Social Security numbers, copies of birth certificates, marriage certificate, armed forces service records)
* copy of updated will and trust agreements
* location of cemetery plot, deeds
* business records—including partnership records, buy-sell agreements
* list of pension plans, IRAs, Keogh accounts
* list of outstanding debts owed by and to you

Make an appointment with yourself to update the list annually on your birthday. This is information that you want to store in a safe place, but not necessarily in a bank safe-deposit box. In case of emergency it would be handy for your family to know they could find all your records in one accessible place. In the case of irreplaceable records, store copies in the box and place the original in your safe-deposit box. Be sure to include on your list the location of the safe-deposit box and key and the names of deputies authorized to enter your safe-deposit box.

Once you have organized all your personal and financial history you will be in a better position to take steps for the future. The next step is finding out where you stand right now—creating a balance sheet.

YOUR BALANCE SHEET

Now that you know where all your financial records are kept, it should be easy to figure out what you own—and what you *owe*. That's called making a balance sheet, although you may find out that your financial situation doesn't really balance out! Still, it's important to figure out just where you stand financially right now. That knowledge will help you set goals for the future.

Making a personal balance sheet is really a very simple operation. Just take two sheets of paper. On the first sheet list everything you own that would have some value should you decide to sell. Your home, any other real estate, car, stocks, bonds, individual retirement account, value of your pension fund—all should be included on the list. Remember, this is a financial inventory, so if you have an engagement ring or heirlooms that you would never sell, they don't really belong on your balance sheet. Similarly, even if you saved for years for that expensive fur coat, it's not likely to have much resale value for your balance sheet. Be realistic. What we're trying to figure out is how much cash you could raise if you really needed to. Those items are considered your assets.

On the second sheet make a list of everything you owe. That's called your list of liabilities. Start with the largest debt first; that's probably your mortgage. Be sure to include car loans, education loans, and of course the current outstanding balance on your charge and credit cards. Don't be discouraged if the totals on this sheet outweigh the list of assets. That's common for young people just starting out after college. But if you have been working for more than a few years, your assets should be growing fast enough to pay down your debt.

Although a debt-heavy balance sheet is a danger signal, it's important to take a close look at the *kind* of debt on your balance sheet as well as the size of the debt. Certainly your debt will look huge if you've just taken out a mortgage and have not had time to build equity in your home. Borrowing money to start your own business may be a risk well worth taking.

Some debt—like a mortgage—is used to build up equity ownership. That can be considered positive debt as long as you are in a position to afford the monthly payments. But if your balance sheet is overloaded with credit card and charge card debt, it's time to take a closer look at what you're spending your money on.

It simply doesn't make sense to pay the 18 percent (or higher) finance charges on a credit card to purchase things that are not growing in value. That includes clothes, vacations, and restaurant meals. Not only are you paying a higher price by financing these expenditures, but it doesn't make sense from a tax point of view since these finance charges will no longer be deductible in 1991.

When you have compared your assets and liabilities you will get a pretty clear picture of how your financial life balances out. If you already have substantial assets, it might be time for a serious look at your investment program to make sure your money is working at its maximum without taking on unwanted risk.

On the other hand, the balance sheet may show you that before you can start making your money work *for* you, you have to stop making it work *against* you by costing you huge amounts of interest on the outstanding balances you owe. That means paying off some debt and setting some money aside on a regular basis. In that case, the next step is to make a budget.

MAKING A BUDGET

The idea of making a budget and sticking to it ranks right up there with dieting as a popular pastime. I'm willing to bet that more people are likely to stick with their diets!

But here's a revolutionary way to look at a budget. As you total up what you're really spending versus what you're really earning, you might find a negative gap. Most budget watchers say that gap is the amount you must cut back on your spending. Here's a more optimistic way to approach your budget: Why not look at that gap as the additional amount you have to earn to keep up your current lifestyle?

That's a much more positive approach. It's difficult to cut back once you're accustomed to, and feel you can justify, the money you spend. It might be easier to get a second job on weekends or evenings to boost your earnings. Or you may decide to consider switching to a job that offers an incentive or bonus that will increase your pay. Maybe another member of your family could take on a part-time job to cover expenses.

While most people say they are working as hard as they possibly can, and making as much money as they possibly can, sometimes a closer examination of how "smart" you are working can give some insight into ways you can increase your income.

If those alternatives are just not possible, then making a budget will at least show you how much—and where—you have to start cutting back.

To get started on a budget, you will have to keep track of every penny you spend for at least a month or two. That means you will have to carry a small notebook and write down the amounts when you buy cigarettes or your morning coffee and sweet roll. It's the little things (petty cash!) that really add up, so this list may surprise you.

The next thing you will need is a budget planning workbook, available at most office supply stores. The best budget book I've seen is the *Common Cents Money Management Workbook* (P.O. Box 13167, Albuquerque, NM 87192, at about $10.95 plus $1.50 shipping). This workbook explains the process instead of just leaving you to fill in the blanks.

Another excellent source of budgeting help is the *Rubber Budget Account Book* published by the American Institute for Economic Research (Great Barrington, MA 01230, about $5). This booklet explains that budget categories may be flexible, like rubber, stretching in different months to meet unexpected expenses without destroying the entire concept of the budget.

No matter what budget book you use, you will have to go over your checkbook and petty cash notebook for the past month or two so you can create the proper categories. There will be regular monthly expenses such as rent or mortgage, utilities, gasoline or commuting expenses, food (make a separate column for restaurant meals). And don't forget to make a separate column for savings. Even if this column is blank for now, we'll try to include it in the budget later.

There are some expenses that come only once or twice a year, but are big items in your annual budget. You may make life or health insurance payments semiannually. You may shop for clothes only in the spring and fall during sales. Even if these expenses come in big chunks, you need to save for them out of every paycheck. Some items such as gifts or subscriptions come infrequently, but they should not come as a surprise when you need the cash to pay for them.

At the back of your budget book there should be a section for an overall *annual* budget. Go back over your checkbook from last year and total up your annual spending on major categories such as rent or mortgage, transportation, food, medical, etc. That will help you get the bigger picture of how much you need to allot every month just to cover your basic yearly expenses.

The next step is to keep track of your "cash flow." That is, your paycheck or retirement benefit may come in once a month, or every two weeks, or on the first and fifteenth of the month. But generally some big expenses are clustered around the first of the month and must be paid on time. Take a look through your credit card bills to note the date they must be paid to avoid finance charges. The next step is to try to match your incoming money with your outflow.

It's a classic mistake to think that you are suddenly ahead of the game just because a paycheck arrives and you don't have a bill to pay that week. The temptation is to go out and spend the cash that's sitting in your account, when you should be saving it for the bills that will come due at the end of the month. That's where a budget book really helps you plan.

Now it's time to figure out where you have been overspending. It may be the small impulse purchases that keep your budget from balancing. In that case, it's time to take your checkbook out of your purse or briefcase and leave it at home in your desk. Leave your credit cards and automatic bank teller card at home too. Instead, write yourself a weekly "allowance" check and cash it on Monday. If you run out of money before the end of the week—that's tough. You just don't have any more. Be your own firm banker and tell yourself "No!"

The idea of a budget is to help you stop living from paycheck to paycheck. You should always have a savings reserve for emergencies. Sadly, it's estimated that 27 percent of working Americans would be completely out of cash or available credit and would be forced to start selling their assets (homes and cars) within six months if they lost their jobs.

Getting ahead of the money game may seem like an impossible goal, but it can be done with a little discipline and a willingness to work.

Proof of it is the millions of immigrants who came to this country with little more than the clothes on their backs. This is not just an old-fashioned concept; there are many current success stories of Asian immigrants who arrived in just the past 15 years and built new fortunes.

Remember, you're going to treat your budget like a strict diet. Sticking to the money diet may be difficult at first, but like any other diet, success is its own reward. Think of it not as losing pounds, but as gaining dollars!

UNDERSTANDING TAXES

Understanding taxes is an ambitious project for a lifetime of study. The federal tax code now runs to more than 7,000 pages—plus four volumes of IRS regulations explaining them! And the tax code seems to change every year. That's the best argument that can be made for paying for competent professional tax advice. But every taxpayer should understand some of the basic rules that apply to the federal income tax code.

In 1988 Congress passed the Taxpayer Bill of Rights, giving taxpayers some important protection in dealing with the Internal Revenue Service. These rights are explained in Publication 1, "Your Rights as a Taxpayer." The booklet explains both the audit and collection process and the taxpayer's rights in each process.

The bill also created an IRS ombudsman who is part of the Problem Resolution Office. This person can intervene in any IRS enforcement action when "the taxpayer is suffering, or about to suffer a significant hardship as a result of the manner in which the Internal Revenue laws are being administered." The ombudsman can issue a taxpayer assistance order, which is legally binding on the IRS.

You can reach the ombudsman by calling the Problem Resolution Office in your district and asking for Form 911, which you must fill out describing your situation. The Taxpayer Bill of Rights gives the ordinary taxpayer slightly more leverage against the power of the Internal Revenue Service, but it is up to the taxpayer now to understand these rights.

Taxpayer Responsibility

It is your responsibility as a taxpayer to report *all* the income you receive during the year. It is your *responsibility* as a taxpayer to file an income tax return for every year in which you received income. It is your *option* as a taxpayer to list those items that you believe to be reasonable and legally allowable deductions that would tend to lower your tax liability.

Hundreds of tax protestors—many doing time in federal prisons—have disagreed with these statements of obligation. They question things like the taxpayer's obligation to file a return, or whether the tax money should be paid in paper currency or must be paid in gold or silver. None of these arguments has stood up against the IRS. Enough said.

If you do not list all your income on your federal income tax return, you open yourself up to charges of criminal fraud and potential criminal penalties, including fines and imprisonment. If you do not file a return within the alloted time, you are subject to penalties associated with "willful failure to file," which results in an assessment of 5 percent of taxes due—every month—not to exceed 25 percent. There is also an interest penalty charged on the amount due, and you may also face a 5 percent negligence penalty. If you do not *pay* your taxes when they are due, you could also be assessed a "failure to pay" penalty of one-half of one percent per month—up to 25 percent of the amount due—until the tax is paid.

If you receive income from which payroll taxes are not deducted (alimony, self-employment income, dividend income), you must estimate in advance what your tax might be and pay it quarterly. You are required to pay at least 90 percent of the tax owed, or you will be subject to an "underpayment of estimated tax" penalty. The IRS provides worksheets and vouchers, along with the 1040 ES form for those who need to calculate and file quarterly estimated payments.

When it comes to taking deductions, you're in what's called a "gray area." You can be aggressive in using the tax code to your advantage, or you can be more conservative about the items you choose to deduct from income. It probably goes without saying that the more aggressive you are, the more likely you are to trigger an IRS audit.

If you seek advice from a taxpayer service representative at the IRS, be prepared to document the advice and information you were given over the phone. Keep the name of IRS representative, the date of your conversation, and notes from that date. In order to get written advice, you must make your request in writing, so allow plenty of time. The IRS has said that taxpayers who can document erroneous advice will not be charged penalties.

If you and your tax advisor are in doubt about a substantial deduction, you can request a formal "private letter ruling." That means the IRS will give you an opinion on a particular set of circumstances. Both you and the IRS will be bound by the advice given in this document, but it is not necessarily binding on others in the same circumstance. The IRS may charge for this ruling.

An IRS Audit

The very words *IRS Audit* strike fear into the hearts of many taxpayers. There are few things more disturbing than being called in for an audit. In ordinary civil cases the IRS can automatically audit your returns for each of the last three years. If they suspect you of underreporting income by at least 25 percent, they can examine your returns from the past six years. (There is no statute of limitations for suspected criminal fraud.)

So as we noted earlier in this chapter, you certainly need to keep your records for at least the three previous years. You might also want to keep records for two or three prior years because you might need to demonstrate a pattern of income and spending. Once the three years expire, the IRS can "request" that you allow them to keep your records open for one additional year at a time. If you refuse, that might trigger an immediate audit, so most people are inclined to grant the IRS the right to an extension.

If you are called in for an audit, you have the right to be represented by anyone who is qualified to represent taxpayers before the IRS— attorneys, CPAs, and enrolled agents (specially trained tax preparers). The taxpayer does not have to be present at an audit (unless officially summoned by the district director or assistant district director). If you are concerned about the possibility of an audit, you should be sure to have your return prepared by an expert who will not only complete the return, but who is qualified and willing to represent you at an audit.

Correspondence with the IRS

Do not ignore any letters you receive from the IRS. They don't go away! A letter from the IRS could signal an audit or an "adjustment" on your income tax return. Most of these letters are sent out when the IRS notices a discrepancy between information they have received and what you reported on your return. Verify your records, *respond in writing,* and keep a copy of all correspondence. Do not call the IRS; it is better to have all written records.

Taxes and Privacy

Under the Privacy Act of 1974 IRS officials are forbidden to disclose information about you and your tax return. However, there is a law that authorizes the IRS to divert tax refunds in the child support enforcement cases, education loan defaults, and VA loan defaults.

Taxes and Social Security Numbers

In 1988 Congress mandated that every child who is two years old must have a Social Security number in order to be claimed as a dependent on another taxpayer's return. The Social Security Administration has begun allowing parents of newborn children to apply for a number when filling out birth certificate forms at the hospital. Form SS 5 is used to obtain this number.

These are your basic responsibilities as a taxpayer. Depending on your financial circumstances you will want to seek professional help in determining your obligations to the Internal Revenue Service. While dealing with taxes and the tax bureaucracy can be intimidating, it should not deter you from keeping current in your filing status.

CHAPTER 3

Checking It Out

The first step in everyday money management is setting up a system to handle your spending. You may want to give yourself a weekly "allowance" for everyday spending needs, but conducting all of your personal business in cash can be quite a burden. If you need currency, there's a handy automatic teller machine on almost every corner. But for paying bills and handling transactions, checks generally represent a safer and more convenient form of money transfer.

CHECKING ACCOUNTS

Establishing your own checking account is the first step toward gaining control over your personal finances. A checking account gives you a dependable record of your spending for budget and tax purposes, and it can even be a source of interest income.

Opening a checking account is a simple procedure, but choosing which *type* of checking account is best for you can be a little more complicated. Most banks and S&Ls offer several kinds of accounts to choose from—with different service charges, balance requirements, and numbers of free checks allowed.

The first step is to choose the bank or S&L you want to use. That's partly determined by looking at the current deals they offer, but remember that you're also trying to establish a long-term banking relationship. At some point you may need a mortgage or home equity loan, a credit card, or investment advice. If you can find a local institution that offers these services *plus* attractive checking options, you'll begin to create that special relationship.

As you accumulate money, you may want to shop around for higher rates on certificates of deposit in other institutions either nearby or perhaps out of state. But even in these days of impersonal banking and automatic machines, it pays to establish a relationship with one financial institution. It makes no difference whether you choose a bank or savings and loan for your checking account, since both now offer similar products at competitive rates.

If you just want to use your checking account to pay a few monthly bills, look for a low-cost basic checking account. Usually there is a small monthly fee, averaging about $2.50. Some banks charge only if you fall below a minimum monthly balance, usually about $300. These accounts typically offer unlimited free checking, although some institutions limit free checks to approximately ten each month and then charge about 25 cents for each additional check. Most will allow unlimited free ATM (automatic teller machine) deposits, withdrawals, and balance inquiries if you use machines in their system. Usually you can open a basic checking account with a deposit of as little as $100.

Banks and S&Ls really start to get competitive when they try to attract checking accounts of higher-balance customers. They want to establish a "relationship" with you, the customer, so they will offer a good deal on checking if you use their other products or leave additional funds on deposit. With these checking accounts you may get entirely free checking privileges if you have a minimum balance of perhaps $1,500. The bank doesn't pay you any interest on the minimum, but they will charge you a monthly service fee if you don't keep the required minimum in your account. If you are willing to leave more money on deposit, the bank may offer you more privileges such as paying a fixed, low rate of interest on your balance, no-annual fee credit cards, and higher ATM withdrawal limits. Banks market these as "premium" checking accounts.

The next step when it comes to earning interest on your balance is a NOW or Super-NOW account. (NOW stands for negotiable order of withdrawal, i.e., a check.) These accounts usually pay a low floating rate of interest depending on the amount you leave on deposit. There is generally a monthly maintenance fee and a charge for each check written.

If you really want the best combination of liquidity and high interest rates, you might be interested in a *money market deposit account*. It generally pays a market rate of interest that is fairly competitive with short-term CDs. But in exchange for this higher interest rate, there is a government restriction that applies to MMAs at every institution. You can only write three checks per month on a money market account, although most institutions allow unlimited withdrawals at the teller window or ATM.

With a MMA you always have access to *all* your money, but you don't have the convenience of unlimited checking. A combination of two accounts might serve you best—basic checking for your monthly needs plus a money market account for other funds that you want to keep available but earning interest.

It's important to remember that since banking was fully deregulated back in 1986, each bank or S&L sets its own rules for these accounts when it comes to fees, balances, and interest rates. These checking costs are set in such a way as to attract your business and still make money for the bank. It's your job to choose the account that best suits your needs. Here are some guidelines:

- Ask for complete details on any service charges, including those for minimum balances or additional checks.
- Ask the cost for having checks printed.
- Ask if there is an additional cost for having your checks returned to you after they have been cancelled by the bank.
- Ask for the minimum balance to avoid a service charge.
- Ask for the interest rate paid on balances, and if there are higher rates paid on higher balances.
- If you are opening a money market account, ask how the interest rate is set and how frequently it is changed.
- Ask if there are additional charges for each use of an ATM machine.

Finally, remember there is really no such thing as "free" checking. If you leave a minimum balance in your checking account and it is not earning interest, that is really a cost to you. Calculate that you might have earned at least 5 percent on that money and figure out if giving up that interest is worth all the other services the bank is giving you on one of these premium checking accounts.

If you are watching every penny, it pays to figure out the real costs. But don't let these complex calculations deter you from getting started with a simple checking account. If you are concerned only with convenience, then open a basic account and get started on your task of daily money management.

THE BALANCING ACT

No matter which type of checking account you choose, it's important to keep track of your balance. That will help you avoid "bounced" checks, which not only annoy merchants and are illegal if done intentionally, but can ruin your credit record.

When you open your account, you will be given a choice of check size and checkbook registers. If you need to carry your checkbook with you daily, then you will probably choose the smaller size. But if you find that you will be paying most of your bills from home, you might want to choose a checking system that has a larger register (record book) and three checks to a page. Try to avoid those books where you get just a stub to record the transaction instead of a separate check register. They make it more difficult to keep track of your spending.

When you first open your checking account, you will be making a deposit. Keep careful record of the deposit amount in the column on the far right of your check register. Additional deposits are added in this same column as you make them. Some larger desktop checkbook registers allow you to keep a record of where those deposits come from (i.e., paycheck, commission, gift, or dividend). They may also provide a line where you can indicate the reason for the check, noting payments like contributions, medical expenses, or dues. That information could be useful at tax time.

Every time you write a check, make sure to fill in the name and amount in the check register. Don't make a practice of tearing out a few checks to keep in your wallet. That's the quickest way to lose track of your money. Also, if you withdraw money from an automatic teller machine, be sure to immediately enter the amount in your check register.

Every time you write a check or make an ATM withdrawal you should subtract the amount from your current balance. That way you will always know how much you have left. If you are constantly drawing your account right down to the zero level, you might want to ask your bank for a *check overdraft line of credit*. That means you can't accidentally bounce a check; the bank will automatically transfer funds up to a certain limit. A warning though: These overdraft lines of credit can be expensive, with interest charges of 18 percent or more, unless you arrange for an automatic transfer from your own savings or money market account.

Once every month the bank will send you a statement of your checking activity. The envelope will contain all your cancelled (paid) checks and a computerized statement of your account activity. Take a few minutes every month as soon as you receive your statement to reconcile the figures in your checkbook with the figures the bank has sent you. Yes, you can trust the bank, but can you trust your own addition and subtraction? It's important that your balance match the figures the bank says you have on deposit.

First, go through your returned checks and check each one off in the space provided in your check register. Then notice which ones haven't been cashed yet. You may have written them just a few days ago, or sent one out of town so it took longer to get back to your bank. Also make sure that every deposit you made that month appears as a credit on your statement. Finally, make a note of any service charges the bank debited your account during the month; you will have to subtract them from the balance in your checkbook.

On the reverse side of your monthly statement you'll find an easy worksheet. Take the amount of your balance from the monthly statement and put it on the top line. Add in any deposits that you made in the last few days that were not yet credited on your monthly statement. Then total up all the outstanding checks (the ones written but not yet returned by the bank in your envelope) and subtract that amount from the line above. (These instructions are clearly written on the back of your statement.)

The bottom line amount on this statement reconciliation should match the balance in your checkbook. If there is a substantial discrepancy, go back over your records to see if you forgot to deduct a service charge or made a mistake in subtracting. Some people will spend hours trying to figure out where they made a mistake if they are only a few pennies off. Others figure that if they are within a dollar or two of the bank's figures their checkbook is "in balance."

Deciding whether to keep records to the absolute penny is a personal consideration, but it is an absolute requirement that you match your checkbook register to the bank statement *every* month to keep your financial affairs in good order.

EASY ACCESS

When you are depositing money or writing checks, you should be aware of exactly how long it takes for your money to be available to you—or to the person who is receiving your check. For years it was up to the bank or S&L to decide how quickly your funds would be available to you when you deposited a check in your account. Banks wanted to protect themselves in case the deposit was a "bad check" and was returned to them unpaid. So they routinely delayed making the funds available to you, the depositor, and in the process earned interest on the money.

Now all banks, savings and loan associations, and credit unions must follow specific rules in making your money available. Just how quickly you will have access to the money depends on the type of check, amount, and location of the bank on which it is drawn. For example, if you deposit a U.S. Treasury check, it will clear sooner than a check written to you by a friend on an out-of-state bank.

Since September 1, 1990, the rules call for funds to be made available *the next business day* if you deposit a government check, cashier's check, or certified check. The next-day availability rule also applies to checks written on another account at the same institution. Surprisingly, the next business day rule also applies to cash and direct deposit funds. This was designed to allow banks to process deposits—even those as good as cash—through their accounting systems before paying out the proceeds.

If you deposit a check drawn on a different, but local, institution, the funds must be available to you on the second business day after deposit. And banks can hold onto funds from checks written on nonlocal or out-of-state institutions for up to the fifth business day after the day of deposit. (Business days include all days except Saturdays, Sundays, and federal bank holidays.) Also note that the time of day you make the deposit may affect the day on which you have use of the funds. Many banks consider deposits made after 2:00 PM to be part of the next day's business. Deposits at an automated teller machine *not belonging to your bank* must be available on the same schedule as other deposits.

In practice, many institutions will advance funds to you even earlier than the requirements if they know you well and know the maker of the check. Or you may have a special personal or executive-type checking account on which they credit your account immediately for each deposit. But if you are writing checks against your deposit, it's important to keep in mind that it could take days for an out-of-state check deposit to clear. If the funds are not available, your check could be returned marked "not paid—funds not available." That's embarrassing.

In fact, whenever a check is returned unpaid (bounced) for any reason, it's not only embarrassing, but it's a potential blot on your credit. The person to whom you've written the check has the right to charge you an extra fee for sending it back through the system for collection a second time. In many states you can be prosecuted for writing a bad check. And if you write a bad check to a large company, the company might report it when it gives details of your account to the credit bureau.

HOW TO PAY YOUR BILLS (AND YOURSELF!)

Once you have opened your checking account it's important to set up a system for paying your bills. Some people religiously pay every bill the day it arrives. Others find it more convenient to set the bills aside in a drawer and pay them twice a month. If you decide to bundle them up and wait for a convenient moment, you should be aware of payment deadlines for each bill to avoid interest and service charges. For example, your mortgage or rent may be due on the first of the month. But a credit card bill may have a closing date of the 25th of the month to avoid an interest charge on the outstanding balance.

When you established a budget, you became aware of your cash flow. That is, perhaps you get paid every week, or every two weeks, or on the first and fifteenth of the month. Timing your bill-paying sessions to coincide with your check deposit will help you to avoid spending money just because it is sitting in your checking account.

Bills should not surprise you. You should be aware at all times of just how much you have charged on various accounts. That's difficult to keep track of if you have too many charge cards. The answer may be to limit yourself to one travel card and one bankcard. Otherwise, with too many cards you tend to build up balances that you are unable to pay in full every month. Now that consumer interest is no longer deductible on your income tax return, it simply doesn't make sense to pay 18 percent or more in finance charges on your outstanding balances.

While we're talking about paying bills, it's important to remember the most important monthly bill you have—paying yourself. Just as you know the rent or mortgage *must* be paid on the first of the month, you should also pay yourself first. It's just a matter of figuring out a set amount that you intend to set aside as savings every month. The amount doesn't matter as much as getting into the habit of a regular savings plan.

You can deposit the money regularly in a bank savings account. There is a way to actually "bill yourself" for a set amount of savings every month using money market mutual funds. (See Chapter 4.) When you open a money market mutual fund account you'll get a computerized statement of your deposit. At the bottom is a stub to send in with your next deposit. Most funds also send you a return envelope. So when you make your monthly deposit and get that confirmation, you can simply tear off the stub and put it in the drawer with your other regular bills. Put it *on top* of those bills and pay yourself *first* every month. You'll be surprised how it adds up.

CHECKING ALTERNATIVES

Americans write about 47 billion checks every year, yet millions of Americans don't have a personal checking account at a bank. Instead, they use money orders, postal money orders, and cashier's checks when they need a written record of a transaction. And many others who do have personal checking accounts venture into the area of bank checks when selling a home or buying an expensive product such as a car or boat. These special forms of checking have their own costs and rules— things you should know in advance.

A *certified check* is simply a check drawn on your own personal checking account but officially guaranteed by the bank or S&L in writing on the check to be "good funds." That means the bank guarantees that it is holding money aside in your account to pay the check when it is presented. After you write the check and sign it, you take it to your bank, where a teller will stamp it with a code and sign it, officially guaranteeing payment. You no longer have access to those funds in your account; they are reserved for payment of that check. Charges vary, but most institutions will charge a fee of $2 to $10 to certify a check.

Certified checks are usually required by a contract, such as when purchasing a car for "cash." They are much safer for the seller because the bank is, in effect, guaranteeing the check. So once a certified check is written, you will not be allowed to stop payment on it. If a certified check is lost or stolen, you will have quite a bit of convincing to get your bank to refuse to pay it.

A *cashier's check* is most often used as an alternative to a certified check because you don't need to have an account at a bank to purchase a cashier's check. A cashier's check is actually a check drawn on the bank itself and signed by an authorized employee of the bank. In order to purchase a cashier's check you will have to give the bank the money. If you have an account there, they will just take it out of your checking or savings account. If you don't have an account, they will gladly take your cash and issue a cashier's check. But don't try to convert a personal check on another bank to a cashier's check; most banks will require cash on the counter or in your account in order to create a cashier's check for you.

The fee schedule for a cashier's check depends on the institution and the amount of the check. If you are a customer, the fee could be as low as $2 (some institutions allow one free cashier's check a month). If you are not a bank customer, the fee could be $10 or more for each check. It's almost impossible to stop payment on a cashier's check unless you have proof of some type of fraud. That's why so many mail-order and telemarketing rip-off schemes urge you to send a cashier's check. They'll be long gone with your money before you can prove fraud.

A third alternative to a personal checking account is a *money order*. These may be purchased at banks, S&Ls, currency exchanges, and even at the post office. Money orders are usually for smaller amounts, generally under $1,000. While a cashier's check or certified check is made with the name of the payee on the top line, when a money order is issued the name of the payee is left blank. Only the cash amount of the money order is imprinted on it, usually by a special machine. Until you fill in the name of the payee, a money order is just like cash.

You can use a certified check, cashier's check, or money order to pay almost any kind of bill. The recipient feels secure that the check is good and is unlikely to be "stopped." But when you *receive* a certified check, cashier's check, or money order it is not necessarily the same as receiving cash. There could still be delays in gaining access to your funds.

Banks and other financial institutions may have a sort of double standard for cashier's checks. While they require cash or good funds in your account to issue a cashier's check, they don't always give you cash immediately when you present a cashier's check for deposit. They are supposed to follow the rules set by Congress in the 1987 Expedited Funds Availability Act. That law states that if you deposit a cashier's or certified check, the funds must be available to you the *next* business day. In practice, most institutions will give you access to your cash on the same day if the check is drawn on a local bank or S&L and the amount is under $5,000. But expect to wait one day if the check is from an out-of-state institution.

You will have a tough time cashing any of these instruments if you don't have a bank account. Without an account you will have to use a currency exchange or check cashing service—and depending on the size of the check, the fees can be substantial.

As you can see, there are plenty of ways to live without a personal checking account. You can use cash, money orders, or cashier's checks. But when you add up the costs of using these special banking instruments, you might find it cheaper in the long run to search out a low-cost personal checking account at an area bank or S&L.

CREDIT UNIONS

Many consumers do their banking business at their local credit union. There are more than 15,250 credit unions nationwide, and most are federally insured by an agency of the U.S. government, much as deposits in banks and S&Ls. Some credit unions are fairly small, with only about 100 members and assets of less than $100,000. But others are much larger—for example, the Navy Federal Credit Union, which has 920,000 members and more than $3.5 billion in assets.

Credit union members must have a "common bond"—a shared association such as employees of a certain manufacturer, a union group, members of a religious organization, or a local community. When the credit union receives its charter, it specifies what its common bond will be, and only those who qualify can join the credit union. Family members are allowed to become members of most credit unions.

Usually the first account that a member opens is a *share account,* which is similar to a passbook savings account. It pays a competitive, fixed interest rate. Strictly speaking, this is not considered a deposit, but an "ownership share" in the credit union. Your deposit gives you a vote in the affairs of the credit union. The share account is perfectly liquid in that you can take the money out at any time, just as you can with a regular savings account.

Another popular account in the credit union is a *share draft account,* which operates as a checking-type account. Most pay a competitive interest rate and have no limits on the number of checks that can be written. The monthly fees to hold this account will typically be very low because a credit union is a not-for-profit association.

In fact, that not-for-profit status is one of the great advantages of a credit union. Members tend to find that the interest rates paid on deposits are slightly higher, and the interest rates charged on credit union loans may be slightly lower. That's because a credit union tends to operate on a lower cost basis. Members of its board of directors are unpaid volunteers. The credit union spends less for advertising and often operates out of facilities provided free by the company or business whose members are eligible to join. And the credit union does not pay taxes on its earnings because it is a nonprofit organization.

All credit unions make personal loans to members—either secured by property such as automobiles and homes, or unsecured. Although you must be a member and have an account at the credit union to qualify for a loan, the amount of the loan is not related to the amount you have on deposit.

Many larger credit unions provide additional services such as direct deposit of government checks, credit cards, ATM cards, and traveler's checks.

If you belong to a company or organization that sponsors a credit union, it's worth looking into its services and rates. They often operate with much less red tape than a larger financial institution, and they are usually very convenient.

CHAPTER 4

The Chicken or the (Nest) Egg—Safe Investments

It's not "chicken" to leave your money in the bank in insured deposits. In fact, it may be the smartest thing you can do. Not one penny has ever been lost in a federally insured deposit account. And along with our other smart money investments for chickens—U.S. Treasury bills and conservative money market mutual funds—these are investments that give you an invaluable return: peace of mind.

INSURED DEPOSITS

Leaving your money in an insured deposit account has one real advantage—safety. But when you opt for safety, you give up the possibility of huge gains. Instead, you are guaranteed a regular and reasonable return on your money. That return is called the interest rate.

Interest rates are set by each individual bank or savings and loan, depending on market conditions. If they want—or need—to attract money, they may raise rates. But basically, financial institutions set the interest rates they pay by looking at general economic conditions, the outlook for inflation, and what other, competitive money market instruments are paying. It is up to you, the depositor, to compare the rates and terms offered by each institution and decide where to put your money.

The first thing you must do is check to see that you are indeed investing in a federally insured account. On the window of a bank you will see the sign FDIC—Federal Deposit Insurance Corporation. This agency, backed by the full credit of the United States government, guarantees all deposits up to $100,000 in banks and savings and loans.

It is important to understand the rules governing deposit insurance. You are allowed to have several accounts—differently named—in any bank or S&L and still qualify for deposit insurance on each account, depending on how the account is titled. For instance, your interest in a joint account and a separately owned account are *each* insured up to $100,000. However, the insurance limits are not increased by rearranging the names on a joint account, nor will you increase the insured limits under your name by having several different types of accounts such as checking, savings and money market. In practice, if you have large sums of money it would be wiser to use several institutions or, as we will explain later in this chapter, purchase U.S. government Treasury bills directly.

Some institutions have started to offer an investment product that looks like a deposit account but is really a sort of "loan" to the financial institution. These interest-paying "notes" are not insured but may appear attractive because they often pay higher rates. In fact, some failed S&Ls are being sued by their customers who bought uninsured "notes" thinking they were insured CDs. When you put your money in a financial institution, be sure it is in a federally insured deposit account.

Does it make a difference whether you put your deposits in a bank or savings and loan institution? Not any more. For many years, when interest rates on savings were regulated by the federal government, savings and loan institutions were permitted to offer a slightly higher interest rate. That was because their mission was to ensure a flow of mortgage funds to the housing industry. But with the advent of deregulation in the early 1980s, interest rates were no longer set by the government. And eventually savings and loans were allowed to make other loans besides home mortgages. (Some say that's what got the industry into trouble—making loans in new and risky aspects of the real estate business in order to earn high interest rates that they could then pass on to depositors.)

The bottom line for depositors is that ever since deregulation, banks and S&Ls have been able to offer competitive rates and services. So you should choose the institution you are most comfortable with when it comes to establishing a relationship.

With all the recent headlines about bank and S&L failures, it's no wonder that savers are getting a little uneasy. First, it's important to remember that all accounts are insured up to $100,000. That's a guarantee direct from the United States government. Your only risk is that there could be a slight delay in getting access to your money if your bank or S&L is closed or merged. That's why many depositors examine the financial condition of the institution as a consideration in opening an account. Every bank or S&L is required to give you a "statement of condition" explaining its financial situation. Frankly, those statements are often difficult to understand and do not always give a clear picture of the institution's potential problems.

If you would like to check further into the financial standing of your bank or S&L, there are two services that offer that information to the public. Veribanc (P.O. Box 2963, Woburn, MA 01888) rates every bank and S&L based on its most recent federal financial reports. The safest are rated "green," those warranting caution are rated "yellow," and troubled institutions get a "red" rating. Veribanc has also developed a "star" rating—much like the movie reviews. These are special safety ratings applied to institutions offering the highest yields to attract deposits. Three stars is the top rating, down to one star, which indicates potential problems at an institution. Some get no stars, which means that no information is available or they don't even qualify for the one-star rating. Veribanc will send you a list of the soundest institutions in your area. The cost is $20 for a short report on any institution.

Veribanc also offers an "instant ratings" service where you can call a toll-free number (800-44-BANKS) and an analyst will give you an immediate comment, including color code and star rating of any bank or S&L. This is especially handy when a bank or S&L offers a high rate for a period of just a day or so, and you wonder whether it's a safe place to stash your cash. The cost is $10 for the first institution and $2 for each additional inquiry on the same phone call. They accept MasterCard or Visa for this service and will follow up by mailing the rating information.

A similar service is offered by Shesshunoff Information Services (P.O. Box 13203, Austin, TX 78711). They'll send a six-page report on any bank or S&L, plus a guide to how to understand the numbers in their report. Both of these services are helpful when you are debating sending your deposits to an out-of-state institution offering higher rates than those available locally.

DEPOSIT OPTIONS

Once you decide to leave your money in the safety of an insured deposit in a bank or S&L, you still have some choices to make. There are several different types of accounts, each paying a different rate and offering you different restrictions on access to your money.

Passbook Savings

The simplest account is called a *passbook savings account,* which can be opened with a minimum of $100 (even less for children's savings accounts) at most institutions. You are generally given a passbook in which deposits, withdrawals, and interest are noted by the bank each time you use the account. Interest paid on passbook savings is usually the lowest rate offered on any savings account because the costs to the bank are higher with this type of account, and because you have access to your money at any time.

You may remember that years ago the interest rate on passbooks was fixed by federal law. All that has changed since the banking industry was deregulated in the 1980s. In earlier days, savings and loan institutions were allowed to pay an extra one-half of one percent higher interest to attract money for mortgage lending. Back then, S&Ls paid 5^1/2 percent and banks were allowed to pay only 5 percent on passbook savings. Today, with deregulation, all institutions compete equally, and most pay around 5 percent, although quite a few have been paying less than 5 percent on passbook savings.

Since the passbook savings rate is usually the lowest insured rate around, you would think that it would attract few deposits. But that's not the case. There is currently more than $418 billion sitting in pass-book savings accounts at this writing, losing about $42 million a day in interest they *could* be earning in higher-yielding CDs. Many depositors just don't know any better, and the banks are delighted to have this low-cost money on deposit. But we'll show you some other, equally safe, ways to earn higher rates.

Money Market Deposit Accounts

More than 60 cents of every dollar on deposit at banks and thrifts today is in money market deposit accounts. These accounts offer flexibility and current market rates along with federal deposit insurance.

Money market deposit accounts generally pay an interest rate that is competitive with short-term certificates of deposit—and usually at least one full percentage point higher than the rates paid on passbook savings. You have access to *all* of your money at any time by simply writing a check on your account. There is no penalty for withdrawals. But to keep you from using this type of account as an interest-bearing checking account, you are limited to three checks per month—plus additional withdrawals that can be made from automatic teller machines.

Many institutions require a minimum of $2,500 to open a money market deposit account, although you can certainly find accounts with lower minimums. Some charge a monthly maintenance fee of about $5 to $10 but waive the fee if you keep a required minimum balance in the account.

A money market deposit account is a good place to stash your cash temporarily because it always pays a market rate of interest. That is, if rates are rising in general, your money market interest rate will also climb. Many institutions will pay higher rates on larger deposits. Most institutions change the rates on their money market deposit accounts on Tuesday or Wednesday after watching the rate changes at the weekly Treasury bill auction. So while you won't get a promise of a fixed annual yield on your money market deposit account, you will get a quickly changing current rate that reflects money market conditions.

Certificates of Deposit

Many savers prefer to lock their money up at a fixed rate for a fixed period of time in a certificate of deposit, commonly referred to as a CD. These CDs come in maturities ranging from just a few months to as long as ten years. In ordinary times, longer-term CDs pay higher interest rates as a reward for leaving your money on deposit for a longer period of time. But sometimes, when the banking system is tightening up on credit, you will get equally high or higher rates for short-term certificates of deposit.

When you shop for a certificate of deposit, you will be attracted by advertisements for "high rates." The *rate* is the stated interest you must be paid. If your CD is paying *simple interest,* that means the interest will not compound. Other CDs compound the rate daily, monthly, or quarterly.

If you open a $10,000 CD at 9 percent for one year, you will earn $900 in simple interest. But if the account pays 9 percent interest compounding *daily* then you will earn $941 in interest for the year. Over a long period of time compounding—earning interest on your interest— can make a big difference in how your money grows. Of course, compounding won't be very important to you if you decide to withdraw the interest every month.

Remember, the *rate* is the stated interest you must be paid, but the *yield* takes the benefit of compounding into account. And since yield is figured on an annual basis, if you are quoted an annual yield for a six-month CD, that figure makes the unlikely assumption that you would be able to renew that CD at the same rate in six months. By the time your CD matures in six months, rates are likely to have changed.

The most popular maturities for CDs used to be six months and two years. Those were the maturities allowed when deregulation started back in October 1983. But lately financial institutions have started offering CDs with "odd" maturities such as seven months in order to stagger the rollovers of money on deposit. Comparing rates and yields on CDs of different lengths can be very confusing, so it is best to ask your banker exactly how much money will be in your account at the end of one year, or at maturity for your CD.

Jumbo CDs If you have collected over $100,000 in savings, you will be faced with additional options to earn even higher rates (on the theory that costs to the financial institution are lower when they accept deposits in huge chunks). Typically, rates on these jumbo CDs, as they are called, could be as much as 1 percent higher—although at the height of the financial crisis for savings and loans in Texas you could get an extra 250 basis points (2½ percent) interest because those institutions had such a great need to attract funds.

The important thing to keep in mind if you are buying a jumbo CD (above $100,000) is that you are moving above the federally insured limit. The account is insured up to $100,000. So you might want to remove the interest from your account every month and deposit it elsewhere.

If you have this size account, however, there are other places you may want to put your money with equal safety and high market rates of interest.

Staying Short vs. Paying Penalties The higher interest rates on long-term CDs can be very attractive—as long as rates don't move even higher. That's why chicken money belongs only in short-term CDs of six months to one year in maturity. That way when your CD matures you can always roll it over into a new CD at then-current market rates. You may have to settle for a lower rate at maturity, but at least you won't get locked in to a below-market rate for years and years—or be faced with a penalty for cashing in your CD early.

In return for giving you a slightly higher rate on a CD than on a fully liquid money market deposit account, institutions can charge you a penalty for taking your money out of a CD before its term expires. Generally speaking, the penalty is three months' loss of interest—although since 1986 there are no specific federal regulations about penalties and it is up to the individual institution to set its own rules.

Sometimes, if rates are rising quickly, it may pay to take the penalty and break out of your CD to reinvest the money in a new CD at a much higher rate. In order to decide if this is a good move you have to figure out how much interest you will earn over the term of the new CD and offset that against the penalty you will be paying for breaking out of the old CD.

Chasing the Highest Rates Rates on CDs are set by individual institutions depending on prevailing economic conditions, competition, and their need to attract deposits to fund loans. Sometimes rates will be higher in one city or one part of the country because of local conditions.

That has led many savers to send money to institutions across the nation to earn the highest rates. In fact, you can even subscribe to a weekly service—*100 Highest Yields* (P.O. Box 088888, N. Palm Beach, FL 33408-8888, 800-327-7717)—to keep track of which bank or S&L is offering the highest rates on money market accounts or CDs.

Other savers contact stock brokerage firms that arrange purchase of out-of-state CDs. Typically the brokerage firm will commit for $40 or $50 million worth of CDs at a particular institution at a very attractive rate. Then they'll offer the CD rate to their retail customers in smaller amounts—under the $100,000 insured limit. You will be given a choice of institutions, rates, and length of maturity when you buy your CD through a brokerage firm.

Brokers definitely make money on this service. Usually they collect a fee from the institution, or they take a bit of the yield as their fee. For example, they may take down a block of CDs yielding 9.75 percent and then reoffer them to their customers at a yield of 9.70 percent. So if you want to shop for the absolutely top rate, it may pay to do it yourself instead of going through a brokerage firm.

If the customer buys a $10,000 CD through a brokerage firm, the firm sends the confirmation and collects the money. But the CD is recorded on the books of the bank or S&L as belonging to that individual. Interest is paid through the brokerage account monthly or at the end of the term for shorter CDs.

When using a brokerage firm to buy a CD, it's important to be very sure that the CD is indeed registered in *your* name and thus falls under the $100,000 insured limit. Check the forms carefully to make sure all the paperwork is in order in case you ever have to make a claim for your funds.

No one has ever lost a penny in insured deposits. But in several instances there have been small delays in getting funds transferred in cases where federal regulators were forced to take over a failing institution. Many, although not all, institutions are offering higher rates because they are in precarious financial condition and need deposits. If you are earning an extra one-half of one percent on a $10,000 six-month CD paying 10 percent, the higher rate will give you an extra $25 in interest earnings. You have to ask yourself whether it's worth the paperwork, postage, and potential aggravation to earn that money at an out-of-town institution.

TREASURY BILLS, NOTES, AND BONDS

Perhaps the safest of all chicken money investments is to buy short-term Treasury securities direct from the United States government. Treasury bills are simply interest-paying IOUs of the U.S. government, sold weekly as the government needs to borrow money to run its daily operations.

When tax receipts don't cover the expenses of the government, then the government must borrow money. In fact, with the government running huge budget deficits every year, it needs to do a lot of borrowing. So the government frequently sells both short- and long-term IOUs called Treasury bills, notes, and bonds.

- Treasury *bills* have maturities of one year or less.
- Treasury *notes* have maturities of between one and ten years.
- Treasury *bonds* have maturities of from ten to thirty years.

Treasury bills with three- and six-month maturities are sold at a regular weekly auction held on Mondays (except when a Monday is a bank holiday). On any given Monday the Treasury may sell about $12 to $15 billion worth of Treasury bills—some to pay off old, maturing Treasury bills, and others to raise new cash for the Treasury Department to pay for government spending. One-year Treasury bills are sold once a month, as are two-year Treasury notes. Then every three months the government sells longer-term Treasury notes and bonds—usually in the second week of February, May, August, and October.

The interest rates the government must pay on each of these Treasury securities is set by a sort of auction process. Major government securities dealers make interest rate bids, saying they are willing to purchase a certain amount of securities as long as the interest rates are high enough. The interest rate they demand is based on the current outlook for economic growth, inflation, borrowing demand in the credit markets, and the available money supply.

If the securities dealers demand too high an interest rate, others will undercut them and get to buy the government's securities. So the competing bids set the lowest acceptable interest rate at each auction, keeping the government's borrowing costs down.

Treasury Bills

Individuals may buy Treasury bills at the weekly Treasury bill auctions by submitting a *noncompetitive bid*. That is, individuals simply fill out an application form, submit a check, and agree to accept the average interest rate determined at the auction. You will not know the exact rate of interest you will earn until *after* the auction.

The best way to purchase Treasury securities at auction is to submit your application to the nearest Federal Reserve Bank (there are twelve Federal Reserve banks around the country). See the following list for addresses and telephone numbers. You can do this in person or call the bank and request an application to purchase Treasury securities through the mail. All applications must be made by the morning of the day of the auction. (Check for the exact deadline in your time zone.)

Type of Security	Frequency of Auction
3 and 6-month bills	Weekly
1-year bills	Every fourth week
2-year notes	Monthly
All others	Quarterly

Treasury bills are sold every week in three- and six-month maturities (13 and 26 weeks). They are sold in minimum denominations of $10,000, with additional amounts in multiples of $5,000. To purchase

Treasury bills you will need a certified check or cashier's check made out to the Federal Reserve Bank in your district. The application form is very simple. You will need to give your name, address, and Social Security or taxpayer I.D. number.

You will also have to include the name of your bank or financial institution, your checking or money market account number, and the bank's *interbank routing number,* which you can get easily by calling your banker. You need this information because the interest on Treasury securities is no longer sent to you by check. Instead, it is deposited directly into your checking or money market account. You can also have the interest sent directly to a money market mutual fund.

When you purchase Treasury bills you will be asked if you want them to automatically *roll over.* That means that when the Treasury bills mature they will be automatically renewed at the interest rate set on that week. You can arrange for your T-bills to be rolled over automatically up to eight times for three-month bills or four times for six-month bills. Or you can ask that the proceeds be sent directly to your bank or money market account at maturity.

Treasury *bills* have an unusual way of paying interest. You give the government a check for $10,000. When the interest rate is determined at auction it is called a *discount interest rate.* The government immediately sends your interest check directly into your bank account for the full amount of interest you will earn during the six months. If you elect not to roll over at the end of the three- or six-month period, the government will send you back your original $10,000. In effect, your interest was paid up front—allowing you the use of the interest for the entire three or six months.

For example, suppose you purchase a $10,000 six-month Treasury bill that pays a discount interest rate of 10 percent. Your interest check would be $500—received into your bank account within a week (10 percent of $10,000 for one year is $1,000; for six months it is $500). So all you really have invested for the six months is $9,500.

Since you have the use of the interest money for six months—unlike a bank account where you would be getting the interest day by day—your true rate of return on Treasury bills is actually higher than the announced rate each week. In the example above, the announced discount interest rate was 10 percent, but the actual investment rate of

Federal Reserve Locations for Purchase of Treasury Bills, Notes and Bonds

Board of Governors of the Federal
Reserve System, Washington D.C. 20551
(information only) (202) 452-3000

ATLANTA
104 Marietta Street, N.W.
Atlanta, Georgia 30303
(404) 521-8500
   Birmingham Branch
   1801 Fifth Avenue, North
   Birmingham, Alabama 35202
   (P.O. Box C-10447
   Birmingham, Alabama 35283)
   Jacksonville Branch
   515 Julia Street
   Jacksonville, Florida 32231
   Miami Branch
   9100 Northwest 36th Street
   Miami, Florida 33178
   (P.O. Box 520847
   Miami, Florida 33152)
   Nashville Branch
   301 Eighth Avenue, North
   Nashville, Tennessee 37203
   New Orleans Branch
   525 St. Charles Avenue
   (P.O. Box 61630)
   New Orleans, Louisiana 70161

BOSTON*
600 Atlantic Avenue
Boston, Massachusetts 02106
(617) 973-3000

CHICAGO*
230 South La Salle Street
(P.O. Box 834)
Chicago, Illinois 60690-0834
(312) 322-5369
   Detroit Branch
   160 Fort Street, West (P.O. Box 1059)
   Detroit, Michigan 48231

CLEVELAND*
1455 East Sixth Street (P.O. Box 6387)
Cleveland, Ohio 44101
(216) 579-2000

   Cincinnati Branch
   150 East Fourth Street (P.O. Box 999)
   Cincinnati, Ohio 45201
   Pittsburgh Branch
   717 Grant Street (P.O. Box 867)
   Pittsburgh, Pennsylvania 15230

DALLAS
400 South Akard Street (Station K)
Dallas, Texas 75222
(214) 651-6111
   El Paso Branch
   301 East Main Street (P.O. Box 100)
   El Paso, Texas 79999
   Houston Branch
   1701 San Jacinto Street
   Houston, Texas 77002
   (P.O. Box 2578
   Houston, Texas 77252)
   San Antonio Branch
   126 East Nueva Street
   San Antonio, Texas 78204
   (P.O. Box 1471
   San Antonio, Texas 78295)

KANSAS CITY
925 Grand Avenue
Kansas City, Missouri 64198
(816) 881-2000
   Denver Branch
   1020 16th Street
   Denver, Colorado 80202
   (Terminal Annex-P.O. Box 5228
   Denver, Colorado 80217)
   Oklahoma City Branch
   226 Dean A. McGee Avenue
   (P.O. Box 25129)
   Oklahoma City, Oklahoma 73125
   Omaha Branch
   2201 Farnam Street
   Omaha, Nebraska 68102
   (P.O. Box 3958
   Omaha, Nebraska 68103)

MINNEAPOLIS
250 Marquette Avenue
Minneapolis, Minnesota 55480
(612) 340-2345

Helena Branch
400 North Park Avenue
Helena, Montana 59601

NEW YORK*
33 Liberty Street
(Federal Reserve P.O. Station)
New York, New York 10045
(212) 720-5000
 Buffalo Branch
 160 Delaware Avenue
 Buffalo, New York 14202
 (P.O. Box 961
 Buffalo, New York 14240)

PHILADELPHIA
Ten Independence Mall
Philadelphia, Pennsylvania 19106
(P.O. Box 66
Philadelphia, Pennsylvania 19105)
(215) 574-6000

RICHMOND*
701 East Byrd Street
Richmond, Virginia 23219
(P.O. Box 27622
Richmond, Virginia 23261)
(804) 697-8000
 Baltimore Branch
 502 South Sharp Street
 Baltimore, Maryland 21201
 (P.O. Box 1378
 Baltimore, Maryland 21203)
 Charlotte Branch
 401 South Tyron Street
  (P.O. Box 30248)
 Charlotte, North Carolina 28230
 **Culpeper Communications and
  Records Center**
 P.O. Drawer 20
 Culpeper, Virginia 22701

SAN FRANCISCO
101 Market Street
San Francisco, California 94105

(P.O. Box 7702,
San Francisco, California 94120)
(415) 974-2000
 Los Angeles Branch
 950 South Grand Avenue
 Los Angeles, California 90015
 (Terminal Annex-P.O. Box 2077
 Los Angeles, California 90051)
 Portland Branch
 915 S.W. Stark Street
 Portland, Oregon 97025
 (P.O. Box 3436
 Portland, Oregon 97208)
 Salt Lake City Branch
 120 South State Street
 Salt Lake City, Utah 84111
 (P.O. Box 30780
 Salt Lake City, Utah 84125)
 Seattle Branch
 1015 Second Avenue
 Seattle, Washington 98104
 (P.O. Box 3567
 Seattle, Washington 98124)

ST. LOUIS
411 Locust Street
St. Louis, Missouri 63102
(P.O. Box 442
St. Louis, Missouri 63166)
(314) 444-8506 or 8507
 Little Rock Branch
 325 West Capitol Avenue
 (P.O. Box 1261)
 Little Rock, Arkansas 72203
 Louisville Branch
 410 South Fifth Street
 Louisville, Kentucky 40201
 (P.O. Box 32710
 Louisville, Kentucky 40232)
 Memphis Branch
 200 North Main Street
 Memphis, Tennessee 38103
 (P.O. Box 407,
 Memphis, Tennessee 38101)

*Additional offices of these banks are located at Lewiston, Maine 04240; Windsor Locks, Connecticut 06096; Cranford, New Jersey 07016; Jericho, New York 11753; Utica Oriskany, New York 13424; Columbus, Ohio 43216; Columbia, South Carolina 29210; Charleston, West Virginia 25328; Des Moines, Iowa 50306; Indianapolis, Indiana 46206; and Milwaukee, Wisconsin 53201.

return was 10.66 percent. And you can increase your overall rate of return by putting that interest check in a money market fund for the six months.

Treasury Notes

If you are willing to tie your money up for a slightly longer period of time, you might consider buying Treasury *notes*. Two-year T-notes are sold during the third week of every month in $5,000 minimums. The procedure to purchase them is the same as for T-bills, although you do not need a certified or cashier's check for T-notes; a personal check or maturing Treasury securities will be accepted in payment.

Every three months the Treasury sells notes with slightly longer maturities—usually three, four, seven, or ten years. These are sold in $1,000 minimum denominations.

When you buy Treasury notes, you get an interest check every six months—again deposited directly into your account as per your instructions when you bought the note. Every time you purchase a Treasury security—or when one rolls over—you will receive a computerized confirmation statement listing all of your holdings in Treasury securities. You should also check your bank account to make sure the interest was deposited correctly to your account.

When you purchase Treasury bills and notes, you should plan to hold them until maturity, when the government will pay you the proceeds in full. If you need to sell them before maturity, there is a complicated process to go through to sell them in the government securities market. There are also additional costs involved, especially since you are probably selling an *odd lot*—anything under $100,000 in this huge market.

Treasury Bonds

Longer-term Treasury *bonds* are sold every three months or so. Like Treasury bills and notes, bonds can be purchased directly from the Treasury through the Federal Reserve banks. Although all these securities carry the direct, full-faith obligation of the U.S. government, the longer-term bonds carry a bit of extra risk for the chicken investor. The risk is not that the bonds won't pay off, but that you are tying up your money for the long-term at a fixed interest rate. If rising inflation or a credit crunch forces rates higher in the future, you could be stuck with your low interest rate bonds or be forced to sell them at a loss. (See Chapter 10.)

So chicken money should stick with short-term Treasury bills, or in some cases shorter-term Treasury notes, which offer you the safest investment along with the liquidity to be able to get your money out within a relatively short time.

Your bank or financial institution may offer to purchase the Treasury securities for you, but it is better to buy them yourself directly from your Federal Reserve Bank. Not only will your commercial bank charge a fee for this service, which you can avoid by "doing-it-yourself," but by buying direct, you have opened up your own direct account at the Treasury. That is a special advantage for people who have accumulated more than the $100,000 that is insured at a bank or S&L. By buying Treasuries direct you are, in effect, getting the government's direct IOU for the entire amount of Treasury securities that you purchase.

Are U.S. Treasury securities any safer than your insured deposit in a bank or S&L? Theoretically, no. They are both backed by the full faith and credit of the United States government. The real reasons for chicken money to invest in Treasury bills are: the direct guarantee from the government for Treasury investments in any amount; the liquidity that allows you to get your cash at maturity or to sell out early in the government securities market; and the assurance that with short-term T-bills you will always get the current, free-market interest rate.

MONEY MARKET MUTUAL FUNDS

There is another alternative for "chicken money." In addition to insured deposit accounts or Treasury bills, you might want to consider a *money market mutual fund*. These are pools of money managed by mutual fund management companies in order to allow small investors to earn current money market rates.

In Chapter 14 we'll explain how to use mutual funds to invest in stocks. Mutual funds combine money from hundreds of small investors to offer them the benefits of professional management and diversification. Huge management companies have grown to offer a variety of funds to suit individual needs—everything from general stock funds, income funds that include preferred stocks, bond funds, aggressive growth stock funds, international stock funds—the list goes on and on.

Most mutual funds involve a degree of risk. But each one of these fund management companies also offers a *money market mutual fund*—a good investment alternative for chicken money. Money market mutual funds are designed to purchase short-term money market instruments and pass on the high interest rates to investors whose small savings might not otherwise earn the highest rates. The funds pool investors' money to earn the higher rates on jumbo CDs or to buy commercial paper (interest-bearing IOUs sold by large companies as a way to borrow money for their daily operations) or Treasury bills. These are huge multi-billion dollar daily markets traded by professional securities dealers.

When you open a money market mutual fund you'll do it by mail since very few of these companies have local offices. Consult a mutual fund directory (see Chapter 14) and call the fund's toll-free phone number. Ask the company to send an application and a prospectus—a booklet describing the fund's investments and charges.

Every time you mail the fund a deposit, they'll send you a computerized confirmation of your account, along with a stub and envelope to mail your next deposit. You will also receive a monthly or quarterly statement of all your account activity, including the interest that was credited to your balance.

One of the main attractions of money market mutual funds is their liquidity—you can take all or part of your money out of the fund at any time. Money market mutual funds can offer unlimited checkwriting privileges, although many require a minimum of $100 per check. You can use the check writing privilege to pay bills such as income taxes. Your money on deposit in the fund continues to earn daily interest until the check clears.

Most money market mutual funds also allow you to transfer money out of your account and into other stock and bond mutual funds managed by the same company. That makes it convenient to switch into and out of the stock market with merely a toll-free telephone call. (More on mutual fund switching in Chapter 14.)

Because money market mutual funds invest only in very short-term money market instruments or "paper," the interest rate earned on the fund changes daily. As the general trend of market interest rates moves up or down, so will the yield on the fund. The shorter the maturity of the paper owned by the fund, the more quickly the fund's yield will respond to changes in the general level of interest rates.

Money market mutual funds are required to have an average maturity of 90 days or less for the entire investment portfolio. When fund managers think rates are about to move higher for a while, then they buy only very short-term paper maturing in a few days. If managers think rates will drop, they will extend the maturities to lock in the higher rates currently available.

Money market mutual funds are not covered by federal deposit insurance. But no individual has ever lost a penny in a modern money market fund. The government requires that 95 percent of the investments of a money market mutual fund must be in securities that receive the highest rating from at least two rating agencies. And for that ultimate, extra measure of security there are some money market mutual funds that specialize in investing only in the safest short-term money market instruments such as Treasury bills. Capital Preservation Fund (800-4-SAFETY) is a fund that buys only short-term U.S. Treasury bills. You can open an account for a $1,000 minimum investment and add to it in any amount at any time. Other money market funds specialize only in short-term U.S. government securities and securities of government agencies. These offer the highest degree of safety.

As a money market mutual fund investor you do not risk the loss of your money because of market price fluctuations; your risk is only the ups and downs of interest rates. Since rates change daily, you can't predict how much interest you will earn on your fund. Money market funds are a good place to park money when rates are rising. In hindsight, however, you might have wanted to lock your money up for a longer period of time in bonds or CDs if rates start to fall.

There is a small charge for investing in a money market mutual fund. Generally the fund management company charges about one-half of one percent of the fund's assets every year—a charge that is taken right out of the fund and therefore lowers your yield slightly. Many investors think that is a very small price for access to the current money market rates and liquidity offered by money market mutual funds.

U.S. SAVINGS BONDS

For many years U.S. savings bonds were considered a patriotic but low-paying investment that really made little financial sense. But all that changed in 1982, when the government decided to pay a market rate of interest on Series EE bonds. Now savings bonds have a combination of attractive interest rates and special tax features that make them a suitable investment for many different investors.

Here's how they work now. Series EE bonds are still purchased at a discount. For example, you pay $50 to purchase a $100 savings bond. As the interest builds up over a period of years, the bond reaches its face value at maturity. There is no longer a fixed number of years until the bond reaches maturity, because the interest rate paid each year will vary. A higher interest rate will make the bond "mature" to its face value much faster. Currently you are guaranteed a *minimum* interest rate of 6 percent, so it cannot take longer than 12 years for your savings bond to mature.

In practice, though, savings bonds earn a much higher rate of interest and mature much faster than 12 years. That's because the government sets a new rate of interest every six months. The rate is guaranteed to be 85 percent of the interest rate being paid on five-year Treasury notes. The savings bond rate changes every November 1st and May 1st and is publicly announced. Since Series EE savings bonds went to the variable-rate system in November 1982, the lowest six-month rate paid was 5.84 percent, and the highest was 11.09 percent. For information on the current six-month rate, call toll-free 800-US BONDS.

You are not required to hold your savings bonds to maturity. In fact, you can cash them in after six months, but you won't earn the higher rates of interest. Bonds cashed in before five years earn interest on a fixed, graduated scale. That's an important fact to keep in mind: You should plan to hold bonds for at least five years or more to earn a competitive return. If you continue to hold your Series EE bonds *after* they mature, they will continue earning the market rate interest for 30 years. The accumulated interest simply increases the amount each bond is worth *over* its face value when you finally redeem it.

Besides paying market rates of interest, Series EE bonds have one other important investment advantage. You do not pay income taxes on the interest you earn each year until you cash the bonds in. The proceeds are exempt from state and local income taxes, too. That means you can buy them several years before retirement and defer taxes until after you retire, when you will presumably be in a lower tax bracket.

The tax feature also makes Series EE bonds an excellent gift for young children. Under current tax law, children under the age of 14 must pay taxes on their interest income above $1,000 at their parents' tax rate. But Series EE bonds defer income taxes until the bonds are cashed in. That can be done when the child reaches the age of 14 and pays income taxes at his own lower rate.

Starting in 1990, Series EE bonds also have a special benefit for parents saving for a child's college education. In this case, the bonds must be bought in a parent's name, not the child's name. For 1991, if the parents have a combined taxable income of under $62,900, all the interest on the savings bonds is tax-free if the proceeds are used to fund a child's college tuition. (The bonds do not qualify for the tax break if the proceeds are used for room and board.) This tax-free feature gradually phases out as incomes move above the $62,900 level and disappears completely when joint parental income reaches $94,350 for joint filers, or $57,700 for singles and heads of household. These levels are indexed upward yearly. To get the tax break the bonds must be cashed in and used for tuition in the same year.

It is important to note that you *can* elect to pay income taxes on U.S. savings bond interest every year. And then you can subsequently switch reporting methods and elect to defer taxes, as most people who purchase savings bonds choose to do.

Series EE bonds are easy to purchase through your bank or savings and loan. They are sold in face amounts of $50, $75, $100, $200, $500, $1,000, $5,000, and $10,000. The actual purchase price is half the face value amount. You can also purchase Series EE bonds through a payroll savings plan that takes regular deductions from your paycheck. More than $3 billion worth of savings bonds are purchased through payroll savings every year.

You are allowed to buy a maximum of $15,000 issue price ($30,000 face amount) of Series EE savings bonds in the name of any one person in any one calendar year. Savings bonds may be purchased in an individual name, in the names of two people as co-owners, or in the name of one person as owner, with another person as beneficiary. Upon the death of an owner, if there is a co-owner or beneficiary named on the bonds, they will escape probate although the bonds will be part of the estate for inheritance tax purposes.

You may have heard about Series HH savings bonds. You cannot purchase them directly; they are available only in exchange for the older Series E or current Series EE bonds. Series HH bonds pay interest twice a year, and that interest must be reported for income tax purposes. Series HH bonds pay a fixed 6 percent annual rate of interest.

Series HH bonds have one big tax advantage. When you convert your Series EE bonds to HH (presumably because you now have a need for regular interest income payments) you can still defer paying tax on the accrued interest on your old Series E or EE bonds. You won't have to pay the tax on the gain on your old Series E or EE bonds until you cash in or sell the HH bonds, or until they reach maturity. You *will* pay income taxes on the interest you get from the HH bonds each year.

You can get an application to convert from Series E or EE to Series HH bonds at your bank, S&L, or at any Federal Reserve Bank.

United States savings notes, a form of savings bonds commonly called "freedom shares," were issued from May 1967 through October 1970. At that time, they were sold with a one-half percent higher interest rate than was then allowed on Series E bonds. They therefore had a slightly different discount at the time of purchase and were originally scheduled to mature in four years and six months. However, since then the maturities have been extended. Freedom Shares are no longer sold, but if you hold those older freedom shares, they continue to pay interest at current savings bonds market rates.

Savings bonds purchased years ago, before the current market rate system was established, also earn market rates of interest up to certain cutoff dates. Series E bonds issued before December 1965 continue earning interest until 40 years after their issue date. Series F bonds, Series EE bonds, and savings notes (Freedom Shares) issued after November 1965 will stop earning interest exactly 30 years from their issue dates. Series H bonds issued between 1959 and 1979 also have a 30-year final maturity. Series HH bonds issued since 1980 stop earning interest 20 years from the issue date.

You can find out exactly what your old bond is worth by writing the Superintendent of Documents, U.S. Government Printing Office, Washington, D.C. 20402 and asking for the Table of Redemption Values for Savings Bonds. Many banks also keep this redemption value chart on hand to advise customers.

U.S. savings bonds are guaranteed as to principal and interest by the full faith and credit of the United States government. If they are lost, stolen, mutilated, or destroyed they will be replaced without charge and will bear the original issue dates. All these features, plus the market rate of interest, make them an ideal investment for chicken money.

Credit, Buying and Borrowing

CHAPTER **5**

Your Credit

Your credit is one of your most powerful financial assets. Used wisely, credit offers you the opportunity to not only live well now, but to build wealth for the future. Used carelessly, it can create a negative credit record that will be a roadblock every time you want to expand your financial horizons.

It's up to you to decide how your credit history reads. Everyone starts out with *no* credit. You build a good credit record simply by borrowing money and repaying it on time. If you only use cash for your purchases, rent an apartment instead of buying a condo or home, and have no credit cards, you will have no credit history. The minute you decide to borrow money, you can be sure that your repayment history is being reported to one of the four or five national credit bureaus.

Credit bureaus are private, for-profit businesses. The credit bureau industry maintains files on an estimated 170 million Americans and generates 500 million credit reports a year. If you are an active user of credit, your history will be in the files of more than one company.

A credit bureau is simply a computerized information-gathering business; they make no credit decisions. Lenders and merchants send computerized information to the major credit bureaus every month, describing the outstanding balances and payment history of every borrower. Credit bureaus also research public records for judgments, liens, foreclosures, and bankruptcy filings. In turn, businesses can call on the credit bureaus to get current information on anyone's credit history.

Credit bureaus do not *deny* credit; they merely *report* the information they have gathered. It is the lender who makes the decision to grant you credit—whether a credit card, personal loan, or mortgage—based on the information that is in your computerized credit file.

YOUR CREDIT REPORT

Income and assets have very little to do with your credit report. You may have a large income or substantial savings, but these are rarely reported by the credit bureau. The only thing that shows up on your credit report is your record of borrowing and repayments.

It's important to check your credit record at least once a year to see if the material being gathered is accurate. Credit records may be confused with those of someone else who has the same name but a different Social Security number. These mix-ups often occur when two people with the same name—father and son, for instance—live under the same roof. It is especially important to separate your credit record from that of an ex-spouse.

You can get your current credit report by writing to your local credit bureau. You will find it listed in the phone book under "credit bureaus" or "credit reporting agencies." In fact, you might find several credit bureaus listed, and you should check with all of them because they could have different records. If you do not find a local listing, try writing to one of the nation's largest credit bureaus: Trans Union Credit Bureau, 444 N. Michigan Ave., Chicago, IL 60611 or TRW Credit, 505 City Parkway West, Orange, CA 92668.

If you have recently been denied credit, you are entitled to a free copy of your credit report. Otherwise you will be charged a small fee—usually from $5 to $25. Generally the credit bureau will send you an application form on which you must give your name, current address, recent past addresses, and Social Security number. They will also require your signature before giving out your credit record. The credit report is a complicated, computerized document with various code numbers. But along with the report you will be given an explanation of the code system. You will also be able to see who has recently inquired about your credit history.

Disputing Your Credit Report

What happens if you spot a mistake in your credit record? Typically you're in for a long, agonizing process, even though the Fair Credit Reporting Act creates procedures for changing your credit report.

First you should write to the credit bureau and challenge the information. Include a copy of the report that was sent to you and your explanation of why the information is wrong. For instance, if there is a public record such as a divorce involved, it is up to you to give a copy of the document to the credit bureau.

The credit bureau is obligated to verify the questioned information and report back to you within a "reasonable" period of time—generally 30 days. The credit bureau will contact the merchant or lender about the disputed record. If the information cannot be verified, it must be deleted from your report. The bureau must also send a notice of correction to anyone who inquired about your credit in the last six months.

You have to be persistent at challenging an item on your credit record. Sometimes it helps to make an appointment and visit the credit bureau in person. Be sure you keep track of the names and dates of the people you contacted at the bureau. And once the credit bureau says your record has been changed, be sure to ask for a copy of your new record just to make sure.

The Associated Credit Bureaus, Inc., the industry's trade group, says disputes are common. They say that four million consumers looked at their credit files last year, and one million—25 percent—challenged some of the information they found. They do not keep track of how many actual changes were made on credit records as a result of consumer complaints.

If the credit bureau refuses to change the information on your credit report, you have one other option. The Fair Credit Reporting Act says you can add a statement of up to 100 words to your credit history to explain the problem. That statement must be sent out when a lender asks for your credit report.

Bad Credit Stays with You

What happens if the negative information on your credit report is *correct?* If you missed payments or had a lien filed against you, the bad news stays on your credit record for seven years. Bankruptcy stays on your credit record for ten years. There is nothing you can do about it. And negative information may be reported for an indefinite period of time if you apply for a mortgage over $50,000 or life insurance with more than $50,000 face value, or if you apply for a job paying more than $20,000 a year and the prospective employer asks for a credit report.

Solving Disputes Without Destroying Credit

Once you understand how important your credit history is—and how computers keep track of *every* payment and loan you have—you will realize how important it is to keep your credit clean.

That means if you have a dispute with a merchant over something you purchased, you should not retaliate by withholding payments. The merchant has the ultimate weapon: He will simply report your nonpayment to the credit bureau, destroying your credit not only with that one company, but with any future charge or mortgage loans you might seek.

The Fair Credit Billing Act does allow you to dispute a credit card bill for amounts over $50 if the transaction took place in your home state or within 100 miles of your home. But you must notify the seller *in writing* explaining the problem and sending copies of all relevant documents such as the charge slip, merchandise guarantee, or newspaper ad. Keep a copy of your letter and originals of any documents you send.

During the dispute the merchant is not allowed to charge you interest or a late fee on the unpaid balance. And the merchant cannot report the unpaid balance to the credit bureau while the dispute is being resolved.

Keeping Track of Your Credit

If you're getting a little paranoid about your credit report after reading this chapter, you might consider subscribing to a service that is designed to ease your mind. TRW has created a service called "Credentials." For an annual fee of $35 the service will notify you any time anyone requests your credit file. It will also give you a copy of your report at no charge on request.

The TRW service has one more feature that would be useful if you are about to apply for new credit or a mortgage and don't want to spend time filling out a lot of applications. When you join the Credentials service you fill out a standard credit application. It is then stored electronically and transmitted to any credit grantor that you designate. And they will send you copies so you can bring them in to any bank or credit grantor in person. The $35 fee includes membership for your spouse as well. For more information, write TRW Credentials Service, One City Blvd. West, Orange, CA 92668 or call toll-free 800-421-9200.

Consumer Investigative Reports

There is another group of companies that specialize in investigative reports often used by life insurance and mortgage companies. They want to know more than your history of borrowing or repayment; they are seeking information about your general character and lifestyle. They may commission these reports before deciding whether to grant you a substantial amount of life insurance or a large mortgage.

These investigative reports, issued by companies like Equifax, Inc., may compile information by talking to your neighbors, coworkers, and friends. Generally, you will be asked by the life insurance or mortgage company to give permission for this type of investigative consumer report. It should not be confused with a credit bureau report.

While there is a credit report on file for almost anyone who has ever used any form of credit, there may or may not be a consumer investigative report. If you would like to check whether Equifax has an investigative report on file for you, contact its national office: Equifax Services, Two Midtown Plaza, 1360 Peachtree St., N.E., Suite 1100, Atlanta, GA 30309 or call toll-free 800-456-2505. They will direct you to the nearest local office that would have your file, if there is one. They are obligated by law to let you know if they have a file on you.

HOW TO ESTABLISH CREDIT

Now that you have an idea how valuable your credit is, how do you go about establishing credit? There's a credit contradiction in our society. Once you have established basic good credit you may receive solicitations for credit cards in the mail, offering you huge lines of credit. But first you have to get started. And getting started is often a problem for students, those in a first job, and those just divorced or widowed.

The first step is to establish a checking or savings-type account at a credit card-issuing bank. Not all banks are bankcard issuers, but you should find at least one in your city. Then keep a regular balance of several hundred dollars in your checking account. At the time you open your account, or within several months, the bank should grant you a bankcard. They may demand that you keep a compensating balance in your savings account for a while, and ask you to sign an agreement allowing the bank to dip into that account should you default on your bankcard payments. (Or, see information on the cash-up-front card later in this chapter.)

Once you have that bankcard you must *use* it! You may prefer to make your purchases by check or cash, but for the purposes of establishing credit you must actually use your card and pay off the balance regularly. That payment history will be reported to the credit bureau and then you are well on your way to establishing a good credit history. In the future it will be easier to get additional credit cards, a car loan, or a mortgage loan. If you still have difficulty obtaining that first credit card, you should read the section on pages 77–78 explaining the "cash-up-front" bankcard.

Understanding Credit Terms

It's important that you understand everything about the credit you are applying for—the total amount to be repaid over the life of the loan, the rate, and the monthly payment. Laws that went into effect in 1989 require credit card issuers to clearly explain in advance the annual percentage rate and the way monthly interest and minimum payments are calculated.

Anyone who grants credit to you has a legitimate interest in getting paid. Especially when it comes to a large loan such as a mortgage, a creditor may ask for your income tax records as well as looking into your credit history. Many credit grantors use a scoring system, or "points," to determine who gets credit. Some factors considered are income, length of time at the same job, amount of other outstanding debt, home ownership, and length of time at same residence.

If you are planning to apply for a major loan such as a mortgage, it would be a good time to repay all the outstanding balances on your credit cards, if possible, because those will stick out when the lender looks at your credit record. You should also check your credit record before applying for a loan to make sure there are no errors.

If you are denied credit or employment because of something negative in your credit report, the company must give you the name and address of the credit bureau it used. That will give you a chance to contact the credit bureau and find out what's in your report.

Getting and maintaining good credit is a key element in your financial plan. And making sure your credit report is accurate makes excellent financial sense.

WOMEN AND CREDIT

It is particularly important for women to have credit in their own name, even if they are married and are able to use their spouse's credit card. By establishing credit in your own name you can avoid a credit crisis if you are divorced or widowed. So make sure that you have a card issued in your own name—*Jane* Doe, not Mrs. *John* Doe.

However, just having a card in your own name does not mean that a separate file is established for you at the credit bureau. Contact the credit bureau and ask for a report of your own credit—and one for your spouse. The Equal Credit Opportunity Act requires credit grantors to report the payment history of any account to credit bureaus in *both* names, not just the one that appears on the credit card or billing statement. So now a wife may have a credit history reported separately in whatever legal name she chooses to use.

If an account was opened before June 1, 1977, the credit report may not reflect individual listings for each spouse. Contact the credit bureau to make sure that each credit report is separate, although many items such as mortgage payments and consumer loans will be listed on both credit records.

If some of your individual credit references have been omitted, write to the credit bureau explaining the situation. You should also write to the credit grantors—the merchants or card issuers—asking them to confirm that the credit is indeed in your own name and to report it separately. They may ask you to sign a separate credit request.

If you are divorced or widowed, your previous credit history will stay with you. But you should certainly notify the credit bureaus about a divorce so that your spouse's subsequent credit actions will not be recorded on your file. Once you are divorced or widowed, a creditor cannot close your account or change its terms unless you demonstrate an inability or unwillingness to pay. However, the creditor can require you to submit a new application if the original charge account was based on your former husband's income.

If you are divorced and applying for credit, you do not have to reveal alimony or child support payments unless you want to have them considered as part of your income. If you do choose to have them considered as income, the credit grantor must include them. However, the grantor may verify the regularity with which those payments are made.

You cannot be asked about your marital status if you are applying for credit in your own name—unless you live in a community property state where both husband and wife are considered co-owners of all property acquired during marriage and responsible for each other's debts and obligations. This is also the only circumstance under which a husband's signature can be required when a wife applies for individual credit.

Having credit in her own name can be critical for a woman, because you never know when life's circumstances will change. It's best to start early building a strong individual credit report.

CHOOSING A CREDIT CARD

Credit cards are a huge industry. According to the American Bankers Association, consumers held 134 million Visa cards and 90 million MasterCards in 1990—and charged $246 billion in purchases on their bankcards. One bankcard, one travel/entertainment (t&e) card, plus charge cards at some local department stores should be enough to cover most of your credit needs.

If you have too many cards in your wallet, the temptation to overspend can get out of hand. One way to tell if you have too many credit cards is to see whether you are able to pay off the balance in full on each card every month. On occasion you might make one large purchase that will take some time to pay off, but that should be the exception, not the rule.

Credit card finance charges are among the highest interest rates consumers can pay, and the interest is no longer an attractive tax deduction. So your goal should be to use credit cards as a convenience, not as a source of long-term financing.

Although there are really two major bankcards (Visa and Master-Card), they are issued by hundreds of different banks and savings and loans—each with its own fees, interest rates, and credit limits. With bankcards you have the option of paying the entire balance due every month, or paying a minimum amount and paying finance charges on the remaining balance.

This is called *open-end credit,* meaning you have a certain limit of authorized credit that you can draw upon as needed. The card issuer figures the minimum monthly payment based on your outstanding balance, usually using the assumption that the debt will be totally repaid in 18 months.

Bankcards are different from travel and entertainment cards such as American Express and Diners Club, which require that you pay the balance in full every month. They do not finance your balance, and you may lose your card privileges if you do not pay the balance in full. Many of these t&e cards now allow you to convert your balance to a revolving credit system.

Both bankcards and t&e cards offer "premium" cards—gold or platinum versions of their regular cards. These cards typically offer higher credit limits, some fringe benefits, and a much higher annual fee. These cards are generally marketed "by invitation only" and require a higher net worth or annual income. The premium cards appeal to the status conscious, but at a substantial cost. If what you really need is a higher credit limit, don't be afraid to call the card issuer and request a higher limit on your regular card. That could save you the annual expense of the premium card.

In order to distinguish themselves, many cards offer additional benefits on their gold or premium cards. They will extend the manufacturer's warranty on products purchased using the card, or they will add an additional warranty against loss or theft. With some premium cards you can automatically decline the collision/damage insurance when you rent a car using the card. And the premium cards may allow you a larger cash advance.

Once you have established a good credit payment record, you might be surprised to be solicited by mail with attractive offers from credit card issuers. Choosing the best one for you becomes your responsibility. There are a number of issues to consider.

The Fair Credit and Charge Card Disclosure Act of 1988 applies to bankcards as well as department store credit cards and charge cards such as American Express and Diners Club. It requires the card issuer to disclose its annual fees, finance charges, grace period, and billing procedures *before* a consumer makes application and goes through the issuer's credit checking program. The new rules will allow consumers to comparison shop *before* applying for a card.

If you can't pay your balances in full every month, you should look for the credit card with the lowest interest rate. That can make a difference of as much as five percentage points in the interest you are paying.

But it's not just the *rate* on the card that matters; it's also important to note just how and when the rate is applied to your charges. Many cards will give you a *grace period* of 25 days from the date of billing before they start charging interest on your balance. Other cards will charge you interest immediately from the date the transaction is posted to your account. That means consumers who do not pay their bills in full every month will pay higher finance charges, although the posted rate on the card may be lower. The short—or nonexistent—grace period might wipe out the advantage of the lower interest rate.

If you pay off the entire balance on your card every month, the interest rate will not matter very much. Instead, you should look for a card with no annual fee. Many bankcards charge $20 to $35 a year just for the privilege of carrying the card, but it's easy to find banks that do not charge for issuing the card.

Affinity Bankcards

In recent years bankcard marketing has created a whole series of products offering additional services and benefits to bankcard holders. Some bankcards allow you to earn mileage on a popular airline program for every dollar spent. Sears entered the world of charge cards with its Discover card, which offers a very small cash rebate, depending on the amount of purchases charged to the card.

Many cards are issued by banks that affiliate with charitable and fraternal organizations. For example, Citibank issues cards for each of the NFL football teams. Some of these cards are distinguished merely by their artistic design. If it weren't for the annual fee, someone would probably start collecting them as "adult" trading cards—a step up from the old bubble gum cards! Other affiliation cards offer to make a fractional donation to the affiliated charity or organization for each purchase charged to the card. The AT&T Universal card is a Visa or MasterCard that doubles as a long distance discount calling card.

Getting the Best Credit Card Deal

Bankcard Holders of America is a public-interest group that offers consumers advice and information on choosing the best bankcard. For $1.50 the group will send you its "Fair Deal" list of low-interest and/or no-fee bankcards, including toll-free numbers to call for an application. (Bankcard Holders of America, 560 Herndon Parkway, Suite 120, Herndon, VA 22070.)

Statistics show that the average American owns eight credit cards and may be paying annual fees on most of them. With a little careful choosing you can lower the averages—and your credit costs.

CREDIT CARD BILLING DISPUTES

If you use your credit card regularly for major purchases as well as everyday shopping, you will eventually find yourself in some sort of dispute with a merchant. Having made your purchase on a major credit card can work to your benefit in these situations because in many cases the card issuer is obligated to help you handle your dispute.

If there is a billing error, there are specific rules the credit card issuer must follow to correct the problem. They are clearly stated—in very small print—on the annual disclosure form that the credit card company must send you. If you do find an error in billing, you must notify the credit card company *in writing* within 60 days. Be sure to include not only your name, address, and account number, but the amount of the suspected error and the reason why you feel it is in error. While the dispute is being investigated you do not have to pay the bill and you will not incur finance charges.

If the dispute is a result of a problem with the merchant or merchandise you purchased, you may be able to get a refund in the form of a chargeback on your credit card. For example, if you are charged for merchandise you did not receive, or if it was defective or misrepresented, you can ask the credit card company for a chargeback. Again, this request must be filed in writing immediately after the disputed charge appears on your bill. Each card issuer may set a different time limit for filing a dispute on this basis. Check the back of your credit card statement for specific information.

Under federal law, if your credit card is lost or stolen and used without your authorization you can be held liable for the actual amount of the charges up to $50 per card. But if you report the loss before the card is used, federal law says the card issuer cannot make you responsible for any unauthorized charges. Your homeowner's insurance may provide additional insurance to cover the first $50 for which you are responsible.

If you are carrying a wallet full of credit cards and it is lost or stolen, you could still have substantial liability for $50 per card. You should keep a separate list of all the credit cards in your wallet, the card number and expiration date, and the toll-free number of the credit card issuer, which appears on your monthly statement. If your wallet is ever lost, you will not have to try to remember which cards you were carrying. You can simply go down the list and notify the issuers immediately.

There are many services that offer a credit card registry to insure you against loss if your cards are stolen. However, since the limits of liability are so strict, you are probably better off making your own list, saving the fees you would pay to these registry services, and spending the money on something more worthwhile.

BAD CREDIT AND BANKRUPTCY

If you do get into credit troubles you are creating a problem that will stay with you for at least seven years—like the proverbial broken mirror that brings seven years of bad luck.

You'll know you're headed for trouble when your credit card balances start building up to the point where you can only make the minimum payment every month. Then you may find yourself applying for a new credit card to finance new purchases. That's the danger signal. One unexpected problem such as illness or loss of overtime in your job pay, and you'll be unable to make even the minimum payments. That's when you start to ruin your credit record.

If you find yourself overspending on credit, seek help immediately. Most major cities have a local, nonprofit consumer credit counseling service. To find the one nearest you, check your telephone book or write to the National Foundation for Consumer Credit, Inc., Suite 507, 8701 Georgia Ave., Silver Spring, MD 20910.

Beware of "credit counselors" who work at for-profit credit clinics and offer to consolidate your bills and restore your credit. They often charge a fee and do nothing—making your credit situation even worse.

Or you wind up paying very high interest rates that only add to your problems.

At a competent not-for-profit credit service the counselors will help you in two areas. First they'll want to see your outstanding debts—all of them. Then they'll work out a budget for you and sort out how much you can afford to pay monthly. They will then call your creditors and explain the situation. Creditors are not obligated to work with a counseling service, but often they will make accommodations because they want to get paid something—and because they know you are getting professional help.

Sorting out your current mess is just half the problem. The counseling service will work with you—individually or in group sessions—so you can understand why you got into the overspending mess in the first place. It might have seemed like you had good reason—buying furniture or a new wardrobe. But credit counseling often brings out personality factors that induce you to use credit as a form of self-reward. Plan to take part in the counseling program so that you don't get into this mess again.

You should be aware of some of the protection available to you under the Fair Debt Collection Practices Act. The act says that collectors cannot threaten consumers, or try to intimidate them by repeated phone calls, or make the situation public by calling the boss at work in an attempt to embarrass the consumer. It also says that the creditor cannot deceive the borrower by sending official-looking documents that look like a court order or a summons.

If you are really over your head in credit trouble, personal bankruptcy may be the last resort. But you should examine every possible alternative before considering bankruptcy. It immediately ruins any credit you still have, and since it stays on your records for *ten* years, it will ruin your future chances of getting credit. And if you get into credit trouble again, you cannot file for bankruptcy a second time within six years of the first filing.

In 1978 the federal bankruptcy law was changed, making it somewhat more lenient. (Individual states have their own bankruptcy rules, which must coordinate with federal statutes.) You may be allowed to keep more of your individual assets, but bankruptcy should still be considered only after all other alternatives have been exhausted.

For individuals, the most stringent bankruptcy plan is called Chapter 7, under which you file for release of all debts after liquidation of all assets except those protected by law. Federal law provides that individuals can retain $7,500 of equity in a home and about $2,000 in personal property.

Chapter 13 of the bankruptcy code provides a court-approved structured payout to creditors over a period of three to five years. This route to bankruptcy can only be taken by people who have a regular income. The whole idea of Chapter 13 is to allow debtors to retain their personal property while paying off at least a portion of their debt designated by the court.

Both Chapter 7 and Chapter 13 filings are fully reported to the credit bureau—including the full list of creditors and the amount to be paid each month. At the end of the Chapter 13 plan, the bureau will report it as completed, although it will stay on your credit record.

As you can see, bankruptcy is a complicated procedure that certainly requires legal assistance. Be careful, however, about answering newspaper ads offering "quick bankruptcy" and promising that bankruptcy is a way to "obtain a better credit rating." Bankruptcy never improves your credit situation, and ultimately it is never the easy way out.

REESTABLISHING CREDIT

If you have paid off your debts and mended your ways, bad credit reports will still haunt you as you try to reestablish yourself financially. It's difficult to live without a credit card these days—especially when it comes to renting a car or making advance hotel reservations. There is one possible solution.

A few financial institutions will issue you a bankcard as long as you leave cash on deposit with them to cover your charges. These cash-up-front credit cards look like any other MasterCard or Visa, except that your charge privileges are limited to the amount you have on deposit—from $500 to $5,000.

Key Federal Savings Bank of Maryland has issued a quarter of a million bankcards to people who are bad credit risks, and they say they rarely get stuck because of the cash-up-front feature. The card works like any other bankcard, with some fairly stiff credit terms. You are charged interest from the day your purchase is posted—currently at a high 21.9 percent interest rate. There is no annual fee, but putting your cash up front still makes this a fairly expensive card. They do pay you interest of 5.25 percent on any credit balance in excess of $500.

Like other bankcards, you can even get a cash advance of up to 50 percent of your secured credit. And as you build up a good record of payments, they will start to advance you additional unsecured credit.

This type of card is a great first step toward building a credit history because the financial institutions report your payment history to the credit bureau. Once the credit bureau starts showing a positive report, you may receive offers from other, regular card issuers. In fact, Key Federal says that thousands of its cardholders have been able to switch to other, less expensive credit cards.

These cash-up-front cards are not available to just anyone, even if you are willing to make the cash deposit. Only about 60 percent of applicants are accepted for the program. They turn down people who already have huge current delinquencies.

These cards are also an excellent way for people without a credit history—students or the newly divorced or widowed—to establish credit.

For more information on the cash-up-front credit card, write to Key Federal Savings Bank, 626 Revolution St., Havre de Grace, MD 21078, or call 301-939-4840 and they'll send you an application.

CHAPTER

Loans

FAST CASH

It's late at night or on the weekend and you suddenly need cash fast. Where can you get it? You might want to consider keeping a small amount of cash in a safe place at home, just for emergencies. But you should also know where you can get extra money quickly.

The first obvious source is accessing your checking account, even after regular banking hours, through an automatic teller machine. Make sure to get your ATM card and personal identification number (PIN number) when you open your bank account. You may not use the ATM regularly, but it is good to have in case of emergencies.

You should also check to see if your bank offers emergency overdraft provisions for your checking account. That would allow you to withdraw extra money through the ATM, or to walk into the bank and write yourself a check for cash greater than the amount of your current checking balance.

Fast cash does not come cheaply, and using a bank overdraft provision is probably one of the more expensive forms of credit. But it is instantaneous, if you have made advance provisions with your bank or S&L.

Your travel or bank card can also be a source of fast cash. For years you have been able to use American Express cards to cash personal checks at any of the 6,000 American Express travel service offices.

Now if you have an Amex card you can walk into any one of their offices, present the card, and—with proper identification—get cash directly from American Express. If you have a green American Express card, you can get up to $1,000 within a seven-day period. They will give you the first $200 in cash and the balance in traveler's checks. Holders of American Express Gold cards can get up to $2,500 in cash and traveler's checks, and Platinum cards will get you up to $1,000 in cash and $10,000 in traveler's checks in any 30-day period.

American Express cards also work in most bank ATM machines, allowing you to draw cash up to the limit set by the bank that owns the machine. American Express has its own Express cash machines at major airports that dispense both cash and traveler's checks. If you're out of town and wondering what machine will accept your American Express card, you can call toll-free 1-800-CASH NOW for the location of the nearest ATM machine that accepts Amex cards.

You can also get cash by using your Visa or MasterCard. If you take your card to almost any bank you will be allowed to draw against your line of credit. If you have a gold card you automatically have a $5,000 line of credit, and if you don't have a current balance you may be allowed to draw up to your complete line of credit. You will need proof of identity before they will dispense cash.

Now the bankcard companies are making it even easier to use your card to get cash through the ATM networks around the country. All banks that issue MasterCards must offer their cardholders ATM cash through a new national network that includes most ATM machines. If you see a CIRRUS logo or MasterCard logo on an ATM machine, all you have to do is insert your MasterCard and punch in your PIN number. Visa cards work in the Plus network machines along with other local networks.

You can withdraw cash as a charge against your credit card up to the limits established by the bank that owns the machine. Many place a limit of $200 in cash withdrawals a day, even though your line of credit on the card may be much greater. The system works around the world; if you are in a foreign country the withdrawal will be in local currency, but will be charged against your account in dollars.

Remember that you are paying for the convenience of this fast cash. Many bankcards start charging interest from the moment the withdrawal is posted, and the interest rates you pay on these quick "loans" are charged at the same rate as for outstanding balances—usually in the 18 to 21 percent range.

Sending Cash

Now what happens if you need to send fast cash to someone out of town? There are several alternatives. Western Union is the best-known money transfer service, although American Express is getting into the business also.

Last year Western Union handled about 10.8 billion money transfers amounting to nearly $3 billion. The average transaction was less than $300. To use their services you must bring cash or cashier's checks to any of the 13,000 Western Union offices. Or, by using a telephone, you can send up to $2,000 anywhere in the United States using a Visa or MasterCard charge card.

To pick up the funds at the receiving end, the payee must present two forms of identification and identify the sender's name, location, and amount of the transfer. Generally the money is paid out in cash at the Western Union office, although when larger amounts are transferred Western Union may give you a draft that can be cashed at a local bank.

American Express has a new MoneyGram service that competes with Western Union. It claims to have an advantage over Western Union when it comes to *international* money transfers—promising cash will be available at one of its international offices within ten minutes, while Western Union promises the money in two to three days.

Fees for these cash transfer services depend upon the amount of money handled. American Express charges $11 for every $100 wired, while Western Union charges $14 for each $100.

If you need to send larger amounts of money immediately, consider using the Federal Reserve Bank wire transfer system. This allows you to wire money directly from your bank account into another bank account in a distant city. Many banks will require a 12- to 24-hour wait before granting access to the money at the receiving bank.

Fees for wire transfers range from about $15 to $20 for a domestic transfer to as much as $55 for an international transfer. There is one drawback to using the bank wire transfer system: Since it operates through the Federal Reserve Bank, transfers must be made during normal banking hours.

You can't predict exactly when you're going to need fast cash. But if you know in advance how to get cash on a weekend or evening, in or out of town, you're one step ahead of the game.

PERSONAL LOANS

If you are really short of money, you might want to take out a personal loan. To obtain an *unsecured* loan of from $500 to $2,500 you will have to approach either a bank, S&L, credit union, or finance company. You are asking them to lend you money just on your "signature"—your promise to repay. Since they will have no collateral to repossess if you default, the financial institution will check your credit very carefully.

Depending on current market conditions, a bank or savings and loan where you have an account will probably offer the lowest rate on an unsecured personal loan. But it may also take longer to get approval for the loan. Some institutions will not make unsecured personal loans unless you have another account with them.

Finance companies generally charge higher rates (subject to state usury laws), but may be set up to give faster approval—usually within a day or two. They are generally on-line with the major credit bureaus and can check your credit immediately.

Your company credit union may be the cheapest and fastest way to get an unsecured personal loan. As a member of the credit union you can borrow up to the specific limits of the union, and you are not limited by the amount you have on deposit there.

What does a bank or finance company look for in granting an unsecured personal loan?

• First they will want to see what you already owe, and the amount of your monthly payments. Generally speaking, they will decline credit if your monthly payments (excluding mortgage) exceed 20 to 25 percent of your take-home pay.

- They will want evidence of financial stability—easier to demonstrate if you are older (although they are not allowed to discriminate because of age). They will certainly ask for proof of income and length of time on the job (which they will verify with your employer).

- They will ask the reason for the loan. They want to make sure it is going for what they consider a reasonable purpose, which helps them estimate the likelihood of getting repaid.

These same financial institutions also offer *secured* loans—secured by the equity in your home, car, or other personal possessions.

HOME EQUITY LOANS

Many years ago, it was common for people to borrow money on the equity in their homes by taking out a second mortgage. Usually they were unwilling to refinance the first mortgage, probably because rates had moved higher. And lenders were willing to make second mortgages at slightly higher rates because they had the security of the first mortgage in their portfolio.

Today there is still a demand from homeowners to tap the rising equity value in their homes. In fact, borrowing on home equity got a huge boost when interest on consumer loans was phased out as a tax deduction. Since interest on mortgages and property loans is still deductible up to certain limits, tapping into home equity to borrow money became not only available, but attractive as an income tax shelter. Current tax law says you can borrow up to $100,000 on your home equity above your original mortgage indebtedness while retaining full deductibility of the interest expense.

Banks, S&Ls, and finance companies rushed to satisfy the demand, creating home equity loans with all sorts of features designed to make borrowing easy and relatively cheap. Today there is an estimated $6 billion worth of home equity loans on the books of financial institutions, and the number is growing each year.

A word of warning about home equity loans before we begin to look at the terms and features. These loans are suddenly as easy to get as credit cards—and as easy to use. That puts a great temptation on the homeowner to borrow money for basically nonproductive purposes—a vacation, a car, consolidating credit card debts.

Borrowing on the equity in your home should be reserved for value-building investments such as improving your home or paying for a child's college tuition. It's good to know that the equity is available in emergency situations, but using home equity for nonproductive purposes can be dangerous. Remember, if they come after you for nonpayment, they're not just repossessing a car or TV. This time they take your home!

With that solemn thought in mind, you should be aware of the ins and outs of home equity borrowing. All home equity loans require many of the same steps you took in getting a mortgage. All lenders will want to check your credit record, and will want to have a new appraisal of the home (unless you recently took out a mortgage with the same lender). But not all home equity loans or lines of credit are alike in their costs, terms, and repayment plans.

A home equity *loan* is much like a second mortgage. When you are approved, the lender will give you the amount you asked for either in the form of a check or in a deposit to your account with the lender. You will start paying interest from the moment you take out the loan.

A home equity *line of credit* works somewhat differently. You are approved to borrow up to a certain limit. You can draw down the money as needed and repay it at your convenience—subject to certain minimum monthly payments that depend on the amount borrowed. You can borrow on your line of credit and repay as many times as you like. You don't pay interest until you actually use the money from your line of credit.

Most rates on home equity loans and lines of credit are tied to an index usually the prime rate (the rate banks charge their best customers to borrow). But since you are only a "good" customer, and not the bank's "best" customer, your rate will usually be one or two percentage points above the prime rate. That means that your "affordable" home equity loan today, could become a huge burden if interest rates climb dramatically. In the early 1980s few borrowers dreamed that the prime rate would rise above 20 percent, but it did.

If you take out a $25,000 home equity loan when the prime rate is 8.5 percent and if the terms call for prime plus one percent, then your original monthly payment on the loan will be $195.21. But if prime climbs to 11.5 percent, your payment will jump to $256.85 a month. Most home equity loans will have a cap that limits how high the interest rate can go. Some have caps as high as 18 percent. At that rate, your $25,000 loan would have a monthly payment of $369.86. Now you can see one of the dangers of home equity loans—floating rates can cost you a lot of money.

The second danger of home equity loans comes in the fine print — the repayment terms. Often, a home equity loan will seem more affordable than it really is because the terms call for you to repay "interest only" for the first few years. Not only are the payments lower, but they are completely tax deductible. That's a real attraction—until you realize that at some point down the line you must pay off the balance in full.

Generally these home equity loans are structured interest-only for the first five or seven years, and then a balloon payment of the entire loan is due. Will you have the money to pay off the loan in full in five or seven years? Will you be able to qualify for another home equity loan at whatever the prevailing rates are then? Will your credit be good enough then to get a second mortgage or refinance your first mortgage? Will your house be worth enough to justify such a large mortgage seven years from now?

These are the uncertainties of taking out a home equity loan and paying interest-only while you use the money. Remember, if you have to answer no to any of these questions, the lender could foreclose on your home. Some lenders recognize the inherent problems in this situation and either structure their home equity loans to be fully repaid in a short period of time or promise to convert your home equity loan to a second mortgage when the balloon comes due. It pays to make sure in advance that your balloon cannot burst.

BORROWING ON STOCK MARGIN ACCOUNTS

There is one other way to raise money that is often overlooked. You may own stocks that you have no desire to sell because the tax on the profits would be too great, and because you do not want to get out of the investment. These stocks can be a source of quick, cheap money simply by using a margin account—which means that the brokerage firm will lend you up to 50 percent of the market value of your stocks. If your stocks are held by your broker, this is a very simple process. If you keep your certificates at home or in a safe-deposit box, you will have to bring them in to the broker.

The stocks are signed over to the brokerage firm's name. That does not affect your holding period for tax purposes or your receipt of dividends or stock splits. They will be automatically credited to your account at the brokerage firm. If you later pay off the margin loan, you can ask for the stocks to be reregistered in your name and have the certificates sent back to you.

The advantage to using your stocks for a quick cash loan is the low interest rate charged by most brokerage firms. Generally the broker loan rate is tied to the bank prime rate, or the rate at which brokerage firms can borrow money. The firms then charge their customers about $1/2$ to $1^1/2$ percent over their own cost of money. They may even give customers with very large margin accounts a slightly lower rate. Since the brokerage firm can borrow at close to the prime rate, the interest charged on margin accounts is a real bargain compared to interest charged on credit cards.

There is no limit on the amount of cash you can raise this way. Brokerage firms will lend up to 50 percent of the current market value of stocks listed on the New York and American stock exchanges and on many over-the-counter stocks. In fact, at many firms, the larger your borrowing through your margin account, the lower the interest rate you are charged.

There *is* one catch: If the price of the stock starts to fall, the brokerage firm can call you and ask you to put more money into your account. They are limited by federal law to lending only 50 percent of the value of your stocks, and if your stock value drops you are liable to make up the difference.

If you cannot put up the cash to bring your account into the 50 percent balance, they have the right to sell your stock at the market price. So you don't want to use this form of borrowing if your stocks are very volatile or if the market is falling. But it can be a nice source of fast cash at relatively low interest rates if a crisis occurs.

BORROWING NUMBERS

Borrowing money for consumer purchases simply doesn't make sense these days. In the first place, consumer interest disappears as a tax deduction in 1991. In the second place, most consumer finance rates are far above the rate you can earn on your savings by leaving the money in the bank. Still the figures on outstanding consumer credit continue to grow—$694 billion at last count, and that excludes mortgage debt.

If you need to borrow money in spite of the financial logic, you should be aware of the *true cost*—that is, the real amount you will be repaying in interest on the loan. While that seems like a simple observation, there are actually several different ways to calculate the interest on any loan. Even though it may appear at first glance that you are paying the same interest *rate,* the method of calculating the payments could result in big differences in the *amount* you are repaying over the long run.

The one absolute method of comparison is the APR, or *annual percentage rate.* Under the 1969 Truth in Lending Act lenders may calculate their interest rate and other finance charges in any way they want, but the total real costs must be expressed in terms of the annual percentage rate.

Take a $1,000 loan for one year at 12 percent interest. The best deal for the consumer is a simple interest loan on which interest is paid only on the declining balance outstanding. On this loan the APR will be 12 percent, and at the end of one year you will have paid $66.08 in interest. If that same $1,000, one-year loan is quoted as a 12 percent *add-on* rate, the APR is really 21.46 percent, and at the end of one year you will have paid $120 in interest. If the same loan is expressed as 12 percent *discount* interest, the APR is 24.28 percent, and at the end of one year you will have paid $136.36 in interest.

Here's how *add-on* interest works. In our example of borrowing $1,000 at 12 percent per year, the total interest charge would be $120. The lender adds that amount to the principal, making a total of $1,120. That $1,120 is then divided by 12 to give you 12 equal monthly payments of $93.33 each. So with the add-on loan you receive $1,000 in cash and repay $1,120.

Here's the catch. With a simple interest loan you only pay interest on the outstanding balance that declines every month. But with add-on interest you pay interest on the full amount of the loan, even though you have to repay 1/12th of the amount every month. So during the second month you only have use of 11/12ths of the money, and by the final month you only have use of 1/12th of the original loan. Still you're paying interest on the money for the entire term of the loan, so the true interest cost—the annual percentage rate—is much higher.

If a lender uses the *discount* interest method of calculating a loan, it will cost you even more. In this case, the lender figures the interest—$120—and then subtracts the interest from the amount of the loan. The difference is the actual amount lent to the borrower. So even if you are borrowing $1,000, the lender gives you a check for $880. In essence, you are paying the interest up front. And since you do not have the full use of the money for any of the term of the loan, the effective interest rate is higher.

In the case of both add-on and discount interest rate loans you have the use of the original loan amount for only about half of the repayment period. Because of that, the annual percentage rate is roughly twice the stated interest rate on this type of loan. And if this is a multi-year loan, the true APR is even higher—27.87 percent for the discount 12 percent loan if the term is two years.

When it comes to credit card finance charges there's more at stake than just knowing the true interest rate you are being charged. Some card issuers charge interest only on the unpaid balance. Others base their finance charges on the average daily balance. Some cards will give you a 25-day grace period, while others charge you interest from the date of purchase—especially if you already have an outstanding balance due on your card.

These differences may add up to just pennies a month if you owe only a small amount. But if you're making a larger purchase such as a used car, the difference over a few years can be substantial.

Consumers who borrow money may run into one other bit of perplexing interest rate calculations if they decide to repay a loan early. Suppose you borrowed $1,000 for one year for a total repayment cost of $1,120. If you decide to repay the loan in six months, you might think that you owe only $60—*half* the original amount of interest. But that's not the way banks and finance companies figure it.

If you repay a loan early you are certainly entitled to pay less total interest, but the amount you are obligated to pay may not be directly proportional to the time you have kept the money. Instead many banks, finance companies, and insurance companies use something called the Rule of 78s to figure out just how much interest you owe.

Remember that when you took out the loan you had use of the entire amount for the first month; then you made a payment and had use of 11/12ths of the loan amount for the second month. During the third month you had use of 10/12ths of the money. So the bank may feel it is entitled to more interest in the early months because you had use of more money earlier on.

If you add up all those "twelfths" in one year, you get a total of 78 twelfths. The bank counts up how many twelfths of a year you had use of the money. This formula, called the rule of 78s, allows the bank to figure out exactly how much interest to charge you based on the amount of time you had use of its money. It also shows how much interest to rebate to you if you pay off your loan early. Because this method results in higher costs to consumers and penalizes prepayments, many states have outlawed its use.

When you are borrowing money for any reason, be sure to ask for the annual percentage rate. That's the only reliable way to compare borrowing costs. Also ask for the total amount of interest to be paid over the life of the loan. That will help you judge whether it's worth borrowing to buy something you want. And be sure to ask if there is a penalty for prepayment of the loan, or how much interest you will be charged if you repay the money early.

CHAPTER 7

Buying a House

Buying your own home is probably the most expensive—and emotional—purchase you will ever make, so it's important you do your homework *before* you take that big step. Although rising home prices and high interest rates have made it harder to take that first step into the housing market, it remains a goal for most families and many singles. And with good reason. Home ownership provides not only shelter, but a form of economic security. That's why it is considered part of the "American dream."

AN ECONOMIC OVERVIEW

Shelter is one of life's basic necessities. When you pay rent, you are spending money regularly but will have little to show for it in the future. When you buy a home, your monthly payments may be slightly larger, but you are building *equity* (ownership) in a piece of property. In fact, not only are you buying shelter and building equity, but you may be making your best investment.

Traditionally, home prices have risen fast enough to actually beat increases in the cost of living. For many people, the family home has been a better investment than stocks, precious metals, or collectibles over the long run. But there are always downturns in the economy and in the housing market. Recessions lower buyers' incomes and their ability to buy homes. Certain areas of the country may be depressed economically for a period of time so home prices in that region suffer. But overall, the last two generations of Americans have valued their homes not only as shelter, but as a good investment.

That may not always be the case in the future. One reason that home prices beat inflation over the years was that buyers were "subsidized" by fixed, low-interest rate mortgages. Back in the 1970s lenders were still making the traditional 30-year, fixed-rate mortgages—at 7 and 8 percent. But then in the late seventies and early eighties, inflation pushed interest rates into double digit levels. Home prices soared along with inflation, and homeowners who were lucky enough to have those low, fixed-rate mortgages profited. Their monthly payments remained locked in at low levels, and they were repaying their loans in dollars made less valuable by inflation.

Lenders were stuck. But then, in the early eighties, banks and savings and loans were allowed to pay market interest rates on savings deposits. In fact, they had to compete for deposits by offering the highest rates. But they were stuck earning low rates of interest on those old fixed-rate mortgages. The result: big losses. Bankers quickly learned their lesson and developed new adjustable-rate mortgage products, forcing buyers to take some of the interest rate risk. Many financial institutions continued to make some fixed-rate loans, but they saved their best deals for adjustable-rate mortgages. That way they would be protected in the next round of rate increases. By 1990, adjustable-rate mortgages accounted for 28 percent of all new home loans.

Lenders took one other step to protect their balance sheets. Instead of keeping the mortgages in the bank's own portfolio they took advantage of new federal programs to "package" a group of mortgages and sell them in a fast-growing secondary mortgage market. That meant that while the homeowner may have continued to make monthly payments to the local bank or S&L, the actual owner of the mortgage was an investor far removed from the local lender. The resale process allowed local institutions to replenish their supply of funds to make more loans.

These days, without the subsidy of low, fixed-rate mortgages, home price appreciation is not nearly as inevitable. Over the previous 20 inflationary years, the family home had become a substitute for savings and investing—a well of "easy money" to tap for everything from college educations to vacations.

Today home prices still rise with inflation, and in some prosperous areas where housing is in demand, single-family home prices far outstrip inflation. But in spite of those real estate courses on cable television that promise you can make a fortune in the housing market, buying a family home should still be viewed mainly as an equity-building investment in shelter, not a substitute for a regular savings and investment plan—and certainly not as a get-rich-quick scheme.

FIGURING YOUR FINANCES

Before you start looking for your dream house, you should figure out just how much of your dream you can afford. That means figuring out just how much cash you can accumulate for a down payment, and how much a lender will allow you to borrow for a mortgage.

For most conventional mortgages you will need at least a 10 percent down payment. But don't despair if you can't round up the cash. You can turn to several government-sponsored mortgage programs that require less money down. And many lenders will allow you to use a gift of a down payment from a relative if it's documented with a letter.

If you have the down payment you also need to figure out just what price home you can afford. Most lenders say a buyer's monthly mortgage payment should not take more than 28 percent of his or her gross income (before taxes). Lenders also take into consideration your other regular monthly debts and obligations, and that may reduce the amount they figure you can afford to spend on a mortgage payment each month. Some lenders might be more flexible about the percent of your income that can go toward the mortgage.

Many major lenders will tell you *before* you go house shopping exactly how large a mortgage they are willing to finance for you, given your personal economic circumstances. Check with your local financial institutions to see if you can get one of these commitments, subject to appraisal of the home, of course. When you know where you stand financially, your real estate agent can show you homes that fit your spending bracket.

Most lenders will have a chart that shows you how expensive a house your income will support, but here's an easy rule to give you a rough guideline (assuming you don't have a lot of other debt). If you're going to make a 10 percent down payment and mortgage rates are around 10 percent, you should be able to afford a house that's priced at twice your annual income. That means you would be able to buy a $150,000 home if you have annual income of $75,000 and have saved enough money to put $15,000 as a down payment. If you can afford a 20 percent down payment, you might afford a house that costs three times your gross family income.

In addition to saving up the down payment and figuring out how expensive a house you can shop for, you need to attend to one other financial detail before you go house shopping. You should have cash ready in your checking or money market account so you can put up *earnest money* immediately when you decide to make a bid on the house. It's not enough just to submit an offer to the seller; you'll have to attach a check for about 5 to 10 percent of the purchase price. In some regions of the country a check for only $1,000 is considered enough earnest money. Check with your broker to determine local custom.

Earnest money sent in with an offer to buy is the seller's security that you will indeed go through with the purchase once the offer is accepted and the house is taken off the market. The earnest money should be given to the broker, not the seller, to hold until it is either applied to the purchase price, refunded, or kept by the seller in case of a default. You should ask for the earnest money to be put in an interest-bearing escrow account with the interest credited to you. Since the seller has certain rights to the earnest money, you should carefully review all the details of your offer before you submit it to the seller.

HOUSE SHOPPING

About 5 percent of American families purchase a new home every year. Statistics show that they spend, on average, three weeks looking for the "right" home and making their lending decision. Clearly, this most important purchase also has a strong subjective aspect. Beyond all the facts, most families just decide they like one particular house!

When shopping for a house there are many things to look for aside from the financial issues. Probably the most critical is the neighborhood and the local school system. Even if you do not have school-age children, a good educational system raises the property resale value of all homes in the neighborhood. You'll also have to discipline yourself not to fall in love with the most expensive home on the block. It is much wiser to buy a smaller home in an area of more expensive properties.

You will probably be dealing with a real estate agent or salesperson when you search for a home. It's important to be honest with the agent about your financial limitations. However, when shopping for a home—even with *your own* agent rather than the listing broker—you should be aware that the agent actually represents the seller, not you. The broker taking you to see houses is actually a subagent of the listing broker. And it is a broker's obligation to get the best price for the home seller.

Keep that in mind when you make an offer somewhat below your top price. It may be wise not to let your broker/agent know exactly how high you are prepared to go. Of course your broker wants to see you buy a home and wants to see a deal made, but the broker also has a certain obligation to the seller. After all, it's the seller who pays the commission!

Before you make an offer, be aware of what other homes in the neighborhood have sold for recently. If you are moving to a new city you might be pleasantly surprised at different property values—and you don't want to bid too high. You can ask your broker to show you "comparables"—recent sales prices and listing prices of other homes in the area. Be sure to ask how long the property you are looking at has been on the market.

One other word of financial advice when it comes to buying a home: You will pay top price if the house is in top condition. "Move-in" condition is appealing to many buyers, and you may figure that not spending time with construction people and decorators is worth paying a higher price. But the real bargains go to those who can see beyond current disrepair to a sound structure and good layout.

When buying a home, always make an offer subject to inspection by a professional within one week. You can consult the phone book or ask your broker to recommend a professional building inspector to check for structural defects in a roof, and for problems in electrical or heating systems. Many real estate brokerage firms also offer a warranty insuring the structure and major appliances for a period of one year after purchase. The cost is generally $250 to $500.

Negotiating the purchase of a home is one of the biggest business deals you may ever make, and it may also be the most emotional one. The secret is to separate the emotion from the finances. Determine the top price you are willing to pay. In some "hot" real estate markets you may find yourself paying the asking price—or even higher. But if you feel you can purchase the house for less than the asking price, make sure you don't insult the seller by trying to "steal" it.

A reasonable first offer might be 10 or 15 percent below the asking price. Give the seller only a few days to respond. A counteroffer slightly lower than the original asking price means the seller is willing to negotiate. But it's unwise to get into a nickel and dime, back and forth game. Instead you might want to ask the seller to throw in a few extras—the refrigerator or chandelier, for instance. That allows everybody to save face and bring the deal to a conclusion.

Be careful when adding extras to your bid for the house. Personal property such as furniture or draperies, or even a boat that might come with the deal are not financeable as part of your mortgage. The appraised price of the house must justify the amount you are asking for in a mortgage. You may have to make a separate deal for personal property you are purchasing from the seller and present a separate check at the closing.

When you make your offer, you will attach certain conditions, in addition to naming your price. You will want to:

- give the seller a set period of time—two days to seven days—to accept or reject your offer
- make your offer subject to your ability to obtain financing
- establish a set time to take possession of the property—perhaps within 30 days of closing
- set the closing date for a reasonable period of time

- set a penalty cost that must be paid every day the seller is late in vacating the property
- list all the items that the seller has agreed to leave for you—everything from storm windows to lighting fixtures
- include a provision that allows you a final inspection of the house just prior to closing, to make sure no damage has been done as they move out

If you didn't have a mortgage commitment (or cash) lined up before you started house shopping, you will have to make your offer to purchase subject to getting a mortgage. Most sellers will be willing to give you at least 30 to 45 days to get a mortgage commitment. Your broker should be able to help you arrange financing, or you can do it yourself through your own bank or savings and loan. And just when you're delighted about finally making a deal to buy the house of your dreams you'll come face to face with the multiple-choice world of mortgage options.

UNDERSTANDING MORTGAGES

Your mortgage will probably be the largest loan commitment you will make in your lifetime. If you think it pays to shop around for the best deal on a car or a credit card, the potential costs and savings are magnified hundreds of times when it comes to getting a mortgage. For instance, if you take out a $100,000 mortgage for 30 years at 10 percent, you will be paying back more than $215,000 over the life of your mortgage loan. So it pays to understand the details when you take out your loan and to shop around for the best rates and terms.

Your real estate broker will help to put you in touch with local lenders who offer the best deals. You are most likely to get a mortgage loan from a savings and loan, a bank, or a mortgage company. When you shop for a mortgage you will be looking not only for the best deal (rate and points) but also for the most reliable lender—one who will give you quick approval and a firm commitment to the promised deal for at least 45 days.

Rates and Points

Obviously the interest rate on the mortgage is the first thing you will look for. Even one-eighth of a percent can wind up saving—or costing—you a lot of money over the life of a 30-year mortgage. For instance on a 10 percent, 30-year $100,000 mortgage, an additional half percent costs an extra $37.17 per month, or $13,381 over the 30-year life of the loan.

The other key ingredient to compare is the *points* you will have to pay. One point is equal to 1 percent of the total amount you are borrowing. If you are borrowing $90,000, then one point is $900; two points would cost $1,800. The points are paid up front, at the time of the closing and are paid directly to the lender.

Many lenders will ask you to pay two or three points. When rates are rising, lenders want to make sure they make money on the loan deal even if they commit to a fixed rate before closing, so they may even ask for more points. Your tax advisor may suggest that you pay the points with a separate check at the closing so they can be taken as a tax-deductible item.

Points are not considered part of the principal amount of the loan, but they are a cost of financing your house. So you should ask your lender to give you not only the mortgage rate, but the *annual percentage rate* of your loan. The points are taken into account when figuring the APR, and that will raise the true percentage cost of your loan.

The rate and points are the key ingredients in the cost of a loan, and they can change rapidly as the general level of interest rates in the economy moves up and down in response to changing economic forecasts. Since it may take one to two months to close on your purchase (including the time it takes for approval of your loan and other legal details) make sure the lender gives you a firm commitment to your deal. A *commitment* is the lender's promise that—subject to a check of your credit and appraisal of the house—you will indeed get the promised mortgage at the promised rate and terms if you close within a specific period of time, usually 45 to 90 days. This commitment should be made in writing because oral promises do not stand up in court.

Some lenders allow you to lock in the rate and points on the date you apply for the loan; others will not fix the terms until the loan is actually approved. Since approval can take several days or more, you could be running a risk of paying higher rates. Other lenders say they will set the rate only on the date of final closing—an even greater risk. So it's wise to check not only the rate being offered, but the "lock-in" policy of the lender.

Many mortgage seekers have been enticed by ads promising the lowest rates, only to find they cannot get a firm commitment, or that the rates are low, but the points are outrageous. Especially when mortgage rates are rising quickly, you need a lender that will not come up with loopholes to get out of a commitment. For example, in the past during times of heavy refinancing, the appraisal process stretched out for weeks or months. Some lenders took advantage of this delay to renege on their promised low rates. Choose a reputable lender with a long track record in your locality.

Down Payment

The third key element in your home financing decision is the down payment. If you have only a small amount of savings you will have very little choice. Most lenders will demand at least 10 percent down unless you are using special VA or FHA mortgage programs. However, if you have a large sum of money saved up you will have to decide how much you want to put down on the house. There are a number of things to keep in mind.

First, the 1987 tax law allows deductions only on a home acquisition mortgage, plus a $100,000 home equity loan. Thus, if you pay a substantial amount down to buy the house and later decide you want to borrow money on your equity, your interest deduction will be limited.

Second, you don't want to put all your cash down on the purchase of the home, leaving yourself no ready cash for emergencies. You might be wise to put 20 percent of the purchase price down and leave the balance of your savings in a money market account earning interest. That will allow you to keep a reserve for home improvements or emergencies—and to diversify your investment dollars.

For those who consider a home purchase as an investment only, the smaller the down payment, the greater the leverage. If you buy the home with $10,000 down and it appreciates in price by $10,000, you have a 100 percent return on your investment. That's small comfort, unless you intend to sell the house.

The main advantage to making a larger down payment is that the lender will be slightly more accommodating and is likely to approve your loan more quickly. The other advantage to a large down payment is that it will lower your overall interest cost on the mortgage over the years and allow you to own your home outright much sooner. As we'll see later, that can give you a certain peace of mind, but it also limits your tax deductions.

Applying for Your Mortgage

It's fairly expensive just to apply for a mortgage. The lender will ask for a nonrefundable application fee that usually runs about $200 to $300. This covers the cost of the time to take your application, check your credit, appraise the property, and do the paperwork. So while it may be tempting to apply for a mortgage at more than one institution "just in case," it can also be expensive.

You will have to pay some other fees as well. Both the lender and your lawyer will want a title search to make sure the seller has clear title to the property and there are no liens or unpaid taxes. The buyer may want to buy a title insurance policy just to protect against any liens that do not show up in a title search. The buyer will also pay the fee for a qualified appraiser hired by the lender.

The first big hurdle in the application process is filling out the application itself. Here your broker will be of real assistance, but you should also come prepared with the proper information. Decide beforehand whether the property will be titled alone or in joint name with a spouse, relative, or friend. Anyone whose name appears on the title will also be considered a mortgageholder and will have to take part in the mortgage application process.

You will need Social Security numbers, previous addresses, W-2 forms showing income, and, possibly, tax returns for recent years, especially if you are self-employed. If you currently have a mortgage, be prepared to give the lender's name and address and your account number. As part of the application you will also need to make out a personal balance sheet, showing all your assets such as CDs, stocks, other property owned, personal property, and cash value of life insurance. The other half of the balance sheet lists your current outstanding debts—including other mortgages, credit card or installment loan debts, and car loans. Alimony or child support may be considered as income for purposes of granting the loan, although the lender may verify the regularity of payments. If you are responsible for paying alimony or child support, list that figure on your balance sheet as a regular obligation. The lender will contact a national credit bureau to verify this information (see Chapter 5), so before applying make sure that there is no erroneous information on your credit record.

Once you have made an application for your mortgage loan, check frequently on the progress of the approval process. When there is a lot of action in the home-buying or refinancing markets, lenders have been known to let things slide until the last minute—causing real problems right before closing. Remember, your contract with the seller specifies that you must close in a certain period of time or forfeit your earnest money. You should keep track of conversations with the lender to make sure things are proceeding smoothly. Of course, that's one reason to deal with a local institution that has a reputation for reliability.

It usually takes at least a month to close on a home because there are innumerable details to consider before the transaction is finished. That's why you should have a competent real estate attorney assisting you, along with your broker. Your lawyer will check for technical things such as the status of property tax payments and utility bills and will guide you through the proper exchange of documents at the closing.

MORTGAGE CHOICES

The first step in getting a mortgage is dealing with the lender. The lender has the power to choose whether to grant you a mortgage. But, as agonizing as the approval process may be, the second half of the mortgage decision-making process may be equally painful. This time it is up to *you* to decide what type of mortgage best suits your needs.

For many years, the typical single-family mortgage had a fixed rate and a term of 30 years. All of that changed in the early 1980s, when inflation pushed interest rates sky high. While you can still get the traditional mortgage, borrowers are now faced with a bewildering array of mortgage options. Rates are *fixed* or *floating*. And floating rates are tied to all sorts of other indices or rates.

Some rates change annually, others change every few years, and some are planned so that monthly payments gradually move higher. You can pay your mortgage monthly or biweekly. Terms of 15 years are now common, allowing a huge savings in interest over the life of the loan. Many government agencies and states offer special programs for first-time or low-income homebuyers. How do you choose?

The first step in choosing a mortgage is to figure out just how large a monthly payment you can afford. As we noted earlier, most lenders figure you should be able to pay about 28 percent of your monthly income in housing costs. Another way of figuring your allowable monthly payment is to take 36 percent of your gross income and then subtract your regular monthly obligations. The balance is the amount you can spend on a monthly mortgage payment.

Keep in mind that your monthly mortgage payment includes not only the principal and interest you are paying to the lender, but also an additional amount that the lender will set aside to cover real estate taxes and homeowner's insurance. This whole payment is called PITI (principal, interest, taxes, and insurance). If you are buying a condo, the lender will also take into account the monthly association dues.

The lender has a definite interest in seeing that your property taxes are paid on time and that the property is fully insured. So the lender collects this amount from you as part of your monthly payment, sets the money aside in an escrow account, and pays the property tax and insurance bill out of this account. With a fixed-rate mortgage your principal and interest payment remain the same each month, but rising property taxes or insurance rates could increase your overall monthly payment during the life of the loan.

Generally, you will have figured out how much you can afford to spend each month, and therefore how expensive a house you can afford, before you went house shopping. But there are ways to stretch your budget by choosing a more flexible type of mortgage. Or, by choosing a shorter-term mortgage, you can pay off your home early and save hundreds of thousands of dollars in interest.

30-Year or 15-Year Mortgage?

For example, a $100,000 standard 30-year fixed-rate mortgage at 9.5 percent will cost you $841 a month in principal and interest. Over the life of the loan, you will pay out a total of $202,708 in interest. But if you can afford to spend a little more every month—and if you plan to live in the house for a long time and ultimately want to own it free and clear—you might consider a 15-year mortgage. Lenders generally charge a slightly lower interest rate on a 15-year mortgage than on a 30-year. So let's assume you'd get the same $100,000 mortgage at 9.25 percent for 15 years. Now your monthly payment will rise to $1,029 a month for principal and interest. But the house will be paid off in 15 years, and the total interest paid will be only $85,254. You will have "saved" $117,454 in interest over the life of the loan.

A 15-year mortgage might be considered a "forced savings" plan, helping you build equity instead of spending your money elsewhere or choosing a different investment plan. If a young couple just starting out could afford it, they would have their home paid for before the children start college. Older buyers might be glad to have a home completely paid for before retiring.

Of course, home mortgage interest remains one of the few tax deductions available to most consumers, and for that reason many people would rather buy a more expensive house with a higher monthly payment than pay off a mortgage early. After all, to the extent that mortgage interest is deductible, it lowers your annual income tax bill.

Biweekly Mortgage

If you want to pay off your mortgage early but can't afford the higher monthly payments with a 15-year mortgage, you might see if your bank will make arrangements to let you pay your mortgage biweekly. With this system, a homeowner makes 26 payments a year instead of 12 monthly payments. The smaller payments are made every two weeks and work out to about half the regular monthly payment. With this system there will be two additional biweekly payments each year. These extra payments, plus the speeded up payment process, help reduce the principal and cut interest costs.

In our example of a 30-year, fixed-rate mortgage at 9.5 percent, instead of paying out $202,708 in interest over the life of the loan, the biweekly mortgage payer would pay a total of only $132,931 in interest. Since the life of the loan is shortened as the principal is paid down faster, there is a tremendous savings in total interest cost.

Prepaying Your Mortgage

Even if you do not want to rigidly structure additional payments, you should ask if your lender has a penalty for prepayments. If there is no prepayment penalty, you might want to regularly pay an additional amount of principal each month as long as you can afford it. Make sure it is clearly labeled as an *additional principal payment*. Or you might choose to make a one-time additional prepayment if you suddenly receive some money. In that case, be sure the payment is credited toward principal.

At the end of the year, your lender should give you a statement showing the interest you paid during the year and the amount of the outstanding mortgage balance. It should not come as a surprise that the mortgage balance you owe hardly declines in the first few years of the loan. That's because the first years' payments are primarily interest. In the first year you will pay off only about one-half of one percent of your outstanding loan. Only in the last ten years of a 30-year loan will you see a substantial reduction of the outstanding principal balance.

Adjustable-Rate Mortgages

Fixed-rate loans give the homeowner some certainty and control over monthly expenses, but you can generally get a lower rate and points if you are willing to share some of the interest rate risk with the lender by taking on an adjustable-rate mortgage.

An adjustable-rate mortgage makes sense if you believe rates are going to fall in the coming years, or if you only plan to stay in your house for a few years and figure you'll be selling before interest rates rise. Adjustable-rate mortgages may also be the only choice when fixed rates are high and appear to be moving higher. Then lenders tend to offer lower points and sharp discounts on the first year's rates on adjustable mortgages—making them more affordable to first-time homebuyers.

Before taking on an adjustable-rate mortgage you should be aware of the worst-case scenario. If the first year's monthly payment is attractive, what would be the highest you could wind up paying in the next few years, and could you afford it?

For example, a $100,000 30-year adjustable-rate mortgage might have an initial rate of 7 percent even when fixed-rate mortgages are costing 10 percent. The attraction of the adjustable-rate mortgage is obvious. The first year's monthly payment is only $665.30.

Every year, on the anniversary of your adjustable-rate mortgage, the interest rate will be refigured. Before you take out the loan you should understand that the rate will be tied to a specific index. The most popular are the one-year Treasury securities index and the "cost of funds" index for lenders across the country. Generally the one-year Treasury securities index is a bit more volatile, moving up more quickly as rates rise and then dropping faster as rates fall.

Most adjustable-rate mortgages will come with a limitation on how much the rate can be adjusted every year. Usually there is a 2 percent per year limitation. There should also be an overall *cap* on how much the interest rate can rise over the life of the loan—generally from 5 to 7 percent.

Now let's go back to our example of an adjustable-rate mortgage with a 7 percent initial rate. Generally this is a below-market rate designed to attract mortgage seekers. So the next year the rate is likely to rise. In fact, if it rises the allowable two percentage points after the first year, the monthly payment will increase to $801.93.

In the unlikely case that mortgage rates continue rising over the years, the monthly payment could eventually hit the cap. In this example the cap is 6-1/2 percent over the original 7 percent first-year rate. That would bring the rate to 13.5 percent, giving the homebuyer a monthly payment of $1,128.58. That's the worst-case scenario, but if you don't figure it out *before* you sign on for an adjustable-rate mortgage, you might be in for a shock.

Of course, if rates are rising you will have the opportunity to refinance your loan along the way. You might have the stomach for another adjustable-rate mortgage with a low initial teaser rate. Or by this time, you might decide to settle on a fixed-rate loan. Either way, it will cost you additional fees and points to refinance the loan. These are things to consider before you take on an adjustable-rate mortgage.

Graduated Payment Mortgages

There are other types of mortgages structured to allow first-time or lower-income homebuyers into the housing market. With a *graduated payment mortgage,* the monthly payments are structured to be lower in the early years and then to rise gradually as the homeowner presumably develops a higher income and can afford the higher monthly payments.

The interest rate on a graduated payment loan is fixed, but the lower early monthly payments may move up by a set amount each year. The lower first payments do not cover the true cost of the mortgage in those early years, so the buyer may be faced with *negative amortization.* That is, the outstanding loan balance actually *increases* during the first five years or so, instead of declining. So if home values fall in the area, a homeowner with a small down payment and a graduated payment mortgage could actually owe more than the house is worth.

Still, a graduated payment mortgage may be a good way to buy that first home. Lately, many lenders are creating new forms of graduated payments that do not negatively amortize (build up a higher loan balance). Instead, they stretch out the length of the loan slightly in the early years, with later higher payments finally reducing the loan maturity back to 30 years.

FHA and VA Mortgages

The government has created two huge loan programs that benefit homebuyers. The Federal Housing Administration and Veterans Administration loan programs provide insurance to the *lender*—not the buyer—that the loan will be repaid. In fact, about 20 percent of all home loans are guaranteed by the government. Lenders like to make FHA or VA loans because there is less risk; the government is guaranteeing that the loan will be repaid. On the other hand, these loans also involve more paperwork, and so they are more commonly made by mortgage companies.

An FHA loan can be made for as much as 97 percent of a home's appraised value. That means a much lower down payment is possible—from 3 to 5 percent is standard with FHA loans. The qualification requirements for an FHA loan tend to be more lenient, and the actual mortgage interest rate may be lower.

But there are limits on the maximum amount of an FHA loan, ranging from over $124,000 in major metropolitan areas to under $70,000 in rural areas. Rates and points on FHA loans are set by agreement between the lender and the borrower. These mortgage rates fluctuate with the market (although years ago the FHA used to set fixed rates on this type of loan). FHA loans are assumable—a feature that could be attractive if you sell your home in a time of rising interest rates.

FHA loans require borrowers to pay a mortgage insurance premium. On a 30-year mortgage, you will pay a premium equal to 3.8 percent of the loan amount. This money is paid at closing and is usually financed as part of the total loan amount. Most people don't pay much attention to this fee, but a portion of it can be recovered when the loan is paid off or transferred to a buyer of the house.

Veterans Administration loans are available to qualified veterans, unmarried widows of veterans, public health officers, or servicemen and women on active duty. You will need an official VA certificate of eligibility or statement of service to get this loan.

Like FHA loans, VA loans have much more lenient eligibility requirements and may be made with *no* down payment. But there is a maximum amount of $184,000 for a VA loan. With VA loans the borrower pays 1 percent of the loan amount up front to the VA as a loan funding fee. This pays for the cost of the insurance provided by the VA.

VA loans also carry a 1 percent loan origination fee that is paid to the lender. Because of recent high expenses associated with foreclosures on VA loans, there has been some concern that lenders might start demanding either a down payment or higher up-front fees to make these loans.

Private Mortgage Insurance

If you are purchasing a home with less than 20 percent down, your lender will probably require you to purchase private mortgage insurance (PMI). If you are using an adjustable-rate mortgage, PMI may be required if you have less than a 25 percent down payment. Private mortgage insurance works much like FHA or VA government loans. It insures a portion of the exposure of the lender if you default on your mortgage payments.

As its name indicates, though, PMI is bought through private insuring companies. The lender will arrange a policy for you if it is needed. Generally it will cost about 1 percent of the loan amount and is paid for by the buyer at the time of closing. Then each year there is an annual premium for the continued insurance—usually costing about one-half percent of the amount financed. The lender will collect this premium monthly as part of your regular monthly mortgage payment. Like your real estate tax and homeowner's insurance, it is put in a separate escrow account and paid directly to the insurance company by the lender.

Special Loan Deals

Many states offer special mortgage programs for first-time home-buyers or to make home buying possible in low-income neighborhoods. Check with your state housing agency to see if there are funds available under these programs. Often the state will sell bonds at its own lower interest rates and then make the proceeds available in the form of mortgages.

Since these programs may not be widely publicized, there is often money left over in the mortgage funds, just waiting for applicants. There may be income or geographic restrictions for many of the loans, but first-time homebuyers can often access the money to purchase a home in any neighborhood within certain price limitations.

Seller Financing and Land Contracts

In times of tight money, sellers often resort to financing a buyer directly. In fact, early in this century that was the standard form of home financing. No banks or lenders were involved in land deals; the seller simply made a *land contract* with the buyer.

There are some advantages to dealing direct—and some substantial disadvantages. A "motivated" seller might offer a rate concession to a buyer. And, of course, you will avoid the expensive fees that a bank or mortgage broker might charge. But in a land contract your attorney must do all the same work for a title search and title insurance.

Perhaps the biggest disadvantage to dealing direct with the seller in a land contract is the way most of those deals are structured. Typically, if you miss just one payment the seller can call the loan and you could lose your entire investment in the property. Always consult an attorney who is an expert at real estate before structuring one of these deals.

Balloon Mortgages

Many land contracts and even conventional mortgages are structured to expire in a relatively short period of time—from five to ten years. Because this shorter time period would result in very high monthly payments, both parties may agree to adjust the payment schedule. For instance, you could have a seven-year loan with a 30-year amortization (payment) schedule.

When the loan is due in seven years you will still have a huge outstanding balance because you have been paying it down as if you had 30 years to pay off the loan. The balance that is due when the loan matures in seven years is called a *balloon*. There's nothing wrong with structuring a loan that way, except that you will have the responsibility for either paying it off in full or finding another loan in seven years to refinance the balance or balloon. Can you foresee what interest rates or credit availability will be at that point?

Accepting a shorter-term loan from the seller with a balloon payment may be your only way to buy the piece of property you want. But be sure to understand the risk you will face down the road when the balloon comes due.

Buydowns

Monthly payments on a mortgage can be lowered temporarily or permanently by a *buydown*. This feature is generally offered by builders of new homes who use lower-cost financing as an incentive to sell their homes. The builder negotiates with a lender for a large volume of financing to be used for a particular housing development. The builder will pay money up front in order to get the lower interest rate financing for potential buyers. Other times—especially in the sale of VA or FHA homes—the seller will *buy down* the rate for the buyer by paying some points to the lender.

A buydown may last the life of the loan, or for just a few years. The cost of buying down a loan depends on the lender, the general level of interest rates, and the maturity of the loan. When interest rates are at the 8 percent level it will cost about eight points to buy down a 30-year loan to a 1 percent lower rate. When rates rise to 10 percent, it will cost about six points. There is an inverse relationship between higher current rates and fewer points to buy down the interest rate. With mortgage rates at 13 percent, it will take five points to buy down the rate by 1 percent.

REFINANCING YOUR MORTGAGE

If you took out a mortgage when interest rates were high, you've probably been waiting for rates to drop so you could refinance. Generally speaking, if rates drop at least two percentage points below your current mortgage it may pay to refinance—*if* you plan to stay in your present home for a while.

To make the refinancing decision you have to figure out exactly how much you will save on your monthly payment and how much it will cost to refinance your loan. A rule of thumb says that it costs about 3-1/2 percent of your loan amount to refinance. If you are refinancing with your original lender, the costs may be somewhat lower.

The costs of refinancing are similar to those for new loans because the lender may demand a new loan origination fee, new credit reports, and a new appraisal on the house. The lender has probably sold your loan in the secondary mortgage market, so the entire process has to start over from the beginning. Lately, the Federal National Mortgage Association, which buys and packages most mortgages for resale in the secondary market, no longer requires your current lender to get a new appraisal if you refinance with the original lender within a few years of taking out your original mortgage.

Once you know the total cost of refinancing, you have to figure out how long it will take to break even or come out ahead with your new lower monthly mortgage payment.

As an example, if you currently have a $100,000 loan at 12 percent and want to refinance it with a new mortgage at 9-1/2 percent, the total cost of refinancing might be $3,500. At 12 percent you paid $1,029 a month in principal and interest. At 9-1/2 percent you will pay only $841 a month. The monthly savings is $188. If you divide the $3,500 cost by the $188 monthly savings, you see that it will take you 19 months to recover the cost of refinancing. After that you are money ahead.

If you are not planning to stay in the house for at least another two years, it probably won't pay to refinance. Unlike when you originally purchase a house, the points you pay up front to the lender to refinance a loan are not immediately tax-deductible. They must be spread out and deducted over the life of the loan.

Many people refinance from an adjustable-rate to a fixed-rate mortgage—usually after the initial low teaser rate is adjusted upward. The uncertainty can drive you into paying points and fees all over again. But if you refinance out of an ARM you will never really know whether you are coming out ahead. If rates continue to rise, you will be happy that you refinanced, but if rates fall, you might be sorry. When you refinance an adjustable-rate mortgage you are buying peace of mind and a fixed monthly payment you can live with.

Some institutions offer a new kind of loan—*convertible ARM*. Most of these loans allow you to switch from an adjustable-rate to a fixed-rate mortgage at any time from the 13th month through the 60th month of your loan. Check the terms of your convertible loan to make sure you are allowed to switch to a fixed rate at any time. Some older convertible mortgages allow switches only on the anniversary date of the mortgage. Then you need to give the lender advance notice of your intention to convert.

The formula for a fixed-rate mortgage is usually a complicated one, so ask your lender exactly what the rate will be when you convert. The conversion rate may be higher than current market rates. In the long run it may pay to refinance to a completely different conventional loan, although it usually costs only about 1 percent of the loan value to make the conversion from adjustable to fixed. But it may be worth paying higher fees to get a significantly lower long-term, fixed-rate loan.

When you do decide to refinance, you will be "stretching out" your mortgage—and ultimately paying a larger total interest bill. If you lived in a house for four years before refinancing a 30-year mortgage, your payments would now be stretched out over 34 years. As an alternative, if you plan to live in a house for many years, this might be the time to switch to a 15-year mortgage at the new lower rate. Your payments won't drop as much, but you have already figured the old, higher payments into your budget. And you will own the house free and clear in a much shorter period of time.

REVERSE MORTGAGES

Many senior citizens find they own their homes free and clear with no mortgage, but are short of cash for living expenses. For seniors, a home equity loan may not be the solution to cash flow problems, because these loans require repayment out of current income. Instead a *reverse mortgage* can allow seniors to remain in their homes while receiving a monthly check. Several companies have structured reverse mortgage programs to act like an annuity: the homeowner can never "run out" of equity in the home and the checks keep coming until the homeowner (and spouse) die. The monthly income is considered a return of principal and is not taxable, nor does it affect Social Security benefits.

The lenders that structure these programs require an upfront fee, plus they charge for appraisals and title insurance. They also figure in a fixed, reasonable interest rate. Then they use the actuarial tables to figure out the life expectancy of the homeowner. From these calculations they can plan to give the homeowner a monthly check for a fixed amount—without running out of equity in the home. At death, or when the house is sold, the proceeds of the loan are repaid from the sale of the house. If the homeowner lives longer than predicted, the lender can never collect more than the value of the home. Some plans do allow the lender to participate in the price appreciation of the house after the loan is made.

For more information on reverse mortgages you can contact Providential Home Income Plan at 800-441-4428 or the Capitol Holding Home Income Security Plan at 800-942-6550. The Department of Housing and Urban Development (HUD) also works with lenders in some states to grant reverse mortgages. As with all mortgage plans you should have your attorney carefully review all the documents and costs, before signing a contract. But a reverse mortgage is one way for senior citizens to have their home and live in it comfortably.

TAXES AND YOUR HOUSE

When you sell your home you will have to pay taxes on the gain, just as you would on any other capital asset such as a stock or bond. But under the current tax codes you won't get any special treatment for making that gain even if you have owned your home for a long period of time. The gain is considered ordinary income—with a couple of important exceptions.

If you sell your home and buy another more expensive home within a two-year period (either two years before or two years after the sale of your home), you are allowed to defer paying taxes and roll over your profits into the new home. This is *not* a one-time benefit. You can continue to postpone taxes on your primary residences as you "trade up" over the years. If at some point you buy a less expensive house than the last one, some of your deferred profit will be taxable to the extent that it does not go into the purchase of the new house.

Then, after you reach age 55, you have a one-time chance to sell your home and take up to $125,000 profit free of any federal income taxes. That can include the accumulated profit on previous houses that you rolled over into your latest house. In order to take advantage of this one-time, over-55 tax break, you must be 55 on the day you sell your principal residence, and you must have owned and lived in it for at least three of the five years before the sale. Only one $125,000 tax break is allowed per *couple,* so if a widower has remarried, his spouse cannot sell her house and take the tax break if he has already used his one-time exemption.

As you purchase and sell each house, it's important to keep track of your true cost and sales price. The cost is called your *basis,* and it includes more than just the original price you paid for the house. Along the way you spent money to improve the house, perhaps adding a new bathroom, or siding, or a fireplace. These expenditures are considered part of your basis, or cost, and should be added to the original purchase price of your house when figuring taxable gain.

You should keep accurate records, including paid bills, showing all money you spent to improve the property. Regular maintenance does not count as a capital expenditure to improve the property. Thus, painting your house might not be considered an investment that increases your cost basis, but adding aluminum siding would be a capital expenditure.

One other tax tip related to homes: Your house-hunting expenses or even your moving costs could be tax deductible if they are related to a job change. Keep records of those expenses and consult your tax advisor to see if all or part could be considered deductible in your personal situation.

Buying a Car

There are more than 140 million registered passenger cars in America—and chances are that over your lifetime one or more of them will belong to you. Americans of average family income spend more on their cars each year than they set aside in savings. In fact, for the average family, car costs rank fourth—only behind what the family spends on housing, food, and medical care. Clearly, the American love affair with the automobile is an expensive proposition.

Since cars are purchased more frequently and for smaller initial outlays than the family home, less attention is usually given to the overall cost of owning and maintaining a car. Dickering with the dealer and "kicking the tires" to get the best price and save a few hundred dollars has become an all-American pastime. Yet most people do not realize that the estimated average cost of owning and operating a standard-sized automobile during the course of an individual's expected driving lifetime is more than $200,000. That calculation takes into consideration not only the original cost of the car, but maintenance, gas and oil, and insurance.

Clearly it pays not only to get the best deal on the initial purchase price, but to develop a car buying strategy that suits your long-term financial goals. For some people that means buying a luxury car and trading it in every two years. For others it means buying a car and keeping it until it is "run into the ground." At times it may pay to buy a used car instead of a new one.

Under some circumstances it may ultimately be cheapest to pay cash for a car; other times you can do better by leaving your money in the bank and accepting low-interest rate dealer financing. Some people may find they can manage their finances better by leasing a car instead of financing it. Whatever suits your purpose, you should decide on the best strategy and method of financing *before* you walk into the showroom and fall in love with a car.

When you decide you want to buy a new car, you have basically two options. You can do your homework by reading *Consumer Reports, Car and Driver,* and other magazines to determine which cars the professionals consider the best built and easiest to maintain. *Consumer Reports* puts out its annual auto buyers issue every April. You can get a copy by writing to *Consumer Reports,* Back Issues, P.O. Box 53016, Boulder, CO 80322; cost is $4.

If you don't want to do the basic research, you can simply watch the television commercials and make an emotional choice about the car you want. That is obviously not a financially sound option, but you'd be surprised at how many people make this investment decision based on emotion.

Keep in mind that if you choose a car that is in demand, you are less likely to get a great bargain from the dealer. Also check the insurance costs for the model you choose. Generally the most attractive models are the ones most often stolen, so they may carry a higher insurance premium. And, finally, check the availability of service. If you have only one local dealer that services this make of car, you will wind up paying more for maintenance and repairs.

Even if you have made up your mind about the make and model, you should know exactly what the car costs the dealer before you start shopping. Many car magazines publish annual guides to the dealer's cost for each make and model of car. The "sticker price" on the car window is the manufacturer's suggested retail price. In fact, the dealer's cost may be as much as 20 percent less than the sticker price on more expensive cars. And dealer markups are even larger on luxury accessory items.

There are two useful services that will, for a fee, give you the actual dealer cost for any make or model car. Consumer Reports Auto Price Service charges $11 for a computer printout of the price and options prices for any car you choose. (Consumer Reports, P.O. Box 8005, Novi, MI 48050.) You can get a similar printout from Car/Puter International Corporation, which charges $20 for the printout and a referral to car dealers around the country that offer prenegotiated discount prices, similar to "fleet" prices. (Car/Puter International Corp., 499 Sheridan St., Dania, FL 33004, 800-753-6000.) For car costs over the phone, their number is 1-900-226-CARS. Their service costs $2.00 per minute.

The first thing you want to establish when you walk into the dealership is the absolute lowest price you will have to pay for the new car. Don't even start talking about trading in your old car or about financing terms until you have the dealer's rock bottom price on the new car. It helps to have researched the dealer's cost on the make and model car you want, and all the accessories or package deals.

You will run across some other terms that could add to the cost of your car if you're not careful. Dealer "prep" may be added to the sticker price, but it should be included in the base price of the car. Other additional packages such as rustproofing, alarm systems, and something called ADM (additional dealer markup—often seen on hot new imports) are all basically money in the dealer's pocket at your expense.

If you do your homework, you should be able to purchase your car for about $150 to $250 over invoice. Of course, the dealer is unlikely to show you his actual factory invoice, but your research will give you the true figures. Don't feel sorry for the dealer if you make a great deal! Eventually, he will receive an additional payment called a *holdback,* which amounts to about 2 percent of the base sticker price rebated to him by the manufacturer.

If you choose a model that is in great demand, you might wind up paying $400 or $500 over cost, or even paying the actual sticker price, as well as paying for additional luxury items that you really don't want or need on the car. You can keep the markups to a minimum only if you're willing to order the car and wait for it, or deal for a car that is in oversupply on the lot.

Once you lock in the purchase price of the new car, you have two other important financial decisions to consider—financing the car, and getting the best price for your old car.

PAYING FOR YOUR NEW CAR

When it comes to paying for that new car, you are likely to have some confusing choices. You can pay cash, you can finance the car through the dealer, or you can obtain financing through your bank or credit union. You might also have to choose between a cash rebate from the manufacturer (which can be used toward your down payment) and a very low manufacturer's finance rate. Since it can all be very confusing, you just have to sit down and figure out the total costs—over the life of the car—for each alternative.

Generally speaking, paying cash is the cheapest way to purchase a car. Since the dealer always makes money on the financing (if you finance through the dealership), you are saving money by paying cash. There is one exception. Dealers frequently offer below-market financing as an incentive to buyers. If you can pay 2.9 percent or 4.9 percent to finance your car and leave your money in the bank earning 8 or 9 percent, then you will be money ahead.

You may be given a choice of manufacturer's low-interest rate financing or a cash rebate that can be applied to your down payment. Accepting the rebate would lower the total amount you are financing so you can save on finance charges throughout the term of your loan. But then you are often stuck with the higher finance rates being offered by the manufacturer. That's when it pays to check with your credit union, bank, or S&L to find out their lowest financing rates for new cars. If you have an account at a financial institution, you may qualify for a special deal. Some institutions may be looking to make new car loans and offering special low-interest rate deals of their own.

Oftentimes it will pay to take the cash rebate, apply it to the down payment, and then seek financing outside the dealer. For example, if you are buying a $10,000 car with a choice of taking a $1,000 rebate or 2.9 percent financing, the arithmetic is simple. If you take the rebate, the car will cost you only $9,000 which must be financed either at standard dealer rates or through your bank. That financing could carry a rate of 11.9 percent. If you finance the car for two years at 11.9 percent, the total cost of the car, including finance charges, will be $423.24 per month or $10,157.56 total. But if you take the 2.9 percent financing on the $10,000 cost of the car, your overall out-of-pocket cost for the car will be $429.37 per month or a total of $10,304.88.

When making comparisons, figure not only the monthly payment cost, but the total cost of the car over the life of the loan. Also be sure to look at the length of each loan. Often, the special manufacturer's financing deals are limited to two-year loans. You can stretch out your payments over a longer term if you search out another source of financing. Just make sure your loan payments don't last longer than your car! These days many people are financing their cars for as long as five years, even though they may want to trade them in after only two or three years. That leads to a condition called being "upside down." That is, you owe more on the car than it is currently worth on the open market. Longer-term contracts allow you to purchase more car than you could otherwise afford, but they can result in big disappointments at trade-in time unless you plan ahead. Imagine walking in to sell your car and finding out it's worth less than you still owe!

Here's an example. A buyer purchases a $14,000 car, borrowing $11,500 at 12.5 percent. Assume the car loses 50 percent of its original purchase value over the first two years, and about 6 percent of its value each year thereafter. A three-year loan would call for a monthly payment of $384. After 11 months the buyer reaches a position of *positive equity,* meaning that the trade-in value of the car is greater than the amount the buyer still owes. If the buyer had taken out a five-year loan, the situation would be quite different. The monthly payment would be only $258, making the car more affordable, but the buyer would have to wait 37 months to achieve positive equity.

The financing is a big source of profit for a dealer. That's why it pays to shop around. The dealer may get his money at a fixed rate of perhaps 11 or 12 percent from the manufacturer or a bank. He can then reoffer the financing to you at a higher rate. On a $15,000 car, for every two percentage points you pay in interest over the dealer's cost of funds, the dealer pockets an additional $1,500 profit.

Even if you manage to purchase the car at a reasonable price, and search around for the best financing, there are still some hidden ways you can pay more than necessary for your car. After you've agreed on a purchase price and financing, you may be offered some additional "deals." For example, you might be offered an *extended warranty*—which could cost more than $800. The dealer cost on this item may be as little as $250, making it a great source of profit. If you don't take the extended warranty from the dealer, many insurance brokers may offer it at a much more reasonable price.

Another source of profit for dealers is *credit life and disability* insurance—something commonly referred to as "choke and croak" insurance. It may add only a few dollars a month to your payment, but these policies tend to be overpriced. Credit life insurance is designed to pay off your car if you die suddenly; much cheaper term insurance policies can be bought through your insurance agent. The credit life policy is also designed to make your payments if you are disabled. This is really money in the dealers pocket—money better saved to make a few month's payments on the outside chance you become disabled.

TRADING IN YOUR OLD CAR

When it comes to trading in your old car, you basically have two choices—sell it yourself, or give it to the new car dealer in trade. Before you make that decision, you should have a good idea of what your old car is really worth. Prices of used automobiles are recorded in the *N.A.D.A. Official Used Car Guide* put out by the National Association of Auto Dealers. It is commonly called the "blue book."

The blue book lists the value for every make and model car by year. It assumes that the car is "clean" and does not have any major mechanical problems or need other repairs. When you look at the prices in the blue book, you will see two columns that you should pay particular attention to. The far right column lists the average retail price. That's the amount the car should sell for in the retail market (on the dealer's used car lot) if it is in good condition. That's the price you could safely ask if you were advertising it in the newspaper.

The second column of importance is the average trade-in, which appears on the far left. This is generally lower than the average retail price because it reflects the latest average *wholesale* price based on auction reports throughout the area. In other words, this column represents what the dealers receive on the wholesale auction market when they sell cars they took in trade, *not* the amount they paid to retail purchasers of new cars for their old cars.

If you decide to trade your old car in on your new one, you should have already established the price you are paying for the new car. Now you must get the highest price possible for your trade. Many dealers will set a very good price to move new cars off the lot, but then offer a very low price on your trade-in. In this case it pays to check out another dealership. Remember, you should always lock in the complete new-car price first, and then negotiate the trade.

You may decide to sell your old car to a friend or through a newspaper ad. If you have the time and energy to do this, you may get a few hundred dollars more than the dealer would offer. You may also have to deal with a disgruntled car buyer when something goes wrong with the car two weeks after the sale! There are some other caveats when selling your car through a public newspaper ad.

Be sure to retain the driver's license of anyone who offers to take it for a test drive. Every year many cars are stolen in scams like this. Also demand a cashier's check or certified personal check in payment for the car you sell, and do not transfer title until the check has cleared. If you are *buying* a used car from someone whom you do not know, be sure to inspect the car registration form and the current auto insurance form before handing over any money. That way you can examine the registration on each to be sure you are not purchasing a stolen car.

If you are selling your car directly, you may be asked to do some "seller financing"—i.e., allow the buyer to pay you on time. That's truly dangerous. If the buyer cannot get financing through a bank or credit union, his or her credit is certainly not good enough to induce you to become the lender.

BUYING VS. LEASING

Auto leasing used to be reserved for businesses and self-employed individuals, but changing tax laws and rising new car prices have created a boon in the auto leasing business. In 1988 there were 1.3 million cars leased to individuals—a sharp increase over previous years.

The Tax Reform Act of 1986 is largely responsible for this new trend. It eliminated the sales tax deduction and phased out the deduction for consumer interest. The act also affected business car owners by repealing the investment tax credit for cars and limiting the benefits of depreciation by spreading it out over a longer period. Since consumer finance charges disappear completely as an income tax deduction in 1991, one of the great advantages of financing a car has simply disappeared. Many car buyers are not in a position to take out a home equity loan to purchase a car, thereby making the interest deductible. And rising car prices have sent many car buyers looking for the lowest monthly cost to purchase an expensive automobile. For many people, the answer is leasing.

You can lease a car directly through the dealership or you can go to an auto leasing company. A dealership will arrange leases for the cars it sells. Working through a dealer it's no more difficult to arrange a lease than to arrange financing. An auto leasing company will order the car you specify from any manufacturer and also arrange the lease.

Should you lease or buy that new car? You might think of it as a comparison between renting an apartment and buying one. Leasing is like renting. A major advantage of a lease deal is that there is no down payment required, although most leasing companies will ask for the first month's lease payment in advance plus one month's payment as a refundable security deposit. However, just like renting an apartment, at the end of the lease term you wind up with rent receipts but no equity. At the end of most lease arrangements, you return the car to the leasing company and have no used car to sell or use as a down payment on a new one.

Choosing to lease a car does have some important advantages. It may allow you to drive a more expensive car than you could otherwise have afforded. That's because lease payments are generally much lower than comparable monthly finance payments. For example, the monthly payment on a $17,500 car financed through the dealer for five years might be about $350 (plus a 10 percent down payment). But a five-year lease deal could put you in the driver's seat for only $305 a month with no down payment.

And when it comes to higher-priced imported sports cars, the difference is much greater. A monthly lease payment on a five-year lease for a $40,000 Porsche could be about $550, compared to $835 a month loan payment on the same car (plus a $5,000 down payment).

Before you get into specific cost comparisons, you should understand the terms of the lease. The most frequently used form of lease is a *closed-end lease*—meaning that you agree to a fixed number of monthly payments and when the term is up you have no more obligations. This type of lease generally runs from three to five years. At the end of the lease you can either buy the car—usually at a price agreed upon at the start of the lease—or give the car back to the dealer and walk away.

Consumers should avoid *open-end leases* that force them to share with the dealer the risk of resale value at the end of the lease. The monthly payment may appear to be lower, but there is greater risk when the lease expires and you have to worry about what the price the car can be sold for.

Check the terms of the lease carefully. Some contracts will charge you as much as eight to twelve cents per mile if you put more than 15,000 miles on the car per year. Some lease contracts will include a service contract covering all maintenance on the car. A leasing company might even offer to make the auto insurance part of the package.

If you have already decided to lease, comparison shopping will be a little easier. You really want to focus on the monthly lease cost—assuming that all the other terms are the same (i.e., number of months, mileage limitations, similarly equipped car). Not all lease deals are the same. You could get the same price on a new car from different dealers—and the monthly lease costs could vary depending on their interest rate and end-of-lease value assumptions.

Leasing a car makes sense if you cannot afford the down payment, or if you want to use the down payment money to pay off other higher interest debt such as credit card debt. Leasing makes sense if you want to drive a more expensive car for the same monthly payment. Remember, at the end of the lease, you wind up with no equity because you paid less along the way for the use of the car.

LEMON LAWS

What happens if you buy a car that turns out to be a lemon? There is an official definition of a lemon: A car that has had four repair attempts for the same reason, or spent 30 days in the shop in the first year, or in the first 12,000 miles.

Your first recourse is the auto dealer, who should repair the car under warranty. But if you have trouble with the dealer or the dealer's service department, you should definitely complain to the manufacturer. Every manufacturer has a regional or district center that handles complaints like yours. If your dealer won't put you in touch with the regional center, contact the manufacturer in Detroit (or if an import, the national import headquarters posted in your owner's manual).

Most major manufacturers will make adjustments without too much pressure. (It may help if you say you are going to complain to your local newspaper or radio "action line.") If you still can't agree on who's responsible for the problem, federal law regulating warranties requires that consumers use the manufacturer's own arbitration process before going to court. Each of the major U.S. manufacturers has its own arbitration system, and will send you a booklet describing the procedure.

In addition, most states have passed some sort of "lemon law" that gives the buyer a choice between a full refund and a new car. However, the car owner may be forced to go through the arbitration process before the car can be officially written off as a lemon. That process can consume time and patience. As a last resort, after arbitration, you can always file a complaint and take the dealer to court.

PART
3

The Power of Money

Money Powers

BUY LOW, SELL HIGH...AND OTHER RULES FOR INVESTING

When it comes to investing for profit, the experts will tell you there's one simple rule: "Buy low and sell high." That begs the obvious question. What's low and what's high? Figure out the answer to those two questions and you've uncovered the secret of successful investing.

Generations of "experts" have worked on systems to tell you when to buy and sell, but no one has yet come up with a foolproof set of rules. That's what makes risk investing so challenging. Techniques may work for a while, but then something changes in the economy—and only in hindsight can it be seen why the system failed. Even with the advent of computers that can be programmed to follow patterns back into the 1920s, it seems impossible to predict future prices. That doesn't stop people from trying!

There are tradeoffs in the search for investment profits. If you want to take the higher risks involved in searching for the next growth company or the future IBM, you will have to sacrifice current income. A small, growing company will be putting its profits back into research and development—not paying them out in the form of dividends to shareholders.

There is risk, too, in hunting for the highest possible income, or rate of interest, on your money. If the safest government bonds are paying

8 percent, then why must a company offer 13 or 14 percent to get investors to buy its debt? Clearly, offering a higher interest rate than those paid on prevailing instruments signals a higher degree of risk.

In any risk investment, good timing is an essential ingredient in turning the balance of profit or loss in your favor. You can buy "safe" bonds and still lose money if your timing is off. You can take the risk of investing in stocks and earn maximum gains if your timing is right.

Investment success requires understanding the risk—and then balancing the risks against the potential reward. And then it requires knowing when to get in—and when to get out. In the next chapters we will look at investments that involve both risk and reward as well as some investment timing techniques.

OUR MONEY, OUR WORLD

Whether you're trying to beat the market, or get the highest rate on your savings, or just plan for your future, the uncertainties of the economy will affect every decision you make. So it makes sense to understand the "powers" that can change the direction of the economy, and interest rates and the investment markets.

You don't need Economics 101 to get a feel for the forces that influence the economy. There are basically three major power centers that affect the value of our money and investments: the federal government (Congress and the President), the Federal Reserve (which governs the nation's banking system), and the foreign investors who have lent us money.

The federal government has the power to tax and spend. And they have used those powers dramatically in the past 20 years. Every year the government receives more and more in tax revenues as the economy grows, and every year it spends more and more. The federal government hasn't had a balanced budget since 1969.

Every year since 1969 the federal government has run a budget deficit. One year (in 1983) the budget deficit was more than $200 billion. In 1987, 1988, and 1989, each year the federal government ran a budget deficit of more than $150 billion. Those deficits really add up. The total of all our budget deficits since the beginning of our country is called the national debt. It now totals more than $3 trillion!

Some people say we shouldn't worry about the national debt because our children and grandchildren will pay it off. But in the meantime *we* have to pay the interest on it. That's because every time the government runs a budget deficit it has to *borrow* the money. It does that by selling Treasury bills, notes, and bonds. Just think of them as IOUs from the United States government. Every year the government has to pay the interest on those Treasury bills, notes, and bonds. In 1990 the interest amounted to $184 billion—the third largest item in the nation's $1 trillion budget. Only defense and social programs consume more of our tax dollars.

But how do those government deficits affect our personal finances? When the government is borrowing all that money it may soak up funds that could be used more productively in the private economy. And all that government borrowing could push interest rates higher—unless there is plenty of money floating around in the economy, or unless there are willing foreign buyers of our IOUs.

That brings us to the second important power in the economy—the Federal Reserve. The Fed, as the nation's central bank, has many powers, including watching the activities of the nation's banks. But even more important is its ability to move interest rates. The Fed can do that by simply raising or lowering the rate at which smaller banks borrow from the Fed. That's called changing the *discount rate.*

The Fed can also affect interest rates by changing the supply of money—pushing money into the economy or sucking it out of the system. It does that by going out into the government bond trading market and buying securities for its own account. When the Fed buys government bonds it pays for them with newly created money—a sort of "rubber check" that gets deposited into the nation's banking system. That increases the *money supply.*

When the Fed decides there is too much money in the system, it simply reverses the process by selling the government bonds it owns. When the buyer pays for the bonds, the Fed simply "tears up the check," which takes the money out of the system.

If the Fed puts too much money in the system, it can lead to inflation and higher interest rates. If the Fed puts too little money into the system, it can lead to recession and a credit squeeze as struggling businesses try to borrow scarce money. Think of it as sort of a giant Monopoly game. If the banker decides the game is going too slowly, he can give each player more money. But if the Monopoly board were like the real economy, putting more money in the game would simply push the prices of each property higher. And any money you had saved (hoping to land on Boardwalk) would have less buying power. That's inflation.

It's the Fed's job to put just enough money into the economy to keep it going—without inflation. And that's not an easy job when the government keeps running deficits and borrowing money. That's why you often hear the Fed chairman lecturing Congress about getting the budget deficit under control.

Throughout most of our postwar history those two powers—the government (taxing and spending) and the Fed (managing the money supply)—have managed to keep the economy pretty well in balance. The one great exception was the huge inflation of the late 1970s. That's a mistake the Fed seems determined never to repeat.

But over the past few years another power has developed the ability to affect our economy, interest rates, and the stock market. To put it simply, that power is "the rest of the world!" For years America has been buying more and more products from abroad. These imports have given us a wide variety of consumer products, but we've sent a lot of dollars overseas to pay for our imports—far more than we've earned from selling American products to them. The sum total of the difference is our *trade deficit*.

The foreigners who received those dollars have turned around and invested many of them back in America. One of their biggest investments has been *our debt!* Foreigners have used their dollars to buy our Treasury bills, notes, and bonds—helping the U.S. government finance its deficits! In fact we now depend on foreign investors to buy nearly 25 percent of our debt at most Treasury auctions. If they didn't buy our bonds, we would probably have to raise our interest rates much higher to attract buyers. Their ability to buy our debt gives foreign investors quite a bit of power. Our interest rates must remain high enough to attract their money, which we now depend on.

If our government keeps running budget deficits and selling IOUs to finance those deficits, we are likely to become more and more dependent on foreign buyers. That means we have to be very careful of how we treat foreign governments and companies. Putting trade restrictions on imports could become an even more touchy situation. If they don't earn dollars, how will they be able to help us out by buying our debt?

Clearly it is no longer just the government's fiscal (taxing and spending) policies and the Fed's monetary policies that affect our economy. Because of our budget deficits we are now tied closely to the rest of the world — those who are our creditors. As Walt Disney said, "It's a small world, after all."

It's important to understand those three basic powers when you make decisions about your own money. The balance of those powers determines whether we will have inflation or recession, higher or lower interest rates. And because it's not easy to predict these trends with accuracy, you must pay close attention to your savings and investments to quickly take advantage of each new direction in the financial markets.

THE VITAL SIGNS—ECONOMIC REPORTS

Where's the economy headed—economic growth or economic slowdown? Just like a doctor examining a patient, you have to check the vital signs to get a reading on the health of the economy. In this case the vital signs include reports on inflation, output, and prices.

Just as a doctor can read medical tests and give a prognosis, it would seem that if you keep close track of the statistics and reports issued by the government, you should be able to predict the future course of the economy. Unfortunately, it's not that easy. Sometimes the reports give conflicting pictures of the economy. Different parts of the business world may go through spurts or slowdowns at the same time. Still, it's worthwhile to keep an eye on the economic indicators and to know how they are compiled.

One of the most interesting of the monthly reports is the *index of leading economic indicators* which is usually issued during the last week of the month. The index is composed of 11 reports, including the average hours per week being worked by factory workers, the number of new building permits being issued, the number of people making new claims for unemployment insurance, and sensitive materials prices. All tend to forecast future trends in the economy, and taken together they are widely watched.

Despite its imposing title, the index of leading indicators has had a mixed record of forecasting business activity lately. If it declines for three straight months it is supposed to forecast an economic slowdown six to nine months in the future. However, the index has given two false signals in the past ten years, declining for three months in a row in 1984 and again in 1987 after the stock market crash with no subsequent recession. Before 1984, the index had correctly predicted all eight recessions since World War II.

While the index is considered a *leading* indicator because it predicts future trends, the monthly report on unemployment is considered a *lagging* indicator—giving a picture of what has already happened. Issued the first Friday of every month, the unemployment figures count those people who have been making a specific effort to find a job during the past month or who were recently laid off. It does not count those who have simply given up trying to find work.

The highest unemployment rate in modern times was reported in 1982—a 10.8 percent national unemployment rate in the midst of a terrible recession. More recently, in March of 1989, the unemployment rate fell to a low of 5 percent. Although these figures are watched carefully by market participants, they are gathered from a surprisingly small, but accurate, statistical sample of 57,000 families surveyed every month.

The *consumer price index* is released during the third week of every month. It is supposed to track the increase (or decrease) of a fixed "market basket" of goods and services used by the average urban wage earner. The major categories are food, shelter, fuel oil and coal, apparel, private transportation, medical care, and entertainment. This measure of the change in prices (inflation) is often used as a base for calculating increases in labor contracts and for the annual changes in Social Security benefits.

Back in 1980, during a period of extremely high inflation, the consumer price index rose 13.5 percent in one year. In 1988 and 1989 the

CPI had an increase of less than 5 percent each year. Many consumers complain that the CPI does not accurately reflect the increase in prices *they* pay. In particular, many say the CPI does not accurately reflect changes in housing costs, especially the increases brought on by variable-rate mortgages. Of course, there are also regional variations that may account for the difference between the official average inflation figures and those that individuals sense in their daily spending.

Turning toward the industrial side of the economic health picture, there are several important reports that are issued monthly. *Producer prices* (formerly called *wholesale prices*) track the cost of raw materials and unfinished goods used by businesses to create final consumer products. The PPI sometimes, but not always, predicts price increases at the consumer level.

Every month another report shows the amount of *factory capacity* that is in use. At its highest levels—about 89 percent capacity—this report hints that the economy is growing strongly and that with factories working at just about full capacity, there might be an incentive for producers to raise prices—inflation!

Market watchers also follow the monthly *durable goods reports*—an indicator of big ticket items such as refrigerators, washers and dryers, and cars that are being purchased by consumers. These are the kinds of purchases that will be postponed by consumers if they are uncertain about the economic outlook. Of course, if consumers stop buying it is a self-fulfilling prophecy: The economy will then slow down.

Other key consumer spending areas are new car sales, retail sales, and purchase of new homes. Those figures are all watched closely for clues to the future behavior of the economy. Once a month the Bureau of Labor Statistics calculates the *savings rate*—the difference between consumer income and spending. In recent years the savings rate has been about 5 percent. Even if spending slows, when money moves into savings it can have long-term benefits by creating capital needed for building new factories.

The *gross national product* is simply the measurement of all the goods and services produced by the workers of this nation. The report is issued monthly by the Commerce Department, but it shows the figures for a quarterly rate of growth. The GNP report is the barometer of the health and growth of the economy. The four components of this report are consumer spending, business investment, government spending, and net exports.

Economists have some real concerns when we import more merchandise than we export. That means our factories aren't working as hard as they might. It also means we are sending more dollars abroad to pay for imports than we are collecting from sales of our products. That's why the monthly *trade deficit* figures are another closely watched indicator of economic performance.

When a doctor reads the results of medical tests, he can almost always say with certainty whether the news is good or bad. But in the case of the economy the numbers are not always that clear-cut. For instance, rising unemployment numbers should certainly be considered bad news. But if economists are worried about the economy getting too strong and creating the potential for higher prices (inflation), then rising unemployment figures may be seen as good news—a slowdown taking the pressure off inflation.

That's why the stock market will sometimes rise on news of an economic slowdown. Yes, a slowdown is bad for business, but if it takes upward pressure off price and interest rates, then at that particular moment it's *good* for the stock market. On the other hand, once the reports of a slowing economy are common knowledge, a slowdown results in lower corporate earnings and profits. That's taken as *bad* for the stock market, and prices fall.

Usually the market goes down on bad news. Sometimes the market goes down on good news. So clearly what the market needs is *no* news. Everybody knows that *no news is good news!* Unfortunately, there's never a "no-news day"—which is why the smart money keeps track of the economic reports.

RECOMMENDED READING

I'm often asked what type of reading a person needs to do in order to be well versed about what's going on in the economy and the financial markets. Instead of giving a long list of recommended reading, I point out that the front pages of your daily newspaper often have more economic impact on your investments than all the technical data given in the financial pages.

Still, there's something to be said for getting familiar with the business publications that regularly report financial news. In addition to your daily newspaper, the *Wall Street Journal* is considered the bible of daily financial information. Most people in the markets *do not* read every page. After you start investing, you will find which information is interesting and important to you. At first, you might enjoy just the feature articles on the front page along with the financial news summary in column two. The front page of the third section of the *Journal* is usually devoted to easily understood articles about investing geared to the general public.

Investor's Daily is another newspaper that is devoted primarily to stock market investors. Its columns and statistics offer a wealth of information to traders and investors. But if you are not making a full-time hobby of investing, you can stick with the business pages of your own local paper.

Several weekly and biweekly magazines carry articles of interest to stock investors. *Business Week, Forbes,* and *Fortune* are among the most widely read of these magazines. They serve two purposes—providing information about specific companies you may want to invest in and analyzing the general economic outlook.

Another "must read" for sophisticated investors is *Barron's,* a weekly newspaper in tabloid format. Stocks mentioned in its columns often move dramatically, and the paper is full of insights into what the best money managers think about specific investments. *Barron's* also has the complete weekly list of stock and mutual fund prices and economic statistics.

All of this reading is useful if you want to know what everybody else is thinking about the market. Remember, though, that when an investment idea, a company, or a concept is written up in almost every business news publication, it is probably too late to buy the stock. After all, once everybody knows the story, who else is left to buy it? This advice specifically applies to research reports issued by brokerage firms. The information contained in the reports is often given to big institutional customers before it finds its way to your local registered representative. That doesn't mean the information can't be helpful with basic investment questions. It just means it's unlikely you are being treated to a hot new investment idea.

You can often find profitable stock ideas just by being aware in your everyday life. When my son switched to Nike athletic shoes after years of wearing Reeboks, I promptly switched out of my Reebok stock! Many of the best investment ideas are the result of common sense and an alertness to changing consumer trends. Of course, with some investments you need to be aware of industry trends that are not immediately apparent—and that's where reading the trade and business publications helps out.

Once you invest in a company, you should definitely read its corporate annual and quarterly reports. (If your broker is holding your stock, you should ask for the reports to be forwarded to you.) Again, the information in an annual report is old news, but it does give you a sense of the direction management intends to take. The most important part of the annual report is the financial statements—especially the footnotes, where all the exceptions are stated. Unfortunately, it takes a bit of study to understand all the financial figures here. (See Chapter 12 section, "Fundamental Analysis.")

The bottom line of this section on recommended reading is that you can never know *all* of the pertinent information about any investment, but the more you know, the better. And as with any other special interest, the more you read, the more you will understand. If you pick up a cookbook for the first time, or *Popular Mechanics,* certainly you might think it's written in an entirely different language. But familiarity with the subject makes it all understandable. It's no different with the language of money.

CHAPTER 10

Interest Rate Investing

Some investors figure they will avoid risk and stick with fixed interest rate returns. At one time that might have meant buying bonds—an investment considered safe for widows and orphans—and chickens! But not all bonds are alike when it comes to risk and return. And even though the word "bond" brings with it a sense of gilt-edged safety, there are ways you can lose money even in the safest bonds. You should understand how bonds work before you become seduced by the promise of regular interest payments.

Even those who plan to stick with short-term interest bearing investments like certificates of deposit and money market funds need to understand the potential risk before they make decisions about savings. What are the penalties for early withdrawal? Where is the insurance guarantee that you won't lose your money?

That great speculator Bernard Baruch once said: "I'm not so concerned about the return ON my money, as I am about the return OF my money!" That's something all interest rate investors should keep in mind.

BOND BASICS

All bonds have certain things in common: They are IOUs of the issuer, promising to pay a set rate of interest, and to repay your principal investment in a set period of time. But how are those interest rates determined? And how can you be sure you are getting the highest interest rate? Or does that involve more risk?

Before you invest your money in bonds, you have to understand the things that cause interest rates to change. Interest rates on both short-term bank deposits and longer-term bonds are set by free-market forces that assess things like the outlook for inflation, the supply of credit available, and the quality of the borrower.

All interest rates bear some relationship to one another. A bank may have the absolute choice of what rate to pay on its deposits, but if other lenders offering similar instruments are willing to pay higher rates, the bank would soon lose all its deposits. There is a huge, multi-trillion dollar interest rate market that encompasses borrowers in the United States and in foreign countries. Investors today have choices not only between rates offered by local banks and corporations and governments, but may choose to invest their money around the world, depending on the return being offered. But in making these invest-ments, there is more to consider than just the interest rate on your de-posit.

For instance, you might be able to earn much higher rates at a bank in Mexico, but then you would have to switch your dollars into Mexi-can pesos to put on deposit there. Mexican pesos are notorious for los-ing value. So even if you could earn 30 percent in an account in Mexico, you have to take into consideration that when you transfer your account back into U.S. dollars, you could have lost more than 30 percent of your buying power.

So let's come back to America and look at the interest rate choices you are likely to have here at home. Generally speaking, there are two key ingredients that determine relative interest rates: maturity and quality. *Maturity* is simply the length of time you are lending your money. If you place it on deposit for just a few months you are taking a different risk than if you are lending it for 20 years. *Quality* deals with the reliability of the borrower. Can the company or government you are lending money to be counted upon to pay its interest on time and to repay the loan in full at maturity?

The general level of interest rates is set by the economic factors men-tioned above—the likelihood of inflation, outlook for growth, or borrowing demand in the economy. But maturity and quality determine the rates specific borrowers will pay to obtain money and, therefore, the rate you can earn if you lend money.

Short-term interest rates are usually slightly lower than long-term interest rates on the same quality investment. For instance, you will usually receive a lower interest rate on short-term Treasury bills (maturities of one year or less) than you will get on 30-year government bonds.

If you are willing to lend your money for a longer period of time, you will usually get a higher interest rate because economic conditions could change over time. So you are compensated for committing your money for that longer time, by getting a slightly higher interest rate.

There is one exception to this rule that short-term interest rates are lower than long-term rates. Sometimes the Federal Reserve Bank (see Chapter 9) uses its power to tighten up on the availability of credit. It "squeezes" the economy to slow down economic growth and cool off inflationary pressures.

When the Fed decides to restrict credit, the result can be a surge in short-term interest rates as borrowers scramble to obtain money. In these rare times, short-term rates may rise above long-term rates. This is called an inverted yield curve. The high short-term rates usually serve their purpose, which is to cool down the economy. In fact, sometimes an inverted yield curve cools the economy down too much and leads to a recession.

All short-term rates and all long-term rates are not alike. You may deposit your money in an insured account at a bank for six months and get one rate, while if you lend money to an acquaintance for six months to finance a business deal, you will probably demand a higher interest rate. That's because of the *quality* difference in the borrower. One is an insured deposit; one carries a higher degree of risk.

Similarly, if you lend money to the U.S. government by buying 30-year government bonds you'll get one rate of interest. That rate will be slightly lower than the rate you would get in buying a bond from a major corporation, because it is usually perceived that there is less risk in lending to the government. You could even get a much higher interest rate on a 30-year corporate bond by choosing a bond issued by a corporation that is considered less secure perhaps because it already has a substantial amount of outstanding debt. (See the section on junk bonds in this chapter.)

So when you choose to invest to earn interest—a return on your money—you have to make some choices about how long you are willing to tie your money up and about the quality of the borrower.

You can learn a lot about a bond just from its name or title. For example a bond may be titled the XYZ Corp. 8-1/2's of 2010. That means it is an IOU issued by a corporation that will pay 8-1/2 percent interest every year and will repay the entire principal amount at maturity in the year 2010.

Bonds are priced differently than stocks. Generally they are sold in $1,000 face value amounts. If a bond has a $1,000 face value and its selling price is $1,000, it is considered to be selling at *par,* or 100. If a bond is selling at a price below its $1,000 face amount, it is said to be selling at a *discount*. Bonds sell at a discount when new bonds offering higher interest rates are issued, making the old, low-rate bonds less attractive. So if a $1,000 bond is selling at a below-par price of 85 or 90, it now has a market value of only $850 or $900. If a bond is selling for more than $1,000 (presumably because it carries a *higher* interest rate than is currently available), it is said to be selling at a *premium*. A premium bond might be quoted at a price of 105, meaning its market is $1,050.

These price swings develop when the general level of interest rates changes, or when there are changing economic conditions in the country or company that issued the bonds. Price movements can mean significant profits or losses to bond buyers—something you should understand *before* you buy any bonds.

BUYING BONDS—THE RISKS

Bonds are issued by governments and big corporations, and they carry with them a sense of security. There are, however, two distinct ways you can *lose* money on a bond. You should be aware of both of those risks before you invest.

The most obvious way to lose money on a bond occurs when the company issuing the bonds *defaults*—reneges on its promise to pay. That doesn't happen very often, but it *does* happen. A classic example is the default of the Washington Public Power Supply System—a public utility in the Northwest that borrowed money to build nuclear plants. The utility defaulted on interest payments on over $2 billion worth of bonds and is now known by its acronym—WHOOPS!

Before you buy a bond, check the reputation of the issuing company. There are ratings services such as Moody's and Standard & Poor's to do that job for investors. They assign a rating according to their estimate of the risk of default. AAA (triple A) is the top rating, followed by double A, single A, and then BAA. Most banks and institutions won't buy a bond with less than a BAA rating. But even the rating services can make errors in judgment—or fail to move swiftly when a company's financial picture changes. Those WHOOPS bonds were once rated A-1 by Moody's!

While it's most dramatic, default isn't the *only* way a bond buyer can lose money. A second risk in owning bonds (or any long-term, fixed-rate investment) is *interest rate risk*. Here's how you can lose money on a bond, even if it's still paying regular interest.

Let's think back to 1974 when triple A-rated, long-term corporate bonds were carrying interest rates of about 8 percent. That was considered a good rate in 1974 because inflation was relatively low. So you could spend $1,000 and buy an 8 percent corporate bond with a 30-year maturity.

Now let's move ahead a few years to 1980. Well, by then the United States was caught up in a vicious inflation running at 12 to 13 percent a year. So when even triple A-rated companies wanted to borrow money by selling bonds, they were forced to pay interest rates of about 15 percent in order to get anyone to buy them. In 1980 if you had $1,000 to invest you could buy a triple A bond paying 15 percent.

But what about your old 8 percent bond? It was still triple A rated, it was still paying interest, and it would still pay back your $1,000 investment at maturity. But in 1980 no one would give you $1,000 for that old 8 percent bond if you wanted to sell it because with $1,000 they could buy a new 15 percent bond. If you were forced to sell your old bond because you needed cash for an emergency, you would find that it was worth only about $650!

That explains the other risk in owning bonds—the risk that the *market value* will drop. That's what happens to *all* long-term bonds when interest rates rise. The longer the maturity of the bond, the greater the drop in market value. This has nothing to do with the quality of the bond, or the likelihood that it will keep paying interest. The market value drops only because there are more attractive investments available paying higher interest rates. The cardinal rule in bond investing is:

When interest rates *rise,* bond prices *drop.*

Of course, it works the other way too. As the general level of interest rates drops, the market value of the old, high-rate bonds will increase. Don't you wish you still had some of those old 15 percent government bonds that were sold back in the early 1980s? Someone has them socked away and is still collecting 15 percent!

This rule of bond investing holds true whether you buy one bond or ten, whether you buy government bonds, corporate bonds, or municipal bonds (issued by a state or local government). It holds true when you buy fixed packages of bonds such as a closed-end bond fund or a unit investment trust. And with certain special twists it holds true when you buy any package of long-term, fixed-rate investments such as a Ginnie Mae portfolio (a package of long-term mortgages). It holds true even if you are buying discount bonds or zero coupon bonds. (We'll explain all of these later in this chapter.)

You have to remember that when you tie up your money at a fixed rate for a long period of time, you are taking a risk—the risk that rates will move higher and that you have to sell your bonds at a loss. And, yes, you still will have a loss even if you don't actually *sell* those old bonds. It won't be a loss of principal on your original investment, but you should consider it a loss anyway because you will be stuck earning a lower rate of interest than those who waited to invest until rates reached their peak.

What happens if you're stuck with some older, long-term, 8 percent bonds when interest rates move up to 12 percent? Should you sell and then reinvest the money in higher-yielding bonds? That depends on several things. First, you might want to take the loss and use it to offset gains on other investments. That would lower your income tax bill. On the other hand, you will have to pay two more commissions to sell your old bonds and buy new ones. That commission bite can really eat into your principal. It might pay to be patient and wait for interest rates to drop again.

Interest rates tend to move in cycles. Just as no tree grows to the sky, eventually even sky-high interest rates will come down. That's because the high interest rates will do the job of slowing the economy and reducing borrowing demand—which will bring interest rates down. If you lock in rates at the top, you will have a profit on your bonds when rates fall. If you hold the bonds as a speculative investment, you might want to sell and take your profit before rates rise again.

That means you must think about the future direction of interest rates *before* you invest in bonds. Do you think inflation will return, bringing higher interest rates? Do you think the pressures of huge federal deficits will eventually force the Federal Reserve to create more money (inflation)? If you think that's the outlook, then don't buy bonds.

Remember when we noted that to be a successful investor all you had to know is when to buy and when to sell? Well, that holds true for bonds as well as stocks and other investments. You should buy bonds only when you think interest rates are at their peak. Of course, nobody knows exactly where the peak will be, but that's the risk you take when you buy a bond!

THE BOND MARKET

While all bonds behave in similar ways when it comes to the relationship between interest rates and market value, there are certainly many different kinds of bonds for investors to choose from. The U.S. government issues bonds, and so do cities and states. Within each city and state there may be several taxing authorities that borrow money by selling bonds. And of course, there are billions of dollars in bonds issued by corporations that have to raise money for their businesses.

Unlike the stock market, there is no fixed trading floor for most bonds, although some issues trade on the floor of the New York Stock

Exchange. Most bonds trade by wire between dealers at trading firms around the country.

How To Buy Bonds

You can buy individual issues of bonds through your stock brokerage firm or through specialty brokerage firms that deal in either corporate or municipal bonds. If you decide to buy the bonds of only one company or state, you should keep certain considerations in mind.

First, you have little diversification if the issuer should run into problems paying interest. Second, unless you buy a substantial number of bonds, you may have difficulty getting a good price when you sell. Third, it is your job to keep track of interest payments, and on some older bonds that may require that you actually clip coupons that are attached to the bond certificate and present them to a designated bank in order to receive the interest payments.

Finally, it is not always easy to figure out the commission you are paying when you buy bonds. For new issues, the commission is priced right into the purchase price of the bond. The selling municipality or company compensates the broker. But if you buy bonds in the general trading marketplace through a stock or specialty bond broker, there are two ways a commission may be paid.

Sometimes a commission is marked right on the sales confirmation—generally a minimum of $100 per order or $10 per bond. If you don't see a commission specifically written on the confirmation, you can be sure the bond broker is getting paid anyway. In this case the firm has purchased the bonds for its own account and is selling them to you out of its inventory. The brokerage firm is making a profit on the purchase and sale, and part of that profit—though not specifically noted—is going to the salesperson.

Remember, the higher the price you pay for the bond, the lower your overall return. Therefore, you might want to check with other brokers for the price and yields of similar bonds, just to make sure you are not paying too much.

Many people prefer to avoid the hassle of buying individual bonds, and instead choose to invest in bond funds. Whether you buy one bond, ten bonds, or a bond fund, keep in mind that all bonds react to changes in interest rates by gaining or losing value. If you are willing to accept a fixed rate of return for years into the future, then you must still choose which kind of bond you want to buy.

U.S. GOVERNMENT BONDS

As we mentioned earlier, the United States government has a nearly $3 trillion national debt. That's money the government has borrowed over the years. The government borrowings come in the form of Treasury bills (IOUs with maturities of one year or less), Treasury notes (IOUs with original maturities of one year to ten years) and Treasury bonds (longer-term IOUs that may have original maturities of up to 30 years). U.S. Treasury bonds are considered perhaps the safest long-term, fixed-rate investment. Although the market value of Treasury bonds still will fall along with other bond values, Uncle Sam generally is considered the most creditworthy borrower in the financial markets.

Each one of these U.S. Treasury IOUs carries a fixed rate of interest that is set when the government sells the bonds. Treasury bills are sold weekly at regular auctions. Treasury notes are sold at monthly auctions. There is usually an auction of two-year Treasury notes during the third week of every month. Minimum purchase for the two-year notes is $5,000. Generally the Treasury sells longer-term bonds at regular quarterly auctions. The bonds are sold in $1,000 minimums at these auctions. You will not know the interest rate before the auction takes place; individual orders are filled at a rate that matches the average rate accepted by the big institutional buyers—huge government bond trading firms based in the United States and abroad.

Like Treasury bills and notes, the bonds are actually purchased through Federal Reserve banks around the country. You can contact your regional Federal Reserve Bank for information about the date of the next auction. (See Chapter 4 for a listing of regional Federal Reserve banks.)

There is another way to buy Treasury bonds. There are billions worth of outstanding Treasuries that are traded every day in the government bond market. There is no trading floor for the government bond market as there is for the New York Stock Exchange. Instead, this market consists of a network of dealers transacting business over the telephone lines. You can see the market prices of outstanding government bonds listed each day in the *Wall Street Journal* and some local papers.

If you want to purchase outstanding government bonds, you can go through your stock brokerage firm. There will be a commission involved in these purchases, which will lower your yield (return) significantly. So if you're buying less than $100,000 worth of Treasury bonds, it's best to buy them directly through the Federal Reserve Bank at the government auctions.

CORPORATE BONDS

Corporations frequently need to borrow money to build new plants, buy equipment, or even to buy other companies. They may choose to issue new stock to raise capital, or they may choose to borrow the money by selling corporate bonds.

Corporate bonds are IOUs of the company borrowing the money. The interest on the bonds is paid out of the company's earnings. If the company is not having a very good year, interest on the bonds must be paid *before* any dividends are paid to shareholders. Therefore, bondholders are considered to be senior to stockholders. A corporation may have more than one class or *issue* of bonds outstanding. In fact, many corporations have numerous issues outstanding. The bonds generally are sold through *underwriters*—big brokerage firms that sell the bonds to retail customers and institutions such as pension funds.

Before a bond is sold it will be given a rating by either Moody's or Standard & Poor's, the two major rating agencies. Moody's top rating is triple A (AAA). The ratings move downward showing the degree of investment safety—AAA, AA-1, AA, A-1, BAA-1, BAA, BA, B, and on down to C. Anything below BAA is not considered *investment grade* and will probably not be purchased by banks or pension funds. The company's rating is based on the amount of debt it already has outstanding and the likelihood that business will provide enough profits to pay interest on the debt. Each year the corporation will probably be required to set aside a sum of money that will eventually be used to pay off the bonds in full when they mature.

Many corporations decide to pay off a small amount of bonds every year. Others have provisions that allow them to pay off all the bonds before the stated maturity in case interest rates drop sharply. Then the company could issue new bonds at lower interest rates. This is known as a *call provision*. Many people who bought long-term corporate bonds at high interest rates in the early 1980s found their bonds were called in when rates dropped. Then they were stuck trying to reinvest the money at lower interest rates.

When new issues of corporate bonds are sold, the company must issue a prospectus describing the company's financial condition and the legal restrictions on that issue of bonds. Always read the prospectus carefully to determine your rights as a bondholder, including provisions for early call of the bonds.

Once the corporation has sold its issue of bonds, there will be a trading market for them. That allows you to sell the bonds at a profit or a loss, depending on interest rate movements. Many bonds are traded in a special room on the New York Stock Exchange; others are traded only between dealers. You can check the latest prices of listed bonds in your daily newspaper. If you buy bonds from a major corporation and the bonds are listed on the New York Stock Exchange, you should have little trouble selling them under most circumstances. Other more thinly traded bond issues could be more difficult to sell. When you buy corporate bonds you should buy in lots of at least $5,000 face value. Otherwise you will have difficulty finding buyers.

Commercial Paper

Not all corporate bonds are issued in long-term maturities. Corporations sometimes borrow for very short amounts of time (270 days or less) by selling *commercial paper*. Commercial paper can be purchased through brokerage firms and through some banks in amounts of $25,000 or more. Money market mutual funds generally buy commercial paper, so smaller investors who want to take advantage of the slightly higher yields on commercial paper than on CDs should invest in a money market fund.

MUNICIPAL BONDS

Municipal bonds are issued by cities, states, and other local taxing bodies such as a water or sewer revenue system. Municipal bonds have one outstanding feature not found in any other type of bonds. The interest on them is free from federal income taxes. If you buy a municipal bond issued by your own state or local government, the interest may be free from state income taxes also. Each state can determine which of its bond issues will be exempt from state taxes as well as federal taxes—double tax-exempt.

Because of this tax-free feature, municipal bonds pay lower interest rates than U.S. government or corporate bonds. There is no set, absolute difference in the rates paid by municipal bonds and taxable bonds. That depends on the economic climate and the tax laws. For instance, when tax brackets were lowered in the 1980s, the tax-free benefits of municipal bonds became less attractive to many people who found themselves in lower tax brackets. So municipal bonds had to offer slightly higher yields to compete, and the gap between tax-free and taxable yields narrowed.

There are two types of municipal bonds: *general obligation bonds* and *revenue bonds*. This is an important distinction. The interest on general obligation bonds is paid out of the general revenues of the city or state. That gives them a higher priority and level of safety than revenue bonds, which are paid out of the revenues of a particular municipal enterprise. For instance, there may be toll-road revenue bonds on which interest will be paid for by the tolls deposited each day by users.

Like corporate bonds, municipal bonds are rated for safety and quality by Moody's and Standard & Poor's rating agencies. The bond rating of a city or state will depend on its ability to manage finances and other local economic factors. Stick with top-quality bonds, although lower-rated bonds will certainly pay higher interest rates.

Some municipal bonds come with insurance policies to guard against default. These policies are purchased from private insurers by the municipality that is selling the bonds. The cost of the insurance may lower the yield somewhat, but many investors are willing to accept the slightly lower yield for the extra margin of safety.

Because municipal bonds are tax-free, you will want to compare the yields you could get on taxable bonds before purchasing municipals. Municipal bonds can give you a real advantage if you are in the upper tax brackets, but that advantage disappears as your tax bracket drops.

To find the taxable equivalent yield on a tax-exempt investment, simply divide the municipal bond yield by one minus your marginal tax rate. For an example, an investor in the 33 percent bracket would divide the municipal bond yield by 0.67.

Here's a real example. Long-term U.S. government bonds are yielding 8.10 percent. A 30-year, A-rated municipal bond is yielding 7.25 percent tax-free. But a 30-year, A-rated corporate bond is yielding 9.50 percent. Which is the better investment based strictly on yield? That depends on your tax bracket. If you are an investor in the 33 percent or 15 percent tax bracket here's how the investments stack up assuming no state or local income taxes.

		% You Keep After Tax	
		33% —*Bracket*—	15%
Tax-free bond:	Return—7.25%	7.25%	7.25%
U.S. gov't. bond:	Return—8.10%	5.43%	6.88%
Corporate bond:	Return—9.50%	6.37%	8.08%

We're comparing A-rated corporate and municipal tax-free bonds to a U.S. government bond. Of course, the U.S. government is considered the best credit you can buy, so its bonds offer slightly lower yields. Still you can see that if you are in a lower tax bracket you'll do better by avoiding the tax-free bond. Many people make the mistake of buying municipal bonds just to avoid paying taxes to the government. But before you buy tax-free bonds, figure out how the yield compares with the after-tax return you could get on alternative investments.

Short-Term Tax-Free Municipals

Not all municipal bonds are long-term bonds. Sometimes a municipality may issue IOUs for as short a term as six months. They are often called tax anticipation notes or warrants, and are used by the municipality to borrow money for a short period of time while it awaits collection of tax receipts. These may benefit investors in high tax brackets, but they should be purchased in large enough amounts to offset the costs of the commissions involved.

CONVERTIBLE BONDS

Convertible bonds are issued by corporations and are a hybrid between common stock and regular bonds. Sometimes a corporation wants to raise money, but is faced with a tough choice. If the company sells more stock, it gives away more ownership and dilutes the management control of its largest stockholders. Perhaps the company's stock seems unrealistically low-priced and the company doesn't want to sell its stock too cheaply. On the other hand, the company might be forced to pay too high an interest rate if it borrows money by selling conventional bonds. The general level of interest rates might be high, or if this is a newer, less seasoned company, bond buyers might demand a high rate to lend their money.

The company might decide to raise needed money by selling a convertible bond. This instrument works like a bond in that it pays a fixed interest rate for a set period of years. But the bond buyer has the right to convert his bond to a certain number of shares of stock at a certain price. That way, if the company does well and its stock price rises, the bond buyers get a chance to convert into stock and make real profits. But if things continue as they are, the bond buyer gets the security of regular interest payments and the knowledge that if the company fails, bondholders have a prior lien on its assets.

BOND FUNDS

Owning bonds can be an important part of an investment portfolio. They provide a reliable source of regular investment income. But as we have seen, choosing and then purchasing bonds can involve just as much investigation and analysis as choosing a stock portfolio.

That's why many people prefer to buy a "package" of bonds—a bond fund. Bond funds diversify your investment among a variety of issues, and they place some of the responsibility on the fund manager for choosing which are the best bonds to buy.

Most bond funds stick to just one particular type of bonds—i.e., municipal bonds, government bonds, high-quality corporate bonds, or higher risk, lower-quality bonds. Most funds buy bonds with similar maturities—although some funds may contain both long- and short-term issues. Some funds allow you to reinvest your interest; others pay it out to you monthly or quarterly.

Some bond funds have portfolio managers who buy and sell bond issues for the fund. Others just put together a group of bonds, sell units of the fund to investors, and never change the investments in the portfolio. Some funds allow the investor to sell the fund shares at a price that reflects the daily value of the investments in the fund. Other bond funds are listed on the New York Stock Exchange, where supply and demand set the price for the shares—and so the daily price may not match the intrinsic value of the bond investments in the fund.

Before you buy a bond fund it's important to understand exactly how the fund is structured, how you will receive your income, and how easy it is to get *out*. And always remember that—like individual bonds—bond funds will go up and down in market value in the opposite direction of the general trend of interest rates.

Unit Investment Trusts (Municipals)

Many municipal bonds are sold in *unit investment trusts*. These are simply packages of a variety of municipal bonds. The trust itself may have several million dollars worth of bonds, but units in the trust are sold to individual investors usually in minimum amounts of $1,000.

Just as the interest on the individual municipal bonds is exempt from federal income taxes, so is the interest paid out by the unit investment trust. In fact, some unit investment trusts are structured to include only certain bonds from one state, so that the interest is exempt from state as well as federal income taxes.

There may be 20 or 30 different municipal bonds in the trust, but they generally all mature in about 20 to 30 years (for long-term trusts). Once the trust invests in bonds, they are usually not sold until maturity, unless they are called in by the issuer. However, in most unit investment trusts the trustees can remove and sell some bonds if they appear to have potential problems. If the bonds are sold, they cannot be replaced in the trust; the money must be sent back to the unitholders.

When the bonds in the trust mature in the distant future, the original investment will be sent back to the unitholders. In the meantime, the trust gathers all the interest payments from the bonds and pays them out to the unitholders—usually on a monthly basis. Some people elect to receive their payments quarterly or semiannually. In a unit investment trust, the interest payments cannot be reinvested in the unit because it already has a fixed investment in bonds. However, most sponsors of unit investment trusts make arrangements for interest to be deposited in tax-exempt money market funds so the interest can continue to grow in a tax-free environment.

The advantage of a unit investment trust is that it diversifies your municipal bond holdings while passing on to you tax-free interest payments. You pay a fee for this service. The commission you pay to get into the fund is usually about 5 percent of your investment. The overall yield on the fund is lowered slightly by an annual trustee's fee, which costs only about one-tenth of a percent per year.

All of the fees, plus the goals of the fund, will be outlined in a prospectus. It will also tell you about the bonds the fund will invest in and let you know if the fund has made arrangements for your interest earnings to be reinvested in another fund so that they can continue to grow tax-free.

When it comes to establishing market value, these unit investment trusts work much like an investment in a single bond. That is, when the overall level of interest rates rises, the value of the trust falls. That's not a problem unless you want to sell your trust. If you sell in a period of rising interest rates, you could lose some of your principal investment. Of course, if interest rates fall after you buy into the trust, then your investment becomes more valuable.

There are several alternatives when you want to sell your unit investment trust. You can sell it back to the original trustee, who every day figures out the real asset value of the bonds, and therefore of your units. (It is wise to contact the original trustee first, for a valuation of the unit, before dealing with other firms.) Or you may find a market maker in the municipal bond secondary market who must, by law, offer you at least the bid (true asset value) price of your unit. The market maker makes a profit on the transaction by marking up the price before selling it to the next buyer.

If you are buying a tax-free unit investment trust in the secondary market—that is, from a bond dealer and not on the initial public offering of the trust, you should definitely be careful about what you are buying. The prices of these units are generally quoted in relation to the original $1,000 investment. If interest rates have gone up, the unit may look like it is fairly priced at $900 per unit. If interest rates have fallen since the initial offering, the unit may look fairly priced at $1,100 per unit.

But there is a hidden problem in the resale market for these unit investment trusts. Many unit trusts carried high-yielding bonds that were called in by the issuers when interest rates dropped. The money was paid out to the original unitholder, and so the principal value of bonds is no longer $1,000. There are fewer bonds left in the unit, and it is hard to know exactly what the total value is. You certainly can't tell by the price of the unit.

Other high-yielding bonds in the older unit investment trust portfolios may be called in in the future. Then the unitholder will be left with cash, and the difficulty of reinvesting it at lower rates. The answer to these problems is to *avoid buying unit investment trusts unless you are buying them on the original public offering.*

There is an estimated $100 billion already invested in tax-free unit investment trusts, and new unit investment trusts are created every year. As we noted above, when interest rates rise the value of your unit will drop. Many unit investment trust issuers will gladly arrange for you to sell your old unit and book the loss for income tax purposes. Then you can purchase a new trust with basically the same tax-free yield. Of course, you will have to pay the initial entrance fee again when you buy the new trust. But consult your tax advisor to see if it's worth establishing the loss to offset other gains for income tax purposes.

Closed-End Bond Funds

Closed-end bond funds work in much the same way as unit investment trusts. They take a fixed amount of money and invest it in corporate and government bonds, and sometimes in preferred stocks. The fund collects the interest and passes it on to fund shareholders. The big difference is that the closed-end bond fund (there are closed-end stock funds too; see Chapter 14) has a professional manager whose job it is to decide which bonds or income securities should be purchased and sold for the trust. (Remember, a unit investment trust starts out with a fixed investment in bonds and does not buy and sell or change its portfolio around after the trust is created.)

Some closed-end bond funds specialize in corporate bonds, or high-yielding bonds, U.S. government bonds, or international bonds. Other funds specialize in municipal bonds. Except for the kinds of bonds they invest in, all work in basically the same way.

Like unit investment trusts, closed-end funds have a fixed capitalization—or number of shares outstanding. They cannot continually issue or redeem shares. The fund itself has a certain overall value that changes daily based on the value of the bonds held in the fund. If you take the overall value of the fund assets and divide it by the number of shares, you get the *net asset value per share*.

However, the *market price* of the shares of the fund may not be the same as its real net asset value per share. Shares of the closed-end fund are often listed for trading on one of the stock exchanges. Buyers and sellers determine the market price of the shares. In times of falling interest rates, the fund shares may trade at a premium to the true asset value because people are rushing in to lock in the fund's high yields. When interest rates are rising, the shares may trade at a discount to the net asset value. People are looking to other investment vehicles with higher fixed yields.

When the securities in the closed-end fund earn interest or dividends, the monies are paid out to the shareholders—after deducting a small fee for management expenses. Generally there is a payout every four months, although many bond funds pay dividends monthly. Profits or losses taken on securities in the fund are also distributed to shareholders and clearly labeled as capital gains or losses.

Professional management, combined with the ease of purchase and sale of the funds (since many are listed on major stock exchanges), makes them an interesting investment opportunity. For more information about closed-end bond (and stock) funds, you might want to subscribe to the *Closed-end Fund Digest*. The $200 annual subscription rate includes an annual guide to all closed-end funds (*Closed and Fund Digest*, 133 E. De LaGuerra St., Santa Barbara, CA 93101). Chapter 14 explains closed-end stock funds in more detail.

Open-End Bond Funds

Many mutual fund management companies offer open-end bond funds. That means that there is a bid price and an offer price. You can always sell your shares in the bond fund back to the fund management company at the bid price, which is the price of the assets of the fund divided by the shares outstanding. You buy at the offer price—the value of the fund plus a sales charge. In the case of no-load (no-commission) funds, the bid and the offer price are the same.

These open-end bond funds buy the same kind and variety of bonds that closed-end funds and unit investment trusts choose. It is the fund manager's job to monitor the performance of the bonds in the fund and to forecast the direction of interest rates. The manager can buy and sell bonds in order to make the fund perform better. For instance, if he suspects the general level of interest rates will rise, the manager might sell bonds and hold a higher percentage of cash in the fund. Then he will reinvest the cash in higher-yielding bonds.

You can still lose money if you invest in one of these open-end, managed bond funds and then interest rates rise. After all, the fund owns bonds, and rising rates are bad for bond prices. The idea, though, is that you will lose less money because the portfolio manager has taken some defensive steps. One advantage of open-end bond funds is that you can have your interest payments (which are paid out as dividends to you, the fund shareholder) reinvested in the fund at the current net asset value.

Most major mutual fund families have at least one corporate bond fund and one tax-free municipal bond fund. Before investing, read the prospectus to get an idea of the average rating of the bonds in the fund and the goals of the fund manager. For a better understanding of how these open-end mutual bond and stock funds work, read Chapter 14.

GINNIE MAES

What kind of investment is this, that conjures up the image of a sweet little girl? Ginnie Mae stands for the Government National Mortgage Association, which pools federally insured mortgages for resale to investors.

In one sense, a Ginnie Mae certificate acts like a long-term bond, paying regular interest at a fixed rate over a period of years. Since the mortgages that make up Ginnie Mae packages are insured by the federal government against default, Ginnie Maes give investors a high degree of security. The interest rates on Ginnie Mae certificates are usually just slightly higher than the rates on long-term government bonds.

When the Government National Mortgage Association puts together these mortgage packages, they are offered to investors as certificates that represent shares in a pool of home loans. Investors receive part of the homeowners' monthly mortgage payments—a combination of interest payments plus a return of principal.

Ginnie Mae certificates are offered to investors in $100,000 denominations. However, creative brokerage firms and mutual fund companies have made it easy to invest in Ginnie Maes for as little as $1,000. Investment firms set up Ginnie Mae trusts or funds that divide up the units for purchase by many investors.

Most of the brokerage firms and mutual funds selling these products arrange to have the interest you earn reinvested in other, newer Ginnie Mae units or fund shares. And as you receive principal repayments from time to time, that amount, too, can be reinvested at the current rate in new Ginnie Mae units. It's all very convenient.

But it's important to recognize which money is which: (1) the interest earned on these units, and (2) your own invested money—the principal—that is being repaid to you either regularly or in larger chunks from time to time. Unlike a unit investment trust bond fund where you get your entire investment back at maturity, Ginnie Maes self-liquidate. Your entire investment will be repaid on average in about 12 years as people move and repay their mortgages. That means you get your investment back a little at a time. So you want to be sure you are not spending your principal along with your interest as you receive those checks along the way.

You can purchase Ginnie Mae units from your stockbroker. Many mutual fund companies both load and no load (i.e., no up front investment fee)—also offer Ginnie Mae mutual funds. The interest rate paid on the unit depends on the current level of interest rates offered on all other bonds. And like all other bonds, Ginnie Mae investments carry a market risk. That is, you can lose a portion of your principal investment if interest rates rise.

This is a most important concept to understand before you invest. Say you buy $10,000 worth of Ginnie Mae units paying 10 percent. If the general level of interest rates and mortgage rates were to rise, new packages of Ginnie Mae units would carry a higher rate of return. And if you want to sell your GNMA investment, no one will be willing to pay you $10,000 for your old 10 percent Ginnie Mae when they can now invest in a GNMA unit paying a higher interest rate.

But Ginnie Mae units have one additional drawback not found with ordinary bonds. Not only can you lose money with Ginnie Maes when interest rates *rise,* there is a risk when interest rates *drop.* Falling interest rates induce people to refinance their mortgages. When those mortgages are repaid, you get your principal and interest back, and your Ginnie Mae investment unit is liquidated—perhaps sooner than you had planned. Instead of having a secure investment paying a high rate of return, you are left with cash to reinvest at the current lower rates.

If you buy a Ginnie Mae unit from your stockbroker, you will probably pay a commission of at least 4 percent. That's part of your investment that is not working for you. Some mutual fund management companies such as Fidelity and Vanguard offer Ginnie Mae funds that charge only an annual management fee of about one-half of 1 percent.

Buying Ginnie Maes in a no-commission mutual fund offers some advantages. These funds are generally part of a family of mutual funds (see Chapter 14) and will allow you to switch out of your fund and into a money market fund at no cost. So when you think interest rates may rise, you can switch out of your Ginnie Mae fund before you lose some of your investment. Of course, the money market fund will certainly be paying a lower yield than the Ginnie Mae fund. No-load Ginnie Mae mutual funds also allow you to automatically reinvest your dividend and principal payments into more shares of the same fund.

JUNK BONDS

It certainly is a sign of the times that one of the hottest investments of the 1980s was something called "junk bonds." They are simply corporate IOUs—bonds—carrying a very high rate of interest because there is a strong possibility that the company may not earn enough money to cover the interest payments. By definition, junk bonds are rated double B or lower; in practice many have C minus ratings or no rating at all. Over the years many new and smaller companies issued what we now call junk bonds. Their debt was inherently risky for lenders because of the companies' inexperience or venturesome business. Lenders always charged a higher rate of interest to fund these companies, and conservative investors always avoided their bonds.

An entirely new dimension in junk bonds was created in the 1980s, when former Drexel Burnham exec Mike Milken developed the concept of using junk bonds as a way of helping companies structure takeovers and buyouts. Highly respected companies sold bonds to borrow money to finance their takeover deals—loading up their balance sheets with huge amounts of debt.

In these cases the problem with the debt is not the quality or experience of the borrower. The big worry is that in a recession, when the companies' earnings drop, there will not be enough money to pay the interest on the bonds. Defaults of corporate junk bonds jumped to a record $24.6 billion in 1990. That is double the default rate of 1989 and equivalent to 8.5 percent of the high-yield bonds that are outstanding.

The very existence of so much corporate debt on the balance sheets could, in fact, tend to make a recession much worse. If a company was concerned about paying the interest on its debt, it might have to cut employment and spending, thereby making the recession deeper.

Even without a recession, in 1989 about $3 billion worth of high-yielding junk bonds had either stopped paying interest or were in the middle of some type of corporate debt restructuring. The classic example was Campeau Corporation, which issued $5.3 billion in debt (junk bonds) to finance its takeover of Federated Department Stores in 1988. Scarcely a year later the company was forced to scramble for cash to pay its interest bill—putting its crown jewel, Bloomingdale's, up for sale. Ultimately, Campeau Corporation's two retailing units—Allied and Federated Stores—were forced into bankruptcy.

There are billions of dollars worth of junk bonds out in the marketplace. Who owns them? Many risk-oriented savings and loans loaded up on them as a way to earn high interest rates they could pass on to depositors. The 1989 savings and loan bailout bill said that S&Ls could no longer invest substantial portions of their assets in junk bonds and would have to liquidate their portfolios over the next few years.

Some insurance companies have huge junk bond portfolios used to fund their high-paying annuity contracts. That's certainly worth studying before you buy an annuity or insurance product just because of its attractive yields.

Many junk bonds were purchased by mutual funds, which attracted individual investors by offering diversity and very high yields. You'll find these bond funds issued by the best and most reliable families of mutual funds (see Chapter 14), where they are sold with the understanding that, in return for getting the higher yield, the investor is taking a slightly higher investment risk.

Those risks become more obvious in times of economic uncertainty, when junk bond investors may learn the true meaning of Bernard Baruch's wise saying: "I'm not so concerned about the return *on* my money, as I am about the return *of* my money!"

ZERO COUPON BONDS

Zero coupon bonds became one of the buzzwords of the financial community in the 1980s. Buying zero coupon bonds allows you to lock in current high interest rates for a relatively small investment. When the bonds mature at a specific time in the future, you are guaranteed a fixed amount of money. That's the big attraction: a large payoff for a small up-front investment.

The catch is that between the time you purchase the bonds and the time the bonds mature, they will take big swings in value, depending on the general movement of interest rates. If you have to sell your zero coupon bonds before maturity, you could have substantial losses. Or if interest rates decline, you could have a substantial gain on your investment in a short period of time.

What *is* a zero coupon bond? It's a close cousin to a Series EE U.S. savings bond. With a savings bond you buy at a discount—putting up $25 to buy a $50 face value bond. In the case of a zero coupon bond, you put up something less than face value to buy the bond. The purchase price depends on two things: the maturity or length of time until the bond is worth face value, and the promised interest rate on the bond set by the issuer.

Zero coupon bonds can be issued by governments or companies. The most popular zeros are actually created by U.S. Treasury bond dealers who "strip" regular government bonds into two parts: the regular interest payments and the right to full payment of principal at maturity. That's why these zeros are sometimes called STRIPS (Separate Trading of Registered Interest and Principal Securities). Other dealers have created CATS (Certificates of Accrual on Treasury Securities) and TIGRs (Treasury Investment Growth Receipts). In spite of the menagerie of names, all these zero coupon bonds basically work the same way.

What makes zeros different from other bonds is that you do not receive regular interest payments every six months. Instead, the value of the bond grows or appreciates based on the amount of interest you would be earning if you were receiving a check. That brings up the first problem with zeros. Most zero coupon bonds are taxed as if you *were* receiving those interest checks. In other words, you are taxed on money you don't actually receive until you sell the bond at its higher value later on. That's why most zero bond purchases are made in tax-sheltered accounts such as IRAs where you don't owe annual income taxes anyway.

The one exception to this rule is zero coupon municipal bonds. They are tax-free anyway, so if you buy a zero coupon municipal you are not liable for the tax on the accreted value every year. Several states have created a college savings bond program based on the sale of zero coupon state municipal bonds. You buy them at a discount and are assured they will grow to face value in a set number of years—and you do not owe taxes on the growth every year. The state also gives you a discount on tuition if the proceeds are used to pay for an in-state college education.

In a perfect world, your zero coupon bond would gain value every year as the accumulated interest payments build up in the bond. And that is what happens if interest rates stay exactly the same while you own your bond. But like other long-term bonds, zeros gain or lose market value depending on the general movement of interest rates.

If long-term rates rise, then new zeros with higher implicit interest rates will be issued. That makes your old, lower-interest zero worth less on the open market. If the general level of interest rates falls, then your zero coupon bond will become more valuable. But there's an extra bit of leverage involved in zero coupon bonds. Because you pay a discounted price to purchase them, each swing in interest rates produces bigger price moves in your zero coupon bond. In other words, *zero coupon bonds are very volatile.*

A general rule is that if interest rates change by 1 percent, the market value of your long-term zero coupon bond investment will change by an amount equal to the number of years until maturity. For example, if interest rates drop 1 percent you would gain about 26 percent in market value on a 26-year zero coupon bond. Or if rates move up by 1 percent you would lose about 26 percent of the value of your investment. For shorter-term zeros—say ten years' maturity—a 1 percent move in interest rates translates into a 10 percent move in price. That's real leverage!

Of course, you only want to invest in zero coupon bonds when you feel interest rates have peaked and are unlikely to go any higher. And you want to watch interest rates closely so that you can sell the bonds at a nice profit when rates decline. Suddenly, you've become a trader, not an investor. So because of the volatility, you should plan to keep your zero coupon bond investment until it matures. At maturity you are guaranteed to get the full face value; in the meantime its market value can take quite a roller coaster ride!

You might notice that the yields on zero coupon bonds are slightly lower than on other comparable long-term bonds. For example, when U.S. Treasuries are yielding about 8.35 percent, zero coupon Treasuries with the same maturity date will yield only about 8.15 percent. That's because with zeros you don't have to worry about reinvesting an interest check every six months. In effect, you are guaranteed that all interest payments will be reinvested in the increasing value of the bond.

A final warning: When you purchase zero coupon bonds from a broker, a commission is usually built into the purchase price. That may increase your costs and lower your yield, or long-term profit. And if you sell, once again you depend on the broker to give you the best price for your bonds. Buying zeros in small quantities can be expensive, and since prices aren't listed you depend on the integrity of your broker.

The solution—if you plan to trade your bonds—is to invest in a no-load mutual fund that buys only zero coupon U.S. government Treasury bonds. Benham Capital Management (which runs the T-bill-only Capital Preservation Fund) has a series of Target Maturity Funds that buy government zero coupon bonds. There are several maturities of zeros to choose from (1995, 2000, 2005, 2010 and 2015). The longer the maturity, the more shares of the fund your investment dollar buys. But again, the longer maturities are more volatile in price.

There are no fees to invest or sell your shares in the Benham Target Maturities Trusts. The fund does charge a small annual management fee—seven-tenths of 1 percent. You can track the value of your investment in the mutual funds section of the newspaper every day. If rates are rising, your investment loses value. When rates fall, you gain. When you feel rates have dropped enough to give you a good profit, you simply call the fund to sell the shares and send you a check. Or you can switch directly into the Capital Preservation Money Market Fund and wait to make your next investment. Or you can just hold the trust until maturity. (For more information and a prospectus, call 800-4-SAFETY).

PART

4

Mastering the Stock Market

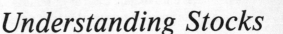

CHAPTER **11**

Understanding Stocks

Whether you start out to buy just one stock or to invest your money in a stock portfolio, there are some basic words, or "jargon," that you need to learn. Just think how confused you'd be if you took your first sewing lesson and didn't understand the term "baste"—or read a recipe book and were told to "baste" the turkey! For a newcomer to car repairs, words like spark plugs and carburetors are a mystery, but with experience these terms and their usage become familiar. It's the same with the language of investments.

STOCK MARKET 101

Let's start with the term *stock*—a *share* of ownership in a company. When a company sells shares, it raises money to make the business grow. Some companies have sold millions of shares over the years. A share is a piece of ownership of the company. The more shares a company has issued, the smaller percentage of ownership your one share represents.

The shares of most large companies are publicly traded—in a market such as the New York Stock Exchange. A company must have sold a lot of shares to the public to be listed on one of the major exchanges. Some larger companies—and many smaller ones—are traded *over the counter* in a market made not in one location, but over the telephones by many brokerage firms willing to buy and sell shares of that company.

If you multiply the number of shares the company has sold to the public over the years by the current market price, you get the total market value of the company. For example, if IBM is selling at $110 a share and has 590 million shares outstanding, the market value is $65 billion. You can tell how big a company is by comparing total market value. A company might have a high stock price but only a few shares outstanding. It would be a far smaller company than one like IBM, which has the largest market value of any industrial company in America.

Once a company sells its stock to the public, it doesn't get any more money if its shares move up to a higher market price. Those shares are owned by individual investors or by mutual funds or institutions. They are the ones who make money if the stock price rises, not the company. The only way IBM could make money as a result of its high stock price is if the company decides to sell more shares to the public. Then a higher price would come in handy; the company would have to sell fewer shares to raise the money it needs. Or if they should decide to take over another company at a fixed price and pay for it in stock. Then, with a higher stock price, they would have to issue fewer shares to buy the other company.

A company does have to worry about *how much* stock it has sold to the public. In many smaller companies, management wants to keep control over a majority of its stock to retain control over the company. Larger companies worry that if they issue too many shares, earnings will be diluted. That is, there will be lower earnings per share, which might lead to a lower stock price.

Every publicly traded company calculates its profits at three-month intervals (quarterly) and at year end. IBM may earn about $5.8 billion in profits for a year. Stock buyers watch to see if those earnings are higher or lower than the year before. Stock analysts also want a reliable way to compare a company's earnings from year to year and with other companies in the same industry. So they divide the total earnings or profits by the number of shares the company has outstanding. In the case of IBM, that's $5.8 billion divided by 590 million shares—or about $9.80 per share.

Most companies' earnings are stated as *earnings per share*. That makes it easy to compare growth in profits from year to year, even if the company sold additional stock during the year to raise capital to invest in the business or to build a new factory.

The next figure stock buyers look at is the *multiple* or *price/earnings ratio* (PE). They take the current market price of one share of the stock and divide it by the expected earnings for one share of stock. Back to our example: IBM is selling at $110 a share and earned about $9.80 per share last year, so it is selling at a price/earnings multiple of about 11.2 times last year's earnings. If next year's profits for the company are expected to be much higher, you would expect the stock to move higher. For instance, if IBM were expected to earn $10.50 a share next year, then next year's price/earnings multiple would be only 10.5 times anticipated earnings.

Stock buyers compare PE multiples of various stocks to decide which one to buy. Mature companies may have a lower PE multiple than small, growing companies. Investors may be willing to pay a higher multiple for the promise of future growth, even though there are little or no current earnings.

The price/earnings ratio of all the 30 stocks in the Dow Jones Industrial Average usually averages out to between 11 and 18 times earnings. (At the market highs before the 1987 crash, the Dow was trading at 22 times earnings. At the market low in 1974, the Dow was trading at 4 times earnings.) But many small speculative stocks trade at price/earnings multiples of 60 times earnings. Many conservative investors just won't buy stocks with high PE multiples; they say betting on future earnings is just too risky.

The next number you should be concerned about as an investor is *dividends*. Dividends are payments made to shareholders out of earnings. Smaller, growing companies may not pay any dividends at all. They simply plow their profits back into the business to make it grow. More mature companies will pay out a portion of their earnings to shareholders in the form of a dividend.

A dividend is stated in a dollar amount, such as IBM's dividend of $4.84 per share. If you own 100 shares of the company you will get a dividend check for $484. Actually, the dividend will probably be paid every quarter, meaning you would get a check for $121 every three months. Some companies pay dividends semiannually; others pay once a year.

If you have $11,000 invested in the company and it pays you a dividend of $484 a year, you are getting a return of about 4.4 percent. Of course, there is always the possibility that the stock price will move higher, giving you a profit and thereby increasing your total return. But you must figure the combination of dividends and stock price appreciation to get total return, and then compare that to what you could get just leaving your money in the bank with no risk of loss.

When the company pays a dividend it will be declared sometime in advance of the actual payment date. You must be a shareholder *of record* to receive the dividend. About a week (five business days) before the record date the stock goes *ex-dividend*. If you buy the stock on or after the ex-dividend date, you are not entitled to receive the dividend. However, on the ex-dividend date the price of the stock is temporarily reduced by the amount of the dividend at the opening of trading. That is, if the company is paying a dividend of 50 cents a share, the price of the stock will drop by one-half point at the opening on the day the stock goes ex-dividend. That allows those who buy the stock without the dividend to pay a fair price.

Although all shareholders of record on the record date are entitled to the dividend, the actual payment may not be made until several weeks later. If you sell the stock before the record date, but the shares are not transferred out of your name immediately, you might receive a dividend check. Then your broker will ask you to return the dividend so it can be passed on to its rightful owner.

Some companies will issue *preferred stock,* which is stock that pays a regular, fixed dividend. Dividends on preferred stocks must be paid before common stockholders receive dividends—and if a company is liquidated the preferred shareholders will get their share of the assets before holders of common stock. If earnings slip, there may not be enough cash on hand to pay even the preferred dividends. But many preferred stocks are *cumulative preferred,* which means the total of accumulated, unpaid dividends must be paid before any dividends are paid on the common stock. Preferred stocks pay the stated dividend perpetually and, unlike bonds, do not mature so you can lock in the high returns as long as the company stays in business.

Sometimes a company will declare a *stock dividend*. That means for every share of stock you own you will get additional shares. The trading price of the stock is reduced by the value of the dividend on the day the dividend is received.

If a company *splits* its stock, shareholders will receive additional shares. If the company has a two-for-one split and you own 100 shares, you will get an additional 100 shares. However, the stock price will simultaneously split in half, so you are not really getting double value. However, when high-priced stocks split, they tend to rise faster. That's why many companies split their shares: It lowers the price and makes stock ownership more accessible to potential buyers.

Sometimes a company will have a *reverse* stock split. It will issue, for example, one new share for every five old shares. This boosts the price of the stock and lowers the total number of shares outstanding.

Selling Short

Although everyone who enters the stock market does so in hopes of making profits, not everyone starts out by *buying* stocks. In fact, some people start out by selling stocks—stocks they do not own!

That's called *selling short*. The idea is the same as our original profit-making premise—*buy low and sell high*. The only difference is that these short sellers work backwards. They sell the stock at a high price and hope to buy it back (cover their short sale) at a lower price.

There are rules for short sellers. Obviously, whenever you sell 100 shares of stock you are obligated to deliver the stock to the buyer. But short sellers didn't own the stock in the first place, so they work through a brokerage firm, which "borrows" the stock to deliver on behalf of the seller. The fee for borrowing the stock is the interest on the money that the stock represents. The short seller pays this interest fee.

What happens to money when selling short? When a short seller sells 100 shares of stock at $55 a share, the proceeds of the sale—$5,500—will be credited to his account, but the money must be left on deposit in the margin account. The short seller also must put up 50 percent of the market value of the stock in a margin account so that the brokerage firm knows there will be money available to buy in the stock at some point in the future.

If the stock drops from 55 to 40, the short seller may want to *cover* his position. That is, he will go into the open market and purchase 100 shares of stock at a cost of $4,000. His profit on the short sale is $1,500. The brokerage firm will deliver the newly purchased stock against the original sale and return the borrowed stock.

It all works out fine if the stock drops in price, but what happens if the stock rises? Then the short seller is faced with the potential of un- limited loss. If the stock was sold short at 55 and climbs to 60 or 70 or 100, eventually the short seller will be forced to buy in the stock at a higher price and take a loss. And in the meantime, as the stock rises, the short seller will be forced to come up with more money in his mar- gin account to make sure there is money on deposit to buy in the stock.

Short selling can be dangerous because there is an unlimited poten- tial for a stock to rise—and, therefore, unlimited potential for loss. But if you sell a stock short at 55, you can only make $55 per share, so there is a limited potential for gain when you sell short. And you would never sell short a low-priced stock, even if you were sure the company was about to report very bad news.

There are also some general SEC regulations for selling short. To make sure that sellers who do not own stock cannot push a company's shares down willfully, you can only sell stock short when the previous differently priced sale was slightly higher—called an *up-tick*. If the stock has dropped in price on all previous sales, you cannot sell it short. That means you have to decide whether a stock is going down and make your short sale *before* the bad news is out and the stock price tumbles.

Selling short is for the pros who can watch stock prices carefully and take the risk. This is a game for the bears who want to profit from bad news. There's nothing unpatriotic about selling short, but there's an awful lot of risk.

MARKET AVERAGES

What is the stock market? For most people, the Dow Jones Indus- trial Average is the number that measures the action on big action days. The Dow is an average of the price of 30 major blue-chip companies that represent about 25 percent of the market value of stocks listed on the New York Stock Exchange. The companies and their stock ticker symbols are shown in Figure 1 below.

Calculating the movements of the Dow Jones Industrials is not as simple as adding up the prices of all 30 stocks and dividing by 30. Instead the divisor is a weighted number designed to keep continuity in the average, in spite of stock splits and dividends.

Started back in May of 1896, the Dow has been quoted daily since then in various forms. In 1928 it grew from 10 corporations to 30, and it still has 13 of the original 30 stocks, some with different names. Companies like Nash Motors, Mack Trucks, and Victor Talking Machines are long gone from the list, but Sears, General Motors, and General Electric are still there.

Figure 1: Dow Jones Industrial Average (DJIA)

DJIA 30 Components

Allied-Signal Inc.	ALD	Int'l Business Machines	IBM
Aluminum Co. of America	AA	International Paper	IP
American Express	AXP	J. P. Morgan & Co.	JPM
American Tel. & Tel.	T	McDonald's Corp.	MCD
Bethlehem Steel	BS	Merck & Co.	MRK
Boeing Co.	BA	Minnesota Mining & Mfg.	MMM
Caterpillar Inc.	CAT	Philip Morris	MO
Chevron Corporation	CHV	Procter & Gamble	PG
Coca-Cola Co.	KO	Sears Roebuck	S
DuPont (E.I.)	DD	Texaco, Inc.	TX
Eastman Kodak	EK	Union Carbide	UK
Exxon Corp.	XON	United Technologies	UTX
General Electric	GE	Walt Disney Co.	DIS
General Motors	GM	Westinghouse Electric	WX
Goodyear Tire	GT	Woolworth Corp.	Z

Source: ©Dow Jones & Company, Inc., 1991. Reprinted by permission. All Rights Reserved Worldwide.

Another more widely used index is the Standard & Poor's (S&P) 500 stock index. Most institutional money managers measure their performance against this list of 500 companies traded on the New York Stock Exchange, the American Stock Exchange, and the over-the-counter market. This is not only a broader list of stocks than the Dow, but it is a market-weighted index. That means each stock influences the index in proportion to the number of its shares outstanding and the market value of those shares. Generally speaking, the S&P 500 should move about one point for every seven points gained or lost by the Dow Industrials. If the Dow has a larger swing, the market is said to be *led* by the blue chips.

If you're trying to beat the market, those are the standard targets. And they don't appear too tough to beat. In 1989 the Dow Jones Industrial Average gained 26.96 percent (with dividends reinvested). The S&P 500 gained 27.25 percent—again, with dividends reinvested. Compare that with the average annual yield for money market funds in the same year, which was 8.9 percent.

And how did the professionals do? According to Lipper Analystical Services, the average stock market mutual fund gained 23.95 percent in 1989. A group of 194 growth and income funds gained 23.18 percent, and a group of 81 funds specializing in small growth stocks gained 22.95 percent. Of course, many money managers outperformed the averages. But the rest are highly paid just to do *as well as* the major indices. In fact, several mutual funds such as the Vanguard Index Trust and the United Services All American Equity Index Fund are set up precisely to mirror the S&P 500. Why would anyone want to do just average in performance? Because, historically speaking, you can make a lot of money that way.

If you had invested $10,000 in 91-day Treasury bills in 1978, your investment would have grown to $15,893 by 1988. If you had invested the same $10,000 in the S&P 500 in 1978, your portfolio would have grown to $37,955 in the same ten-year period. That's not a bad average performance!

You can see that you don't have to make a killing in the market on one individual stock in order to make your money grow. In fact, successful stock market investing can be compared to the fable of the tortoise and the hare. While the hare jumped in and out of stocks, looking for quick profits and listening to hot tips, the tortoise invested conservatively using mutual funds to diversify his risk. Guess who came out ahead in the long run!

The "long run" is the key to stock market performance. It takes a long run to average out the big ups and downs in the market itself. The period from 1978 to 1988, analyzed in Figure 2, took in a huge market upswing and one giant dip. If you are investing for the long run, you can weather those ups and downs. If you are a trader, you want to pick your spots to get in and out. We'll show you some of those techniques in the chap ters ahead. Just remember, though, whether you're an investor or a trader, the stock market involves risks. No one has yet come up with a foolproof system.

STOCK EXCHANGES

If you ever have a chance to visit one of the country's major stock exchanges, spend some time in the visitors' gallery. Stock exchanges around the world are fascinating, and whether you visit in New York, Tokyo, London, or Hong Kong, they all have a few things in common. The stock exchange floor is a place where buy and sell orders are matched.

In the United States, most *listed* stocks trade on the New York or American stock exchanges. There are nearly 2,200 stocks listed for trading on the New York Stock Exchange and slightly more than 1,000 different companies traded on the American Stock Exchange. This is not a fixed number, as more companies apply for listing every year. Stocks may also be *delisted* from trading on the exchanges when they are taken over by another company or fail to meet financial standards for listing on the exchanges.

There are also smaller, regional stock exchanges such as the Midwest Stock Exchange (in Chicago), the Philadelphia Stock Exchange (the nation's oldest exchange), the Pacific Stock Exchange, the Boston Stock Exchange, and the Cincinnati Stock Exchange. These regional

Figure 2:   25 Years of Stock Market History

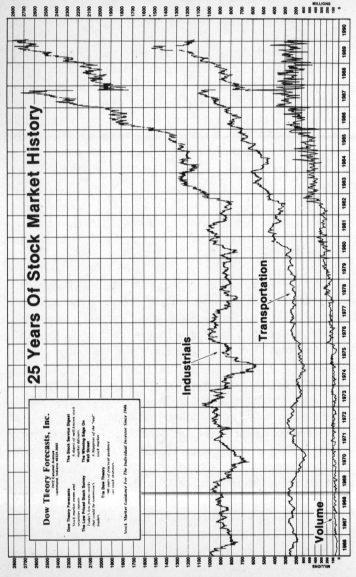

Source: Dow Theory Forecasts, Inc.

exchanges often trade smaller local companies and make alternative markets in some of the larger New York Stock Exchange companies.

On the floor of the New York Stock Exchange there is a *post* where all orders for a particular stock are routed. If you call your stockbroker and place an order to buy 100 shares of IBM, that order will be wired or phoned to the company's representative on the floor of the New York Stock Exchange. The representative will take your order to the IBM post.

At the post a *specialist* matches the buy and sell orders, trying to fill them at prices not too different from the previous trade price. Specialists are obligated to use their own capital to buy or sell shares in that stock if they cannot match orders with each other. Of course, if there is a preponderance of sell orders, they will purchase stock at lower and lower prices. And if a flood of buy orders comes into the post, the specialist will fulfill his or her obligation to sell stock out of his inventory, but at even higher prices. The specialist is charged with making an orderly market.

The specialist system is used to trade the nearly 3,000 stocks listed on the New York and American stock exchanges, but many other stocks are traded in the over-the-counter market, with no trading floor or post where these stocks are traded. Instead, many market makers or dealers working for brokerage firms keep an inventory of stock, and set buy and sell (*bid* and *offer*) prices. Those prices are shown on computer screens at dealer firms around the country. The system is called NASDAQ—the National Association of Securities Dealers Automated Quote system. There may be as few as two or three, or as many as a dozen market makers in a single stock traded over the counter. Their bids and offers, therefore, usually are quite competitive. They may buy and sell for their own accounts as well as selling stock to a broker who phones with your buy order. You will find about 3,000 of the most frequently traded over-the-counter stocks listed in the newspaper every day. They are part of the OTC National Market System.

Some stocks are too infrequently traded to be listed on the NASDAQ computer system. Instead, there are about 11,000 over-the-counter stocks listed in the *pink sheets*—a daily listing of bid and offer prices for hundreds of additional stocks. The dealers list their phone numbers along with their bids and offers. Pink sheet stocks are generally very small companies with thinly traded markets and should be avoided by most investors.

The system of competing multiple market makers is also used on some trading floors. For example, on the Chicago Board Options Exchange trading floor, each stock option trades at a different post. But instead of having only one specialist matching and filling orders, there may be a dozen or more competing market makers, each with a bid and offer price for that option. The Options Exchange contends that the multiple market-maker system offers more competitive prices and adds more liquidity to the trading market. On the Options Exchange, floor members must decide if they are going to trade for their own accounts or execute customer orders in a particular stock on that day.

All of the commodity trading floors use this multiple market-maker system too. But unlike the Options Exchange, most commodity exchange trading floors allow members to trade for both their own accounts and customer accounts. That's called *dual trading* and has come in for some criticism. Opponents of dual trading say it allows a broker to trade for his own profit ahead of any customer orders. Supporters say it adds liquidity to the marketplace. It is likely that restrictions on dual trading will be imposed in the most active commodity markets.

CHOOSING A BROKER

How do you find a stockbroker whose advice you can trust? The first thing to remember is that it's *your* money we're talking about here, and the ultimate decision on investing is definitely yours. Before you even consider investing, you should think about how much risk you are willing to take. As we pointed out earlier, there are bulls, bears—and chickens! Chicken money is nothing to be ashamed of; it's money you can't afford to lose. It belongs only in insured deposit accounts. You don't need a stockbroker's advice for those safe investments.

Still anxious to get into the market? A good broker will be worth far more than what you pay in commissions; the only problem is *finding* a good one! Your best source is a referral from a friend who's bragging about stock market profits. Just as you wouldn't choose a doctor from the phone book, it's not the smartest move to call a brokerage firm and ask who's available at the moment.

When you first call the broker, do it after the markets close, so that the broker will have time to pay attention to your personal situation. (A broker who doesn't stay around the office after the close is either too successful to take on new clients or too depressed about his losses! Find another broker.)

Describe your investment goals and be realistic about the amount you have available to invest. Then *listen* to the broker's reaction and comments. Just because you've taken his or her time to talk, it doesn't mean that you have to invest. In fact, write down some of the recommendations and keep track of their performance. If you miss a few winners, it won't matter much in the long run. In fact, it could be very inexpensive tuition.

Sometimes a broker will call you out of the blue. Brokers, like other salespeople, use "cold calling" to prospect for new clients. You have no obligation to even listen to their ideas, but if you're intrigued you should keep track of their recommendations.

Personally, I think it's worthwhile to meet a broker face to face before doing business. It may be a little inconvenient, but after all, you are establishing a very intimate relationship. When you do open an account, you and the broker should have a clear understanding of not only your investment goals, but of who has the final responsibility for decision making.

I would never give a broker the authority to make trades without specific consent. When you sign the forms to open an account, make sure that you do not give your broker that power. Also read everything you sign so that you know whether you are establishing a cash account or a margin account (which means you are borrowing money from the brokerage firm and could be asked to come up with more cash).

One more thing to get straight right from the start: commissions. We're in the era of negotiated commissions, and that often means the broker has discretion over what you are charged for each trade. If you are an active trader or have a big account, don't be afraid to ask for reduced commissions. On the other hand, if you are just starting out with a small investment, remember that you get what you pay for!

If you talk to enough brokers (and their secretaries or sales assistants) you'll find out that they have some general pet peeves about customers which will make them quickly decide to ignore you. For instance, there's no reason to call your broker several times a day for a quote on the price of a stock you own or are thinking of buying. Unless you are an active trader, this is just an annoying waste of your broker's time.

While you may want to keep track of a broker's recommendations for a while before trading, you can't blame a broker who runs out of patience explaining every investment in detail and then not being rewarded with a trade. Remember, a broker is paid commissions only when you act; the advice does not come free.

When you start trading with a broker you should keep track of all of your confirmations and monthly statements. It is your job, not his, to figure out your gains and losses at the end of the year (although the firm will send you a form totaling profits and losses for tax purposes).

A broker's biggest pet peeve: having to chase a client to pay for stock purchases on time, or to bring in stock certificates when they are sold. If you plan to sell soon, you can make life a lot easier by leaving your stocks registered in *street name*—that is, in the name of the broker-dealer—at the brokerage firm.

What can you as the client expect from your stockbroker? The most important thing is honesty. That means the broker is not unexpectedly "busy" when you want to ask why that stock went down. You can expect an honest explanation of the risk involved in any investment—*before* you buy.

You can expect the broker to create and explain an investment plan for you, not just give you the latest hot stock or takeover rumor. You can expect full information, including research reports or a prospectus, when you are buying a stock. You can expect the broker to notify you if you have purchased a recommended stock and new information comes out on that company.

And you as the client can certainly ask the broker how much commission he or she is making on a deal. That's especially important when buying new or secondary issues, or bonds, or limited partnerships where the commission is not listed separately on the confirmation. The commission generally is built right into these products and may take as much as 8 percent off the top of your investment (about half goes to the firm and half to the individual broker).

The bottom line of any successful broker-customer relationship is trust. If you are uncomfortable with the way your account is being handled or the stocks your broker is recommending, it's your responsibility to either speak up or make a change. There are 457,000 registered stockbrokers in the country; certainly there's at least one perfect match out there for your investment goals.

Discount Brokerage

While every investor needs a brokerage firm to enter orders on the exchange, not every investor needs a full-service stockbroker. If you have done your own research and know which stock you want to buy, you might consider using the services of a discount brokerage firm. That can save you a lot of money in commissions.

Discount stock brokerage firms such as Charles Schwab, Quick and Reilly, and Fidelity Brokerage Services operate nationally. Even if they do not have an office in your city you can always reach them by toll-free telephone number. Discount brokerage firms do not offer many services of full-service brokerages. They will not send you research, and they will not suggest a price at which to buy or sell your stock.

What discount stock brokerage firms *will* do is charge you a much lower commission rate—typically from 25 to 80 percent less than a full-service brokerage firm. There is usually a $40 minimum commission on every trade, and the size of your discount will vary with the size of your order. (You may be able to organize a similar discount with a full-service brokerage firm if you are an active trader.)

Discount brokerage firms will accept your market order or limit order to buy or sell stocks. They will hold your stock certificates in their accounts in street name and will collect your dividends and credit them to your account. Or they will have your stock certificates registered in your name and sent to you.

Discount brokerage firms fully insure your account up to $500,000, as do regular stock brokerage firms. The insurance comes under an industrywide insurance fund called SIPC—the Securities Investor Protection Corporation.

Buying Stocks Without a Broker

Many investors minimize the bite that commissions take out of each transaction by participating in dividend reinvestment plans offered by most major blue-chip companies. That means that investors who already own some of a company's shares can automatically have their dividends reinvested into more shares of the same company. Most of these plans also allow investors to make cash payments into the plans to accumulate more shares.

Usually there is no fee or brokerage commission for this service. The initial purchase of the stock must be done through a broker, but subsequent purchases are made directly through the company. You must register the shares in your name, instead of leaving them with the broker, in order to qualify for these plans. Before making your initial purchase of stock, check the restrictions on direct purchases, which may differ with each company. Those restrictions will be explained by the company's shareholder relations department. Some companies offer this plan only for shareholders with a minimal number of shares.

There is one complication to these dividend reinvestment plans: Reinvested dividends, like cash dividends, are taxed as ordinary income for tax purposes. That means extra record keeping. Also, the investor does not have strict control over the price at which the company chooses to reinvest the dividend. Usually this is done at the market price within days of the declaration of the dividend. Some companies actually offer a discount on the purchase price of stock made through dividend reinvestment plans

CHAPTER 12

How To Choose Stocks

STOCK BUYING STRATEGIES

Whether you are making your own decisions about which stock to buy or getting help from a broker, you should understand exactly how to go about entering your order.

The first thing to decide is the number of shares you want to buy. Generally speaking, you should try to buy at least 100 shares of any stock. That's called a *round lot*. The commissions as a percentage of your investment are always lower when you buy a round lot. If you buy fewer than 100 shares at a time, it's called an *odd lot*. Buying a listed stock in odd lots costs an extra one-eighth of a point, unless the order is placed before the market opening.

If you start out with a small amount of money, that may limit you to a lower-priced stock. Yes, you can buy 10 shares of IBM, but you might have a greater percentage gain if you purchased 100 shares of a low-priced stock. If you have only a small amount of money to invest for a start, and you want to diversify, you should consider buying a mutual fund (see Chapter 14) instead of buying a few shares of several companies.

Once you have picked a stock you will call your broker to enter the order. Typically, you will ask what price the stock is currently trading at. The broker will give you the price of the last sale and perhaps the bid and offer prices for the stock. The *offer* price is the price you will pay if you are buying. The *bid* price is the price you will sell at if you are selling the stock. The difference between the bid and the offer is called the *spread*.

It may surprise you that stock prices are quoted in eighths and quarters of a point—unlike our monetary system, which is based on the decimal system. Some lower-priced stocks are even traded in fractions as small as a sixteenth. When you go to buy a stock the broker may say it is "bid at 20, offered at $20^{1}/_{4}$."

If the stock is actively traded you'll probably enter your order *at the market*. That is, you agree to accept the current price when your order reaches the trading floor. If the stock is thinly (infrequently) traded, or if the market is moving quickly, you may want to specify a *limit price* at which you are willing to buy or sell the stock. If you tell your broker to put a limit of 22 on a stock, and the stock price is quickly moving higher, you run the risk that you won't get your order filled. On the other hand, you won't get surprised with a fill at $22^{7}/_{8}$.

You may want your limit order to be good for only one day. That is, you will buy the stock at 22 if the order can be executed today. At the end of the day your limit order is automatically cancelled. In fact, you can cancel your order even before the day is over. Or you may choose to make it an *open order*—leaving it on the books of the specialist for execution at any later date if the price should return to your limit. If you leave an open order on the books you should keep track of it. The brokerage firm generally will send you a reminder that you have an open order so that you won't be surprised months later when your order is filled.

If you already own stock, you may want to have a little peace of mind in case it drops in price. You could leave an open sell order on the books for a set price *below* the price the stock is now trading at. If the stock falls to that price, the sell order will automatically be executed. This is called a *stop order*. You might want to place a stop order several points below the current price—and raise your stop order as the stock moves higher. That will help to protect your profits.

Some people who watch market charts and technical indicators use stop buy orders. That is, they agree to buy the stock if it rises to a certain price. It may be a price they consider a *breakout*, and so they want to own the stock once it breaks into new high territory. If the stock is trading at $22 a share, this type of order might read: "Buy stop at 24." That is, buy the stock when it gets up to $24 a share.

A *stop limit order* will be filled when the stock gets to that price— and only if it can be filled at that price. The risk with a stop limit order is that the market will be falling (or rising) too fast to execute your order at that specific price. Then your order would not be filled. Most professionals caution against putting stop orders at round numbers because stocks tend to stall at round numbers. A stock might fall to 30 a share and then bounce higher. If you enter a sell stop order at 29⅞ instead of 30, you have protected yourself against getting "stopped out" and then watching the stock return to a higher price.

It's easier to explain the mechanics of selling a stock than it is to give you rules for *when* to sell a stock. There are a number of old maxims:

> "Let your profits run, and take your losses quickly."
>
> "You can never go wrong taking a profit."
>
> "Buy on weakness, sell on strength."
>
> "Trade with the trend."
>
> "Bulls make money and bears make money, but hogs get slaughtered."

As you can see, even the collective wisdom of the ages contradicts itself!

Even before you buy a stock you should have certain objectives based on your reasons for making the purchase. In these days of takeovers, with stock prices doubling within weeks, it is hard to predict the eventual high price of a stock, but when the share price reaches your original objective, it is time to sell.

You might want to sell half of your shares and lock in a profit. Or you might want to use that stop loss order—continually moving the price higher. If you do take your profit and the stock ultimately moves higher, don't look back in agony. One wise trader always said, "Leave something on the table for the other guy." No one ever buys at the bottom and sells at the top. If you can just get the job done in that order— buying low and selling higher—you're way ahead of the game.

Sometimes you will make a mistake and buy a stock that goes down. It happens to the best of professionals. The question is whether to sell or to hang on hoping the stock will come back to your original purchase price. A lot depends on your outlook for the entire market and your understanding of why the stock dropped. Also keep in mind a few basic rules of arithmetic. If you buy a stock at $10 a share and it drops to $5 while you hold on, it has to *double* in price just for you to get even. It might be better to sell out on the way down at $9 and buy another stock. Or wait until the stock falls lower (if it does) and buy it back.

You must take commissions into account when figuring your strategy, but the point is not to get paralyzed into inaction just because the market proved you wrong. It's a fact of life that the market always proves the greatest number of people wrong!

Some people take a completely different action when their stock is dropping. They decide to *average down*. If they purchased 200 shares of a stock at 20 and the price drops to 18, they purchase another 200 shares. If the stock falls further, they may even purchase more. The trouble with this strategy is quickly apparent: You can average yourself into a deep hole!

Averaging down only works to your advantage when you plan for it ahead of time. If you were planning to purchase 600 shares of XYZ stock at 20, then purchase only 200 shares for a start. Keep the rest of the money in reserve, and purchase more shares only if the price falls. That way you won't find all your money tied up in a losing stock. And, of course, every time you make the buy decision as you average down, you must once again reconsider whether your original reasons for purchasing the stock are still valid.

If you average down in a losing position, you may temporarily feel better because it appears you have lowered your average cost. But it takes a commitment of more money to do so. Remember the old saying: "A person who stands with one foot in a bucket of ice water and the other foot in a bucket of boiling hot water can tell you that, on average, he feels fine!"

Another technique commonly used for building a stock portfolio is *dollar cost averaging*. This works more easily with mutual fund shares than with individual stocks because it involves a commitment of a fixed number of investment dollars at regular intervals. Those who practice dollar cost averaging commit to investing a set number of dollars *whether stock prices are high or low.* That means that sometimes your investment dollar will buy a larger number of shares (when stock prices are low) and sometimes one investment dollar will buy a smaller number of shares (when stock prices are high).

The idea is to build up an investment portfolio over the years. And I stress that it can take years for this plan to show profits. It becomes a sort of forced savings plan that has the potential to show real growth. But because this is a long-term program you should not get started if you know you will need the invested money in a short period of time.

One final note: If you decide to trade actively in the stock market, set up a record-keeping system and stick to it. That will make tax time less painful. A notebook detailing purchase date and cost for every stock can be used to match up profits and losses, even if the stock is subsequently sold years later. Then you won't have to go back to your tax records from previous years to establish your cost. Make sure you check your records against the monthly statements sent to you by your broker.

FUNDAMENTAL ANALYSIS

How do you pick stocks that will go up? Generations of market investors have developed theories and strategies. One basic strategy that has proved itself over the years is to buy *value.* That involves analyzing the financial condition of the company and purchasing the stock when the market price has not recognized the true underlying value of the stock.

Omaha-based investor Warren Buffett created a huge fortune for himself and investors in his Berkshire Hathaway Company. He took this small textile company, which was valued at $12 a share back in 1965, and by buying other companies and divisions of other companies he boosted the value of Berkshire Hathaway to more than $8,900 a share in 1989! The company pays no dividends and has always reinvested its profits—by 1988 growing to nearly $3 billion in shareholder equity. Buffett owns 42 percent of Berkshire Hathaway, and his wife owns another 3 percent. He has parlayed a stake of $9,800—mostly earned from paper routes as a boy—into a personal net worth of more than $2 billion. And he did it strictly through his genius in picking undervalued stocks. Now there's an inspiration!

Buffett always said he was a value-oriented investor, preferring to buy companies in good business areas that provided an above average return on equity. Those investors who believed in Buffett's theory and bought Berkshire Hathaway early profited from this investing technique.

What do value-oriented investors look for in choosing a stock? Benjamin Graham and David Dodd wrote *the* book on fundamental investing back in 1934—*Security Analysis*. They stressed the need to look at a company's financial strength as reflected on its balance sheet. Graham defined a "bargain" stock as one that could be bought for no more than two-thirds of its working capital—the money that is cash on hand or could be easily raised from the sale of assets. He figured a company could be liquidated at least for its working capital, and so there was a built-in margin of safety. Back in the 1950s many stocks could meet these standards; today they are very few.

Among the statistics Graham and Dodd considered important was the current stock price as it related to *book value*. Book value is the company's real net worth. It is found by subtracting the company's liabilities from its assets. The result is the book value or *shareholder equity*.

Fundamental analysts often check to see how much of a return or profit shareholders are getting on their equity. To fundamentalists, return on equity is as important or more important than the dividend payout to shareholders. After all, as in the example of Berkshire Hathaway, shareholders can be big winners if dividends are plowed back into a growing business.

Fundamental analysts want to see how much debt the company has. They look at something called the *debt/equity ratio*. There was a time when the standard rule said that a company's current assets should be at least two times as great as its current liabilities. Value-oriented shareholders shunned companies that took on too much debt, reasoning that much of the company's profits would have to be used to pay interest on the debt instead of being reinvested to grow the company.

In the 1980s era of takeovers and buyouts, many companies borrowed money to buy the shares of other companies. Or company managements borrowed money to defend their own position, reasoning that a potential buyer wouldn't want to take on so much debt. A cash- or asset-rich company without much debt became a target for corporate "raiders" who figured they could borrow money to buy the company and then sell off some divisions to repay the debt. Still, many fundamental investors refuse to buy a company with a large amount of debt. They don't see how the stock price can rise when profits must be diverted to paying interest on debt.

You might wonder where a potential investor would gain access to all the information about a company's finances. The first source of information is the company's annual report. Although it is always a little outdated, since the annual report is usually published several months after the company's financial year end, the annual report will give you a great deal of information. When you read an annual report, don't stop at just the glossy pictures of the company's products and the usually cheery letter to shareholders from the chairman or president. In the back of the report will be financial statements that are audited by independent certified public accountants.

There are two major segments to the company's financial statements. The first is a *balance sheet,* which gives a real picture of the company's assets and liabilities. The assets are things the company *owns*—real estate, factories (plant and equipment), and cash on hand. Liabilities are what the company *owes*—money owed to the bank, or borrowed through other forms of debt. The difference between assets and liabilities is the company's *net worth*—sometimes described as shareholder equity.

The second important part of the company's financial statements is the *income statement.* Here you'll find information about the company's current business—the money earned on sales and the expenses incurred. This is where you will find out how profitable the company was last year. Take the income figure and subtract the expenses, and you'll get net income. Subtract taxes paid and you'll get net income after taxes. Divide that by the number of shares outstanding, and you'll get earnings per share.

Be sure to look at the footnotes when you read a company's annual report. It is here that the accountants may express some reservations about the company's financial condition. It's here you will learn about things like lawsuits against the company.

The company's annual report is not the only source of financial information. More up-to-date information can be found in the company's quarterly reports and in several reports that are required to be submitted to the Securities and Exchange Commission. If you are interested in investing in a company, write and ask for the annual report, quarterly reports, and 10K SEC reports, which give more detailed information. The company may also be able to provide you with research reports recently issued by brokerage firms.

There are two excellent sources for basic standardized research reports on all publicly traded companies listed on the New York and American stock exchanges and on the OTC market. Every brokerage firm office will have several thick looseleaf notebooks filled with Standard & Poor's reports on individual stocks. The reports are updated frequently and give a description of the company's business and the outlook for the industry. There is also a history and a small chart of the company's stock price. You will find information about recent earnings and future earnings estimates. There's even an address in case you want to contact the company for more information.

Most brokerage firms also subscribe to *Value Line,* which provides a similar report on individual stocks, along with evaluations of their future prospects. These kinds of reports are basically created for informational purposes. Ask your broker for one of them so you will have all the facts before you make any decisions.

Research reports issued by brokerage firms can be equally helpful, but they are more subjective in nature. That can be a plus or a minus. The investment analyst has talked to management and is making a judgment about the future prospects of the stock based on his or her projections and earnings estimates. Brokerage firm research reports will also give you more information about the industry in which the company operates—sales trends, new products, and technologies. This type of report may focus on several companies within an industry, recommending purchase of one outstanding prospect as defined by the analyst. One drawback of research reports issued by brokerage firms is that, in many cases, the information is presented to large institutional clients before the report can be mailed out to individual retail customers.

You may never delve deeply into a company's balance sheet or income statement, but you should be aware of what these things mean when your stockbroker calls to tell you he has an "undervalued" stock for you to buy.

Be sure to ask *why* the stock appears undervalued. Perhaps the business of the company is currently out of favor among market investors. Everybody might be buying high-technology stocks and leaving basic industrial companies' share prices sagging. It can often be your good fortune to buy stock in a company that is doing well but has not yet been focused on by the investing public. On the other hand, the stock may be undervalued by the marketplace for good reason. Perhaps there is something wrong with the company's business. These are things you can find out by reading the company's financial reports or the ones put out by investment analysts who work for brokerage firms.

Fundamental analysts also look at the general economic picture before investing. They try to determine whether the economy will continue to grow or enter into a recession. They are concerned about the direction of interest rates and Federal Reserve policy that can affect the direction of the economy.

Some analysts watch economic factors such as the *money supply*—basically the amount of money and credit available not only for investors, but for the potential use and growth of the entire economy. If the Federal Reserve has a policy of "squeezing" the money supply (see Chapter 10), the result will be higher interest rates and then an inevitable slowing of the economy.

The higher rates make it difficult for consumers to afford homes and automobiles. As consumer purchases slow down, those basic industries also slow down, and workers are laid off. After a while, the economy enters into a *recession*—an economic slowdown.

While high interest rates may cause the recession, interest rates are eventually brought lower by the recession itself. Lack of borrowing demand by slowing businesses eventually brings rates down. The Fed may eventually decide that business has slowed enough, and then they pump more money into the system to avoid a deep recession—or a *depression*.

If you watch these signs you know that high interest rates are generally bad for businesses because they increase costs and cut demand.

That's bad for stocks. But high interest rates have another effect on the stock market: They create competition for investors' money. Investors look at the total return they can get from stocks—and the risk of loss when they own stocks—and compare it to the possibility of earning high interest rates, risk-free, in a money market fund or bank certificate of deposit.

As interest rates rise, the risk-free investments look a lot better, so investors sell stocks and switch to money market accounts. Of course, eventually so many people sell their stocks, depressing stock prices to such low levels, that bargain hunters step in to buy stocks. They figure the upside potential for stocks is so good, they will forgo the current high rates in the bank.

Investors watch the Federal Reserve and its monetary policies for signals that the Fed is about to loosen up on a tight money stance because when the Fed loosens, it's usually a signal for stocks to rise. That's exactly what caused the stock market to turn abruptly higher in the summer of 1982.

Sometimes stocks can move higher even in the face of rising interest rates. Interest rates may rise on fears of *inflation*—too much money being put into the economy. Then investors may rush to buy stocks as a hedge against inflation—an investment whose value will perhaps beat inflation. During periods of inflationary expectations, stocks in the natural resources businesses may rise fastest.

Clearly there's a lot of information to gather and a lot of economic factors to consider when you become a stock market investor. (Chapter 9 explains many of these economic reports and their potential effects on stock prices.)

No one ever takes all the information and puts it together to come up with one "right" answer to predict market performance. Basically, being successful in the stock market boils down to picking the right company in the right industry, at a time when economic conditions are conducive to future growth.

The secret is to do all of this *before* those factors become readily apparent to other investors. Then your foresight will be rewarded as others decide they are willing to pay higher and higher prices to own shares in a company you invested in.

The last step in successful investing is knowing when to sell. The obvious answer: when "everyone" knows that stocks are going higher and when everyone is in the market, leaving no more anxious investors left to buy!

TECHNICAL ANALYSIS

While some investors base their stock-buying decisions on *fundamental* factors, others see no reason to study a company's balance sheet or industry outlook. They say that buying stocks, or any other commodity, is simply a matter of looking at price patterns and volume figures. They don't care whether the company makes computers or cars, or whether they are buying corn or copper. They simply look at past prices graphed on a chart and then make their buy and sell decisions.

These people are called *technicians*—and although all of their charts and averages are based on readily available trading figures, there are literally dozens of different techniques used to interpret those figures and to predict future prices. And, not surprisingly, different techniques sometimes give contradictory forecasts. Skeptics consider this similar to reading tea leaves, but well-known technicians have a strong following among investors.

Let's start with some of the basics. Suppose you kept a chart of a stock's closing price every day for the last year. Pretty soon you might start to see patterns. Perhaps the stock tends to close higher at the end of the week. Perhaps it moves in a narrow price range, never breaking above, say, $30 a share. Then one day the stock breaks out above that $30 level which has provided so much "resistance," as shown in Figure 3. A technical analyst might consider that breakout into new high territory a signal to buy.

Suppose you notice that a particular stock has been trading in a very narrow range and never seems to go below $26 a share. It seems to have some *support* at that price. Then one day the stock drops sharply below the $26 price level, as shown in Figure 4. Many technicians would consider this a sell signal. Of course, you have already lost a little

Figure 3:

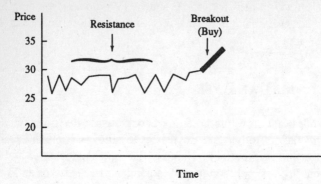

Figure 4:

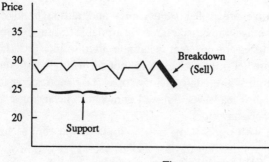

money now that the stock has dropped, but a technician would tell you that following this sell signal could save you from even greater losses now that the stock has broken down through its support.

If you really follow stock charts, you will begin to notice some other patterns. One of the most popular predictors is a *head and shoulders pattern,* as shown in Figure 5. Notice that the stock trades at a level, then moves higher, then backs off and finds support at the previous level. If the stock falls below the support at the right shoulder, analysts will consider it a sell signal.

Figure 5:

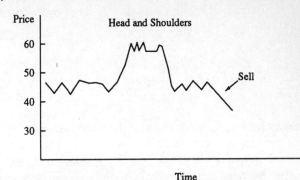

Some analysts construct *moving averages* of stock prices by adding a week's closing prices together and then dividing by the five trading days. That way their decisions won't be distorted by unusual movements on any one day. Other analysts consider volume the most important tool and will buy a stock only when it reaches a new high price level on increasing volume. You can see that becoming a technical analyst could be a full-time occupation! But you don't have to be an expert to appreciate basic price patterns and use their perspective to become a more successful investor.

Fortunately, you don't have to do all the work yourself. Several services offer weekly or monthly books of stock charts sent to you by mail. *Daily Graphs* (213-820-2583) offers a weekly chart of the high, low, and closing prices of 1,600 stocks on the New York Stock Exchange for $15 an issue. A companion book including more than 1,000 American Stock Exchange and OTC stocks is also available. The books include not only prices, but volume figures, moving averages, and other useful technical indicators for the past year.

If you want a longer term perspective, you can buy stock charts that go back 15 years. The Stock Picture (800-633-2252) publishes a booklet of the monthly closing prices for 1,900 NYSE, Amex, and OTC stocks. Each issue costs $30, and they publish every other month.

What you will really need along with the charts are some books to help you interpret them. I highly recommend Stan Weinstein's *Secret's for Profiting in Bull and Bear Markets,* published by Dow Jones-Irwin

($22.95). More advanced students will profit from William Eng's *The Technical Analysis of Stocks, Options, & Futures*, by Probus Publishing ($55).

CYCLES

Many cycles are so familiar we give them little notice. Night follows day, the moon waxes and wanes, and we are secure in the knowledge that eventually spring will follow winter. But while most people generally accept that these natural cycles exist, not everyone accepts the possibility that similar rhythms in political and economic events may be useful in understanding the past, predicting the future—*and* making money!

William D. Gann was one of the most successful speculators of all time. In a trading career that spanned more than half a century—from the 1890s to the 1950s—he amassed a fortune of more than $100 million speculating in stocks and commodities. Gann turned his mathematical theories into profits by correctly predicting the cyclical rise and fall of interest rates and the appearance of booms and panics.

In 1941, Edward R. Dewey created the Foundation for the Study of Cycles. Dewey had been the chief economic analyst for the U.S. Department of Commerce during the 1930s. President Hoover asked him to study the causes of the Great Depression. Unable to come up with a simple answer, Dewey concluded that wars and depressions were triggered by physical forces that created regular cycles, not by politicians and generals.

Today the Foundation for the Study of Cycles, based in Irvine, California, tracks more than 3,000 apparently recurring patterns in nature, politics, and economics. For investors the most interesting cycles are the ones that purport to catalog and then predict moves in the stock market and interest rates as well as long-term cycles in the economy.

Research has established the existence of a 40.68-month cycle in stock prices. Before you think this cycle alone is the key to stock trading profits, you should be aware that there is some uncertainty over the exact beginning and end of each cycle. Still there was enough evidence for the foundation to predict—in March of 1987—that the stock market would peak in early fall.

Many stock market analysts, notably Robert Prechter, have used cycle analysis to make investment predictions—with mixed success. Prechter uses the "Elliott Wave" system based on repetition of patterns to predict market moves. The problem here is correctly labeling past waves on charts of the market's performance, and deciding where we are at any given moment. Two leading Elliott Wave theorists—Prechter and A. J. Frost—disagree on whether the stock market topped out just over 2700 in the summer of 1987 or will reach new highs of around 3200 to 3600 on the Dow Jones Industrials in this cycle.

Perhaps the most interesting of all economic cycles is the long-term Kondratieff cycle. This one is named for a Russian economist who, it is said, died in Siberia. In the 1920s Kondratieff predicted a cyclical downturn for capitalism, a forecast pleasing to Russia's Communist rulers. But Kondratieff also forecast a self-renewing cycle during which capitalism would again flourish. He was banished to Siberia, but his cycle forecast proved correct.

The Kondratieff cycle is expected to take anywhere from 54 years to 60 years to complete. At the start of the cycle there is a period of strong economic growth typically lasting 25 to 35 years. The conclusion of this growth period is usually marked by a major war. Then follows a plateau period of about 10 years as an economy struggles to maintain its previous prosperity. This plateau is characterized by growing inflation and rising debt. Finally there is a cleansing "crash" followed by a roughly 10-year period of low economic growth and stagnation during which debt is wiped out and liquidity returns to the economy. That sets the stage for the next long-term wave of economic growth.

Previous economic declines started in 1929 after the stock market crash 60 years ago (which occurred 11 years after the end of World War I). Turning back the pages of history by another 54 years, you will find the Panic of 1873, which ushered in an era of economic problems— just 10 years after the Civil War. War, plateau, crash, depression. Does it have any lessons for our time?

Donald Hoppe is an economic historian who writes the monthly *Kondratieff Wave Analyst*—a news and investment letter that comments on the current economic situation. Hoppe points to today's international debt problems and S&L bailout woes as similar to the problems of agricultural and bank failures in the 1920s. He says the stock market crash of 1987 was not the "big" one; he figures that will come right on Kondratieff's schedule when the Japanese market tumbles.

The *Kondratieff Wave Analyst* is one investment newsletter I look forward to reading every month for the historical perspective it sheds on current economic and market conditions. (The Kondratieff Wave Analyst, P.O. Box 977, Crystal Lake, IL 60014, $125/yr.)

The Foundation for the Study of Cycles publishes a monthly magazine and numerous cycle charts. Membership costs $59 a year (Foundation for the Study of Cycles, 333 Michaelson Dr., Irvine, CA 92715).

INVESTMENT NEWSLETTERS

Investment newsletters can be a guide to profits in the stock market or a real waste of money. That depends not only on the newsletter you choose, but on whether you're willing to devote the time and attention to following the advice properly. Once again the responsibility for managing your investments falls on you.

There are investment letters that specialize in stocks, options, or commodities. Some are based on fundamental research. That is, they track earnings of companies and industries to project rising or falling stock prices. Other newsletters are technically oriented. That means they look at stock price and volume patterns to predict winners. Market letters may specialize in one group of stocks—medical technology or precious metals. Some identify takeover targets or concentrate on new emerging growth issues.

The advertisements are tempting You'll find them in the business magazines and Sunday financial sections of the newspaper, bragging about past performance and enticing you with hints of their next money-making recommendations. But investment newsletters are no longer required to be registered with the SEC unless the writer is also managing a pool of money. That makes it important for you to check their records independently.

Mark Hulbert, author of the monthly *Hulbert Financial Digest,* tracks the performance records of more than 100 investment newsletters (316 Commerce St., Alexandria, VA 22314, 703-683-5905.) He takes every one of their recommendations and composes a portfolio for each newsletter, reporting the results monthly. Hulbert has been at it for ten years and notes that the best performers over that long run are *The Zweig Forecast, Value Line Investment Survey, The Prudent Speculator, The Chartist,* and *Growth Stock Outlook.* But in 1989 only 10.2 percent of the letters he rated beat the S&P 500 market averages with dividends reinvested.

Checking long-term performance is one way to choose an investment letter. It's also important to choose one that you are comfortable with. Some are jammed with statistics and technical information. Others may be simple to read but not particularly profitable. The best way to choose is to take a trial subscription to several letters for a few months. Even with the discounts offered by most newsletter writers, the trials can be an expensive proposition.

There's an easy way to solve that problem. A company called Select Information Exchange offers a package of trial subscriptions to different investment newsletters for only $11.95. You can choose from a catalog that lists more than a hundred popular investment letters. For a free copy of this catalog write to Select Information Exchange, 2315 Broadway, New York, NY 10024 or call 212-874-7333.

I am often asked to name my favorite investment letters. My criteria for a good newsletter might be different from yours. I read a number of newsletters for market opinions and stock ideas, but those change depending on the trend of the market. Some writers do better in bull markets; others are better at protecting your money on the downside.

One of my favorites in all kinds of markets is *The Wellington Letter,* published monthly by Bert Dohmen, who is based in Honolulu, Hawaii—real proof that you don't have to be right next to the markets in order to be on top of them. Bert has often ranked among the best "market timers" in the country, but to me that is not the real advantage of his investment letter. He takes all aspects of the economy, interest rates, international markets, as well as the U.S. stock market, and ties them together in a logical and understandable package. I consider his letter "must" reading every month (*The Wellington Letter,* P.O. Box

1287, Honolulu, HI 96807 or call 800-992-9989, six months for $195, one year for $375).

To follow more specific market timing and stock recommendations I would suggest trying a few sample letters from the best performing market analysts, using the Select Information Exchange service described above.

CHAPTER 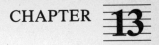 **13**

More on Stocks

The United States is by no means the only country to have active stock markets. There are widely traded stock markets in London, Paris, Tokyo, Hong Kong, and all around the world. You might want to invest in stocks on one of these foreign markets for one of two reasons: Either the economy of that country is growing quickly and stocks are rising there, or you want to take advantage of currency value changes that could enhance your profit. But how does an American investor buy stocks on these markets?

INTERNATIONAL INVESTING

If you have enough money and time, you can establish brokerage accounts in a foreign country and conduct business by international telephone, fax, and telex. However, it's not just the orders that need to be transmitted, you'll also want to receive research reports and market commentary. This whole process can be expensive and is probably not worth it unless a substantial amount of money is involved. You may also be able to execute orders on foreign exchanges through several large U.S. brokerage firms with overseas offices.

American Depository Receipts (ADRs)

There are, however, many foreign stocks that are actually traded on American exchanges. They are traded in the form of ADRs—American Depository Receipts. These are negotiable receipts that are issued by American banks and represent actual shares held in their foreign branches. These ADRs eliminate many inconveniences involved in owning foreign shares because the bank takes care of issuing dividends in American dollars and handles stock splits, stock dividends, and rights offerings.

You can purchase these ADRs through your regular stock brokerage firm. Most ADRs are actively traded and easily quoted. They are subject to Federal Reserve margin regulations. Whether you buy the foreign shares direct or use ADRs, your capital gains are taxed by the U.S. government. Some foreign countries impose a withholding tax on dividends and interest, although that tax can be partially reclaimed.

International Mutual Funds

There are other ways to invest in foreign markets, using professional management and diversifying your portfolio. Most of the major mutual fund companies offer *international funds*—portfolios managed by professionals with access to data and research from around the world. Typically they diversify the fund investments in major international markets—and within each market may hold several different securities, both stocks and bonds.

Families of no-load funds (see Chapter 14) allow you to switch between their international stock and bond funds and other funds in the group at little or no charge. So you have the double advantage of professional management and the chance to get out of the fund very easily if you think the international situation is changing. For example, the T. Rowe Price group of mutual funds has both an international stock fund and a bond fund, along with many other funds. Fidelity has funds for Europe, the Pacific Basin, and Canada, along with an international growth and income fund and an international bond fund. There are even funds that specialize in segments *within* the international markets, such as bond funds that buy only *government* bonds from foreign countries. You can find all the open-end, no-load mutual funds in the guides listed in Chapter 14.

Several closed-end funds hold portfolios of foreign stocks of one particular country. The Japan Fund, the Germany Fund, and the Mexico Fund are examples. Shares of these funds are listed on major exchanges so you can buy them on margin. However, as we explain in Chapter 14, these funds are not always priced at the intrinsic net asset value of their holdings.

Sometimes the shares will trade at a discount to the true market value of their holdings—when people are negative on investment prospects in that country. And it is possible that the shares of the fund could trade at a premium to their intrinsic value—when investors turn bullish on that country. This gives a potential double advantage in making money on foreign stocks if your timing is right.

Timing is particularly important in buying international stocks and stock funds. Not only do you have to guess right about the individual stock and the economy of that country, but you also have to be aware of currency changes. You want to buy stocks in another country when U.S. currency is strong—allowing you to purchase more shares for your dollar. At the same time, you hope that country's economy is improving, which will give you profits within the foreign market itself.

One investment newsletter devoted exclusively to investing in international stocks and mutual funds is *The International Fund Monitor* (P.O. Box 5754, Washington, D.C. 20016, $72/yr. or single issues for $6). This monthly newsletter tracks economic conditions, political events, and currency fluctuations in countries around the world. Every month there is an interview with a leading international fund manager and recommendations of international funds—including funds that invest in single countries.

Eurobonds

American investors also have access to foreign bonds, with the same risks involved in any fixed interest rate purchase. Although the average investor will buy foreign bonds through a mutual fund portfolio, it helps to understand Eurobonds.

These are bonds issued by governments, banks, institutions, and private corporations around the world. They are sold outside their own countries by investment syndicates that are set up to market the bonds to international investors. They may be denominated in foreign currencies or in Eurodollars—dollars held outside the United States. For sophisticated investors, the attraction of these bonds may be the interest rate being paid or the currency in which the bond is denominated.

While most individual investors will never get involved in Eurobonds or Eurodollar CDs, it is interesting to know that there is a huge international borrowing market that is often tapped by big institutions and corporations that do global business.

Foreign Currency Investments

As we noted above, when you invest in the securities of a foreign country, you are also taking a currency risk. Suppose you just want to speculate on the value of the currency itself—against the dollar. You could trade foreign currency futures or options that are listed on commodities exchanges. (See Chapter 16.) Or you could simply go out and buy traveler's checks issued in a foreign currency—and pay a substantial fee. But there are some more efficient ways to translate your dollars into a foreign currency as an investment or speculation on the value of those currencies vis-à-vis the dollar.

Since January 1, 1990, U.S. banks have been allowed to offer CDs denominated in foreign currencies and paying interest at rates those deposits would earn overseas. The deposits are even insured by the FDIC up to $100,000.

Still, these insured deposits do carry a risk. They pay the higher foreign interest rate plus or minus the difference between the value of the two currencies when the CD is opened and when it matures. If the dollar rises, the currency difference is deducted from your earnings on the CD. If the dollar falls, you make money in addition to the interest you're earning.

Several major banks now offer these foreign CD accounts, usually with minimums ranging from $10,000 to $50,000. Many institutions charge service fees, which can cut into your interest or gains. The one bank that seems to welcome smaller accounts ($10,000 minimum) is the Mark Twain Bank in St. Louis, MO (800-926-4922).

Several mutual funds act basically as foreign currency money market funds—allowing you to convert your dollars to investments in Swiss francs, or Japanese yen, or West German marks. If you trade through the discount brokerage firm of Charles Schwab you can invest in the International Cash Portfolio Series, which offers several single-country currency funds and a managed multi-currency fund. Shearson Lehman Hutton offers Global Currencies portfolios, and Fidelity offers several single-currency funds.

A warning to investors in so-called global money market funds. These funds attract investors when short-term foreign interest rates are higher than those in the United States. But the comparison to domestic money market mutual funds is a bit unfair, because these foreign funds often expose the investor to currency risk—especially when exchange rates are volatile. Some funds say they use futures and options hedging techniques to minimize currency losses, but in the quickly changing currency markets those hedges do not always work. For more information on these international currency funds and on international equity or bond funds, contact the *International Fund Monitor* in Washington, D.C. at 202-363-3097.

PENNY STOCKS

Penny stocks are low-priced stocks—usually under $5 a share. They may be just low-priced stocks, or they may be low-quality stocks—or they may be potential investment rip-offs. The first word of advice about penny stocks is: *Beware.*

In 1989 the Securities and Exchange Commission adopted new regulations to protect the public from "boiler-room" sales operations that have cost investors millions in telephone sales pitches for penny stocks. The new SEC rulings require that a broker get a *written* sales agreement from any investor who isn't a regular customer. The broker will also have to get information about a customer's experience and financial condition before any such sales of penny stocks can be binding. These rules apply to stocks selling for less than $5 a share issued by companies with less than $2 million in net tangible assets. It does not apply to customers who have had three or more transactions in penny stocks with the same broker in the past year.

In issuing the regulations, securities officials said they hoped this would save investors "hundreds of millions of dollars a year that has been lost to fraudulent penny stock operations." You can see that penny stocks have the potential to completely wipe out your investment dollars.

On the other hand, huge percentage gains have been made in low-priced stocks. A company might have a new idea or product, or it might be a former high flyer that fell on hard times or even declared bankruptcy. If new management or new products made the company a potential turnaround, there is definitely money to be made in these low-priced stocks. There's just a lot more risk than there is investing in blue chips. A number of low-priced stocks actually trade on the New York Stock Exchange. It should be easy to get financial information on these companies from brokerage firms that might still have analysts following the stocks.

Other low-priced stocks are listed only in the pink sheets. (See Chapter 12.) That means prices are set by a few over-the-counter market makers. The opportunity for manipulation of these low-priced stocks is increased if there are only a few market makers, especially if those market makers are located in Denver or Salt Lake City or on the Vancouver Stock Exchange—the home of the penny stock scams!

A good source for information about low-priced stocks is a newsletter called *The Cheap Investor*. Written for the last eight years by William Mathews, it has an excellent record of picking low-priced stocks that turned out to be winners. (Of course, it was relatively easy to make money in the stock market during the 1980s.) Mathews' monthly letter provides recommendations backed by substantial research. He is not a promoter. You can write to *The Cheap Investor* at 2549 West Golf Rd., Suite 350, Hoffman Estates, IL 60194, $87/yr.

BROKER DISPUTES

What happens when you have a dispute with your broker? It could
be over an unauthorized trade or a pattern of excessive trading in your
account, or perhaps you're just angry that you followed the broker's
advice and bought a stock that went down. It's natural to be upset if
you lose money in the market, but the first step is to honestly assess
who's at fault. Was it your greed, or was it an unethical broker or care-
less order clerk that caused the loss?

After the stock market crash of 1987, the number of broker-
customer disputes in arbitration more than doubled. The New York
Stock Exchange now has 1,256 cases pending, and another 3,990 cases
are lined up at the National Association of Securities Dealers. According to the NYSE, about 50 percent of all cases brought before its arbitration panels are settled in favor of the client. So it appears to be
about an even split in deciding fault in these disputes.

If you feel you have a legitimate complaint, the first step is to talk directly to the broker. State your grievance clearly and keep a record of the
broker's response. If you get no satisfaction, ask to talk to the office
manager immediately. It may help to send a letter stating your complaint. If there is a disputed trade pending in your account, demand to
have the trade liquidated *immediately.* That way you will have a specific
amount in dispute instead of an open-ended possibility of loss.

Most major brokerage firms have a compliance department dedi-
cated to solving this type of problem. You may have to call the firm's
head office to reach the compliance department. Send them a copy of
your letter that went to the local office manager. If you have a reasonable complaint, the problem should be quickly solved within the brokerage firm. But the brokerage firm is not your last resort for a
settlement.

Your next step is *arbitration*—a procedure set up by each of the individual exchanges and the National Association of Securities Dealers to
create impartial panels—including members from outside the securities industry—to judge disputes. All decisions of arbitrators are final
and binding and cannot be appealed in court unless it appears there
may have been fraud in the choice of the arbitration panel.

Proponents of arbitration call it "fair, fast, and final." Indeed the average time for a case to be settled by arbitration is about eight to twelve months. While that may seem a long time, it's far less than a civil court case will take. You don't have to have a lawyer for an arbitration proceeding, but it might be wise to hire one because you will be going up against a brokerage firm that will use its own legal talent.

The cost of setting up an arbitration varies depending on the amount in dispute. It will cost you $100 in filing fees for a claim of $5,000 or less, and up to $400 for a claim of $50,000—plus attorney's fees and research expenses. You can file at any of the exchanges or with the National Association of Securities Dealers.

You may not have much of a choice about taking your disagreement to arbitration. If you look at the form you signed when you opened your brokerage account, you probably agreed to submit any disputes to an impartial panel of arbitrators instead of going to court. In 1989 the Supreme Court ruled that arbitration clauses in brokerage account agreements are valid and the proper course of action to be taken in settling a securities dispute. All arbitration clauses in customer account agreements will be enforced. That makes it even more difficult to sue a broker.

The Securities and Exchange Commission has some rules governing arbitration procedures on all exchanges. The section of the new account agreement that requires arbitration must be highlighted and fully disclosed to the customer. And the agreement cannot place any limitations on what problems go to arbitration or the amounts the firm agrees to pay. Starting in 1990 all arbitration results are made public—allowing investors to know which brokers and firms have consistently been ruled against in disputes with customers.

If a customer wins, an arbitration panel is likely to award specific damages, i.e., money lost in a transaction, and perhaps legal fees. In some cases they may also award punitive damages. But the panel does not set penalties against the broker or firm. Those penalties might subsequently be applied if there is an exchange investigation as a result of an arbitration complaint.

Even if you are compelled to go to arbitration by your brokerage agreement, you might still want the broker or firm to be punished further. If you feel there have been criminal violations of securities rules, you can complain to the Securities Exchange Commission—either the regional office or in Washington, D.C. (202-272-7440, or write to SEC Consumer Affairs Dept., 450 5th St. N.W., Washington, D.C. 20549).

In the case of a commodities disagreement you should also contact the individual exchange—but you might also want to complain to the Commodity Futures Trading Commission (202-254-6387). In addition, the National Futures Association has its own arbitration system. All commodity brokerage firms and trading advisors must agree to arbitrate any dispute brought to the NFA, and the customer has a choice of arbitration panel members from inside or outside the industry. You can reach the NFA at 312-781-1300 or 800-621-3570, 200 W. Madison St., Chicago, IL 60606.

Some exchanges offer their own arbitration panels; others use the American Arbitration Association, a private nonprofit organization specializing in dispute settlement services that are performed in 34 regional offices. If your broker won't put you in touch with them regarding your right to arbitration, you can contact the American Arbitration Association directly at 140 West 51st St., New York, NY 10020.

In any of these situations you are going to have serious expenses of both time and money, in addition to the money you lost in the disputed trades. The best advice is to keep a close eye on the activity in your account and never to give a broker discretionary authority over transactions. But if you have a legitimate gripe, do your best to work it out quickly before the problem compounds.

TAXES AND STOCKS

The federal income tax code seems to change yearly, causing problems for investors trying to figure out the tax angles when it comes to investments. But no matter how the tax code may be changed, there are some basic concepts about investment profits, losses, and taxes that you should understand.

Capital gains are simply gains on investment property (stocks, real estate, etc.) that are sold at a profit At various times our tax code has differentiated between capital gains and "ordinary income"—i.e, income earned as a wage or from a trade or profession. It has been argued that giving a preferential tax treatment to capital gains is an incentive to investment. The tax code also may give different treatment to capital gains depending on how long the asset was held before it was sold as a profit. In the past, periods of one year or six months were considered *short-term* capital gains; assets held for a longer time and then sold at a profit were recorded as *long-term capital gains*. Similarly, losses on investments may be considered long or short-term capital losses—and receive special treatment as a deduction against ordinary income.

A good accountant will keep abreast of changing tax rules and advise you how to balance out your gains and losses for maximum tax benefits.

When it comes to stock and option transactions there are dozens of other rules that apply to specific situations. There are a few key regulations to keep in mind. *Wash sales* are transactions in which the investor sells the stock at a loss and then repurchases the identical security, or options to purchase that security within 30 days before or after the original sale of the stock. If this happens, the capital gains holding period of the original stock is interrupted. If a wash sale occurs and the stock is repurchased, a loss on the original sale cannot be taken as a tax loss.

Investors often are confused when it comes to making stock sales at year end. The current rules state that the sale of publicly traded property is considered to be finalized in the year in which the sale is made—even if the trade date and the settlement date (usually a week later) fall in two different years. That means investors have until the last trading day of the year to sell and establish a gain or loss in a security.

You may have purchased shares in the same company at different times and prices over the years. Before you sell any shares of that stock you should examine your purchase prices. Let's say the stock is now selling at 40. You bought your first 200 shares several years ago at 35. You bought another 200 shares some time later at a price of 45. Take a look at your tax picture. Do you want to establish a loss this year, or do you want to establish a gain to offset other losses you are taking?

At the time of the sale you should clearly designate *which* shares you are selling and ask the broker to have that information printed on your sales confirmation. If you are delivering certificates, make sure you deliver the properly dated shares.

If the securities to be sold cannot be properly identified then the IRS requires you to use a *first in - first out* system of identifying your shares. That is, the first shares purchased are deemed to be the first shares sold. There are a few exceptions, including shares held by brokerage firms where individual certificates cannot be specifically labeled.

You may have inherited stock or purchased it so many years ago that you lost track of the cost. The IRS requires you to make a bona fide effort to establish the cost basis. You can do this by contacting brokers who keep long-term charts. If you can roughly establish the date you acquired the stock, they may help by giving you the price range the stock traded in at that time.

If you have made a good faith effort to establish a price (keep records of your efforts) and still cannot establish a price, then the IRS requires you to estimate the approximate cost. They may review that cost to determine its reasonableness.

If you have old stock certificates and do not know if they have any current value, you should investigate before you try to sell the shares. There are two companies that will take on the job of researching your old stock certificates. Stock Market Information Service is located at 16855 W. Bernardo Dr., San Diego, CA. 92127 (619-592-0362). R.M. Smythe is located at 26 Broadway, Suite 271, New York, N.Y. 10004 (212-943-1880). You should send a *copy* of your certificates to either firm, and for a small fee they will do extensive research to see if the shares have any current value. There have been instances of people finding old certificates in the attic that have turned out to be worth a lot of money. On the other hand, you are more likely to find that you have some attractive wallpaper!

If you are going to be an active trader you must have a professional accountant do your taxes or read up yourself on the myriad rules relating to securities sales. You can help yourself by keeping accurate records of purchase and sale dates and costs, and keeping track of dividend payments. Keep brokerage confirmations and monthly statements in regular files.

Early in the fall each year, *before* the December rush of tax sales, take a look at your entire income tax picture. Determine whether you want to establish some losses or take some gains to offset losses carried forward from previous years. Plan ahead so that your profits won't be distorted by the need to establish a tax position.

And a final word of advice: Never be deterred from taking a profit by thinking of the income tax consequences. Of course, if the tax law is going to change and perhaps bring rates down, you might want to consider postponing a sale. But if you are upset by the fact that the government is going to take about a third of your hard-earned profits, don't use that as an excuse for not selling. After all, would you feel better if you beat the government out of its money by waiting till the stock was trading at a loss?

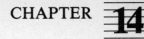

Mutual Funds

One of the secrets to stock market success is spreading the risk. If you do enough homework and get good advice, you can create a diversified stock portfolio for yourself. But many people prefer to buy a ready-made stock portfolio—a mutual fund.

HOW MUTUAL FUNDS WORK

A mutual fund is simply a way of pooling investors' money so that thousands of investors, each with a different amount to invest, can benefit from professional management.

Different mutual funds have different objectives and different risk levels. Some mutual funds specialize in blue-chip stocks, others buy smaller, faster-growing, but riskier, companies. Some funds aim for income, while others stress capital appreciation. There are specialized funds that allow you to invest in technology stocks, or gold shares, or international stock portfolios. Some mutual funds invest in short-term money market instruments, and others are structured to buy longer-term bonds. In fact, the Investment Company Institute, the trade association for mutual funds, lists 22 major categories of investment objectives.

Many mutual funds come in *families*—that is, a group of funds with different objectives that are distributed by one management company.

Perhaps the best known are the Fidelity Group of Funds (the largest), Dreyfus Funds, T. Rowe Price Funds, Scudder Funds, Stein Roe Funds, and Vanguard Funds. Each fund management company may have from six to fifty or more mutual funds under management—each with different goals and strategies. Many of these fund management companies allow you to switch between their funds with no charge.

When buying mutual funds you should check carefully to make sure the objectives of the fund meet your investment goals. Mutual funds not only have different objectives, they may be structured in different ways. Mutual funds, on average, have had an excellent record of market perfomance. Of course, the 1980's was a decade of huge stock market advances, and not all periods may yield an equal track record.

OPEN-END MUTUAL FUNDS

Open-end mutual funds can issue an unlimited number of shares, as more people send money to invest. As more cash comes in, the fund manager can hold it for future investment, or buy more stocks right away. Most open-end mutual funds allow you to start with a small investment (some as little as $100) and add more money whenever you choose. That makes them a great gift for children. You can add money at birthdays and holidays, and they can watch the value of their investment grow. Just as you can reinvest any dividends or gains right back into the fund, you can also easily sell some or all of your shares if you need to take money out. Of course, the value of your shares depends on the daily market value of the investments in the fund.

There are several ways an open-end mutual fund can make money for its shareholders. Since each shareholder owns a proportionate share of the stocks in the fund, when the stock prices rise, the value of the fund shares also increases. Every day the fund figures out the total value of its portfolio of investments and divides that by the number of fund shares outstanding. That gives the price of one share in the fund, which is called the *net asset value* (NAV). You can find price quotations for funds in the newspaper every day, just as you would follow the prices of individual stocks. (See Figure 6.)

Figure 6: How to Read Mutual Fund Quotations

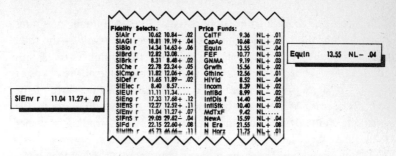

Source: Reprinted by permission of *The Wall Street Journal,* © Dow Jones & Company, Inc., February 9, 1990. All Rights Reserved Worldwide.

There is an alphabetical listing of fund families with prices for each fund. The net asset value is listed in the left column. There may also be an *offer price* that reflects the price you pay to buy the shares and includes a commission. If there is no offer price or if the column reads *NL,* that means it is a no-load, no-commission fund. The right-hand column reflects the gain or loss in the fund's net asset value on the previous day.

A mutual fund can also make money for its investors through dividends and interest earned on its investments. The fund simply passes those dividends and interest on to the shareholders who treat them for tax purposes as if they had earned the money on individual stocks. Generally, the fund itself pays no taxes on those earnings, but passes them directly on to investors.

If the mutual fund owns stocks and then sells them for a profit or loss, those gains (or losses) are also passed directly on to shareholders. If the gain is not passed along, it is held in the fund and increases the value of the fund shares.

Shareholders can easily arrange to have those dividends and capital gains reinvested immediately in shares of the fund, increasing the total amount of shares they own. At the end of the year, though, the fund will send shareholders a statement of the income and capital gains earned on their shares. (Even though capital gains are taxed the same as ordinary income under the Tax Reform Act of 1986, capital gains can still be used to offset capital losses.) Consult a tax advisor to see how those gains and income should be reported.

CLOSED-END FUNDS

Closed-end mutual funds have a fixed, limited number of shares outstanding. The fund still has a per share *net asset value*—the total value of all its investments divided by the number of shares outstanding—but the fund shares do not always trade at the net asset value per share price. If there is a great demand for the shares of the fund, the price of the shares may trade above, or at a *premium* to, the net asset value. If investors turn negative, the fund's trading price per share may be at a *discount* to the net asset value.

Many closed-end funds are managed by distinguished money managers, and the desire to invest with that money manager can push share prices to a premium. Well-known money managers such as Martin Zweig, John Neff, John Templeton, Charles Allmon, and Mario Gabelli all manage closed-end mutual funds. Buying shares in one of their funds is the closest thing to getting their personal money management attention.

With a closed-end fund you can make money in an additional way to all of those outlined for open-end funds. If the value of the investments in the fund rise, the share price should move higher—giving you a gain. However, in addition, if you purchased the fund shares when they were selling at a discount to net asset value, then profits in the fund could attract buyers who might even push the share price to a premium. That's a double "bang for your buck."

The shares of many closed-end funds are listed on the major stock exchanges. You can purchase them through your stock brokerage firm. The commission cost should be the standard—or discount—commission you would pay for any listed security.

For more information on closed-end mutual funds, you might want to read *The Complete Guide to Closed-End Funds* by Douglas Dent and Frank Capiello (Probus, 1989) or contact the Closed-End Fund Digest, 133 E. De LaGuerra St., Santa Barbara, CA 93101.

FEES AND COMMISSIONS

Before you invest in a mutual fund, read the prospectus—a legal-looking booklet that describes the fund's objective, its management, and its charges. Different funds have different costs to you, the investor. Generally speaking, funds that are sold through stockbrokers and financial planners carry a commission, or *load,* which gives the salesperson a fee of from 4 percent to 8.5 percent right off the top of your investment. In the newspapers, an offer price that is greater than the net asset value (NAV) identifies these load funds. That is, the offering or purchase price is higher than the true value per share; the difference is the amount of the sales commission.

Some funds charge no commission when you buy the fund, but do charge a fee when you sell. This may be identified as a *redemption fee,* or deferred sales charge. Generally, the amount of this fee will decline as you hold the fund shares for a longer period of time. Be careful to check for these fees because they are not reflected in the original purchase price. The SEC ruled that open-end mutual funds could not charge back-end loads after October 1990, so many funds had to restructure their charges. However, investors who purchased the funds when they were subject to the back-end load will still have to pay that charge when they redeem those original fund shares. Some funds even charge additional sales fees when you reinvest your dividend or interest payments. Those funds should be avoided.

In addition to any fees charged on purchase or sale of the fund, almost every mutual fund will charge a management fee that can range from one-half of one percent to one percent of total assets annually. The fee covers expenses like the portfolio manager's salary, research expenses, and computer and mailing costs. The fund may also charge a separate fee, taken out of fund assets, to cover the cost of advertising and marketing the fund. This is known as a 12-b-1 fee (after the federal regulatory rule) and has to be disclosed separately. It could be as high as an additional 1.25 percent of the fund's assets.

"NO-LOAD" (NO-COMMISSION) FUNDS

Cost-conscious investors willing to do their homework often turn to *no-load* mutual funds. These funds do not charge an up-front commission, although you do pay the annual management fee, which is taken out of the fund assets. Since there is no commission paid to the salesperson, you won't find stockbrokers pushing these funds. Instead, the fund management company will offer a variety of shareholder services, including toll-free telephone lines with operators trained to answer your questions.

Studies show that there is no correlation between a fund's performance and whether you pay a load or commission to buy it. But there is one obvious advantage to purchasing a no-load mutual fund: Your entire investment goes to work for you right away.

No-load funds are typically purchased through the mail or by a toll-free telephone call. After reading the prospectus, you fill out a simple application form and send a check. You will receive a monthly statement of your fund account and computerized confirmations every time you make a transaction. You can also transact business with the funds using the bank wire transfer system—either to deposit money into your fund account or to have it immediately returned to your bank account. The cost of most of these services is covered by the annual management fee mentioned above.

Most no-load mutual fund management companies also offer a checking service through their money market mutual funds. You will have checks imprinted with your name, just as in a regular checking account. The fund may require a minimum of $100 per check, and may limit the number of checks that can be written every month. You can use these checks to pay regular household bills, major expenses, or income taxes. The advantage is that your money sits in your money market mutual fund earning interest until the check clears.

CHOOSING A MUTUAL FUND

Now that you understand how mutual funds work, you are left with the hardest part—choosing the right mutual fund for your investments. You'll find lots of help easily available. Most of the business magazines like *Barron's* and *Business Week* report regularly on mutual fund performance. In almost every issue *Money* magazine explains no-load mutual funds, reports performance statistics, and gives recommendations.

One critical thing to remember in choosing a mutual fund is that past performance is not always a guarantee of future achievements. A mutual fund is only as good as its portfolio manager—the person actually making the investment decisions. Sometimes when fund managers change, a top-performing fund will turn in a mediocre year. So it's important to know who is managing the fund when you buy it. Also some mutual funds do better in different kinds of markets. One fund may have an outstanding performance in "up" markets, but tends to take big losses in bear markets. Other funds are more defensive, doing relatively better when the market declines.

Another thing to keep in mind when choosing a mutual fund is the minimum investment amounts which may vary with each fund or family of funds. Some funds will allow you to start with no minimum investment. Other mutual funds have minimums as high as $2,500 or even $20,000. There is no correlation between initial minimum investment requirements and fund performance.

In fact one group of mutual funds, the United Services Funds of San Antonio, Texas (800-U.S.-FUNDS), has a unique program for building up an investment portfolio. You can open an account in any one of United Services' thirteen no-load mutual funds for as little as $100—IF you promise to let them automatically deduct at least $20 a month from your checking or savings account to make additional contributions to your mutual fund account. This is an easy way to discipline yourself into a regular investment program. If you're really interested in building a diversified investment portfolio you might want to open an account in the United Services All-American Equity Index Fund, which is designed to match the performance of the Standard & Poor's 500 Stock Index. When the stock market is down, your fixed monthly investment of $20 or more will buy a greater amount of shares. When the stock market moves up, your entire portfolio will increase in value along with this major market index. This is a long-term investment strategy called "dollar cost averaging."

FUND SWITCHING

Many investors prefer to "call the turns" in the market, instead of investing at regular intervals. For this type of investor, timing is essential in successful stock market investing. If you're in the market for the long run, eventually all the ups and downs will be smoothed out. But good timing is what keeps you from buying at the tops and selling at the bottoms. And that can make a big difference in your investment results.

There are all sorts of timing techniques used to predict general market moves as well as the ups and downs of individual stocks. But what happens when you decide to invest in a mutual fund? You expect a professional fund manager to decide when to buy and sell the stocks in the fund portfolio. That's what managers are paid to do. Nonetheless, you still have two big responsibilities: deciding *which* fund to invest in and *when* to buy. There's help available. Several investment newsletters specialize in timing techniques to help you switch into and out of stock market mutual funds.

We explained that no-load funds charge no commissions when you invest and that they come in families—groups of funds with different objectives. There's usually no fee or restriction on switching between the funds in any fund family. However, some funds may restrict the number of switches that can be made between their funds in any one quarter of the year.

Newsletters like the *Telephone Switch Newsletter* and *No-Load Fund-X* choose a list of top-performing no-load funds and advise subscribers when to get into the stock funds and when to switch back to money markets. These monthly letters are supplemented by telephone hot-line update services.

The *Telephone Switch Newsletter* uses a simple system of creating a 39-week average price for a group of five stock funds. When the average moves above the current price, a buy signal is issued. When the average drops below the current price, they tell you to sell (switch out of the stock funds and into the money market funds).

The *Telephone Switch Newsletter* has issued only $10^{1}/_2$ "round trip" signals since they started publishing in 1977, but they boast an annualized compounded growth rate of 18.43 percent. To do that they had to gain an *average* yearly return of about 52 percent! And yes, they did issue a sell signal on October 15, 1987—getting their subscribers out of stocks two days before the big crash! Subsequently they switched back into stock funds on December 6th of 1988, catching the next up move.

No Load Fund-X, another mutual fund switching letter, has a 491 percent total gain since its inception in 1980. That's equivalent to a 21.8 percent annual compounded growth rate—enough to rank this service first in the Hulbert survey of best performing mutual fund advisory letters for the decade of the '80s. This service does not advise switching between stock funds and money market funds; instead it generally prefers staying fully invested in stock funds, switching only to better-performing funds when necessary.

The key to profiting from these services is to follow their instructions regularly and promptly. Of course, no system can guarantee profits, but these two have an enviable track record. You can call each and ask for a recent sample copy and a brochure describing their investment programs. The toll-free numbers for each are: *Telephone Switch Newsletter*—800-950-8765 and *No-Load Fund-X*—800-323-1510.

Other mutual fund timing letters include *The Mutual Fund Strategist, No-load Fund Investor,* and *Investors Intelligence.* You'll find their advertisements in *Barron's* weekly, or you can get trial offers using the Select Information Exchange Service (212-874-7333) as described in Chapter 12.

The real question is whether fund switching beats long-term buy-and-hold strategies. Many of these fund switching services have proved that it *is* possible to beat the market averages through selected buying and selling. Just remember that it takes two signals to make a profit on this strategy: first you have to buy at the right time, and then you have to sell. Actually it may require *three* correct decisions. Because once you're out, you have to decide when to get in again!

FINDING MUTUAL FUNDS

If you're looking for one listing of the names, toll-free phone numbers, and objectives of all no-load funds, there's a directory available for $4 from the Mutual Fund Education Alliance, P.O. Box 11162, Chicago, IL 60611. A relatively new group, The 100% No-Load Mutual Fund Association, also publishes a directory of its more than 100 member funds. This directory costs $1 and the address is 1501 Broadway, Suite 312, New York, NY 10036, 212-768-2477.

In Chicago, the American Association of Individual Investors publishes a helpful guide to no-load funds. It not only lists the funds and their toll-free phone numbers, but gives information about investment objectives and past performance records. This guide is available for $19.95 or free, if you take out an annual membership in the AAII (which I highly recommend). A one-year membership to this association, which will also entitle you to attend its seminars and receive its monthly publication, costs $49. The address is American Association of Individual Investors, 625 N. Michigan Ave., Chicago, IL 60611 (312-280-0170). *The Mutual Fund Letter* is published monthly and not only gives funds by category, but reports monthly performance records, and recommends specific funds to its readers. (*The Mutual Fund Letter,* c/o Investment Information Services, Inc., P.O. Box 3883, Chicago, IL 60654, $99/yr.)

There are several other excellent mutual fund reference guides that are fairly expensive and can be found in most brokerage firm offices or in the public library. Morningstar, Inc. publishes *Mutual Fund Values,* a service that evaluates the performance of more than 1,100 mutual funds with regular updates. The same company also publishes the *Mutual Fund Source Book,* an annual survey of more than 1,700 funds. Another well-known mutual fund advisory service, *Weisenberger Investment Company Service,* publishes an annual survey of mutual fund performance, along with regular monthly updates. Lipper Analytical Services, Inc. compiles the quarterly *Standard & Poor/Lipper Mutual Fund Profiles.* A word of warning: You can get so involved in examining the statistics and picking the "best" mutual fund that you become paralyzed into inaction. If you're ready to take the risks of stock market investing, just pick a fund and get started. Watch the price in your local newspaper every day. Set goals for adding to your investment and, eventually, for selling out. With a mutual fund you have the professionals working for you. And that should make it a lot easier.

Stock Options

While more than 45 million Americans have purchased stocks (and many more are shareholders through company pension funds), fewer than 10 percent of stockholders have ever traded an option. Yet options provide some of the least expensive, risk-limiting ways to invest in the market.

When the Chicago Board Options Exchange opened in April 1973, it pioneered the concept of trading listed options. Now the major exchanges in the United States (and several international markets) trade options on nearly 700 stocks—and the list is growing every day.

Basically, an option on a stock works much the same as the more familiar option on a piece of real estate. You don't buy the entire piece of property; you simply purchase *time*—the right to control the property for a certain length of time. The option gives you the right to purchase the property for a specific price within your option time period.

Investors use real estate options to control a piece of property temporarily while they decide if it is worth buying. Perhaps a shopping center is announced for the land across the street. That would make the property on which you hold an option more valuable. You can either exercise your option and buy the land for later resale, or sell the option itself at a profit, without ever going through the process of buying and selling the land.

If the shopping center across the street doesn't materialize, the land you have under option might become *less* valuable. Then you could try to sell your option at a loss, or just let it expire. You lost the money you spent on the option, but at least you aren't stuck with your money tied up owning the piece of land.

Stock options work under the same principles. In this case, the piece of property is 100 shares of stock. You know whether it is growing more or less valuable because you can track the price of the stock daily. Your *call option* gives you the right to buy the 100 shares of stock at a fixed price during a given time period.

Before the advent of the Options Exchange and listed options trading, people who wanted to buy options on stock had to advertise and contact stock owners directly to make an options deal. Listed options trading on exchanges created standard classes of options with fixed strike prices, and fixed time periods before expiration of each option—plus a publicly recognized bid and offer price.

The strike price is the price at which the option holder can purchase the stock. Thus, today there are option strike prices every $5 a share for stocks priced over $25, and strike prices every $2.50 a share for stocks priced under $25. These prices are set in relationship to the current trading price of the stock. As the stock moves higher or lower, additional series of strike prices are introduced. That gives buyers a choice of strike or purchase prices.

There are fixed expiration months for exchange-traded options. Every option has an expiration in the current month, the following month, plus several additional months during the year. Some actively traded stocks have a different series of options expiring *every* month. That allows option buyers and sellers a choice of just how long an option they want to purchase or grant on any stock. Options expire on the third Friday of each expiration month.

BUYING CALL OPTIONS

When you purchase an option to buy a stock (a *call* option), you have several choices to make. First, you have to decide how long you want your option to last. That is, you must decide which *expiration* month to purchase. Of course, you can sell your option at any time, taking a profit or loss. But if you expect good news to come out four months from now, you would want to purchase a six-month option, giving plenty of time for the news to be reflected in a higher market price. Naturally, the longer the time period of the option you purchase, the more expensive it will be.

The second choice you have to make in purchasing an option is the *strike* or *exercise* price. If a stock is trading at $41 a share, there will be strike prices at $40 and $45 a share. If the stock has moved up and down a lot in recent months, there may also be strike prices at $35 a share and $50 a share. The strike price reflects the prices at which the stock has traded in recent months.

So you have a choice of strike prices: $35, $40, $45, and $50. The stock is trading at $41 a share. The $35 and $40 call options already have some intrinsic value—$6 extra for the $35 option, and $1 extra for the $40 option. That's because the stock is trading above its strike price. These options are said to be *in the money*. The stock is trading below the other two strike prices. Those options are said to be *out of the money*.

Of course, the in-the-money options are more expensive because they already have some intrinsic value. The out-of-the-money options will be less expensive, because all you are really buying is time—the chance to control 100 shares of the stock and hope it will be trading above $45 when your option expires.

The price you pay for the option is called the *premium*. It may have two components: *intrinsic* value (if the option is in the money) and *time* value (the value of any remaining time until expiration). When you pay this premium to buy an option, it is not a down payment. Just like in our real estate example, you are paying full payment for the option or privilege of controlling the property for a fixed period of time and buying it at a fixed price.

How much is an option worth at any given moment? How much should you pay for it? Let's take our example of XYZ stock trading at $41 a share. You decide to buy an in-the-money option—the $40 strike price—that expires in four months. We know the option is worth at least $1 a share (or $100 for 100 shares) because the stock is $1 above the strike price. Now what's the four months' time worth?

That figure is decided by market participants. They take a lot of factors into consideration, such as future dividends on the stock, the volatility of the stock, and the general level of interest rates, which determines their cost of money. If there are a lot of potential buyers anticipating good news, or if the stock is very volatile, or if the market is booming, then four months' time will be worth a lot more money in terms of a call option. If everyone thinks the stock and the market are headed down, then the four months will be less expensive.

Every day that particular option, with that particular strike price and exercise date, will be traded and valued by all market participants. If the price of the stock itself goes up, then of course the value of the option will go up. If there is sudden optimism in the market, then the value of the time left until expiration will increase. Either or both of those components could make your option worth more money. And of course if the stock price drops or people turn negative on the market, your option will lose value.

How do you actually make—or lose—money when you buy a call option? Well, you can sell your option at a profit if its price increases for any of the reasons we described above. The day you purchased it, the option may have been trading at a price of $3^1/_4$. That's $325 for one option (plus commissions, of course). Today it may be trading at a price of 5 ($500). You simply give your stockbroker an order to sell the option at 5 and pocket the profit ($175—less commissions).

There's still time left before expiration of that option you sold at 5, and the new buyer of that option figures there's more profit to be made before the option expires worthless. Of course, the less time there is left, the less value the option will have to a buyer. As you can see, when time dwindles down before expiration, so does the value of your option.

You have another choice in taking your option profits. You can wait until the actual expiration date of the option (or any date before expiration) and *exercise* your option. That means you *call* the stock. You'll have to put up the purchase price. If the strike price was 40, you'll have to put up $4,000 to pay for the 100 shares of stock at 40. Then you can either keep the stock in your portfolio or sell it on the open market.

Most people choose to sell their options at a profit before expiration. That avoids the commissions and hassles involved in exercising the option and buying the stock. Either way, your profit should work out to be the same. Since there is no time value left on expiration date, the value of the option then is only the amount by which the stock is trading above the strike price.

What happens to the call buyer if the stock is trading *below* the strike price at expiration? Then your option expires worthless. Your loss is limited to the entire amount of the premium you paid to buy the option. But you may still be happier than if you had owned the stock. Let's say you paid $300 for the option on the stock at $40 a share. The stock price collapses, and on expiration date the stock is trading at $32 a share. If you had owned the stock you would have lost $800. This way, when the option expires worthless, you lose only $300.

Of course, when you own the stock you can always hang on and hope the price will rise again one day. That's the thing about options: They are only good for a limited period of time. So you have to be right about the stock, and right on in your timing.

What would have happened if the stock was trading right at $40 a share on expiration date? You'd be a loser in that scenario, too. You paid $300 for the option with a $40 strike price. It certainly doesn't pay to exercise your option and call the stock at $40, only to sell it out in the open market again at $40. Your loss is the $300 premium you paid to buy the option.

And what if the stock is selling at $42 and you paid $300 for that option? Then you can sell the option in the market for about $200 on expiration day. With no time left, the option is worth only the intrinsic value to someone who exercises and then sells the stock—a gain of 2 points, or $200. Your loss on this transaction is $100—and commissions.

Options certainly limit your losses. You can only lose the amount you paid to buy the option. That may be a small amount, but it *is* 100 percent of your investment! On the other hand, when you buy an option you gain control—for a short amount of time—of 100 shares of an expensive stock for a relatively small amount of money. If the stock moves up, you can make a huge return on your investment. That's called leverage. And leverage is what gives you the big returns and big risks of buying options.

WRITING CALL OPTIONS

When you purchased that option there had to be a seller—someone who probably owned the stock and was willing to grant you a call option on it at a fixed price for a fixed period of time. Why would anyone do that? Well, the seller received the *premium,* the amount you paid to purchase the option. And the seller may have figured that premium income was a pretty good deal.

The seller, or *writer,* of the option probably owned the stock. If the seller owned 100 shares of XYZ Corp. at a cost of $40 a share, he probably hoped the stock would move higher. But suppose that it has been sitting around $41 a share and now someone comes along and offers to pay him $300 for a call option on the stock.

If he takes the $300 premium, he knows he's obligated to sell the stock to the call buyer at $40 a share during the next four months. He knows the premium money guarantees him a profit of $300 in four months. That's an annual return of nearly 25 percent on his money (if he could do it again two more times during the year). So he decides to write the option.

What could happen to the seller? The stock could sit there for the next four months at around $40 a share, and he would pocket the premium as income because it will not be worth it for the call buyer to exercise the option. Plus, the seller would still own the stock.

The stock could rise—perhaps to $50 a share. If it does, the stock will certainly be called away. The seller pockets the $300 profit but loses out on an additional $700. That goes to the call buyer. Is the seller disappointed? Yes and no. Of course he would have liked all that profit on the stock, but he knew when he wrote the call that he was limiting his profit to $300. He went for the reduced risk—money in his pocket up front. Now he takes the $4,000 he receives for the stock and buys more stock, and writes more calls. The call writer is not aiming for big profits; he wants a regular return on his money.

The call writer has one potential problem, though. What happens if the stock drops in price during that four months? If the stock drops to $37, the call writer is protected. He has that $300 in premium in his pocket. But what if the stock drops to $30 a share? Now he's losing money. He may be afraid to sell the stock and cut his losses because he still has the obligation to deliver 100 shares of stock at $40 a share to the call buyer. What if the stock suddenly rises above $40 again?

As you can see, writing calls is no sure thing. There is still the potential of loss if the stock drops. That's the risk when you write *covered* calls. Covered means you already own the stock when you write the call.

Some people actually write or sell calls when they do *not* own the stock. That's called uncovered, or *naked,* call writing—and it's probably the riskiest thing you can do in the options market. If the stock soars, you're still obligated to deliver it to the call buyer at the low strike price. Your risk of loss is essentially unlimited. This is a difficult game for professionals, and definitely not for amateur speculators.

PUTS

We've just described the basics of buying and selling call options, which are the right to buy the stock for a certain fixed price, during a certain period of time. Now it's time to turn the tables and explain *put* options. They work exactly the same way as call options, except that they give you the right to *sell* the stock or *put* it *to* someone at a fixed price for a fixed period of time.

When you buy a put option, you believe the stock is going down and you want to make a profit. You don't want to sell short (see Chapter 12) because if the stock turns around and goes up you could have an unlimited loss.

But for a few hundred dollars or so you could buy a put option that gives you the right to sell it back to the option grantor at a fixed price. Let's say the stock is selling at $40 a share right now and you think it will drop. You can buy a four-month put option with a $40 strike price for $250. (Put premiums are usually lower than call premiums unless the market is falling rapidly.)

If the stock drops below $37.50 you'll have a profit. You'll probably sell the put option in the marketplace—or you could go out and buy 100 shares of the stock at $37^1/$_2$, where it is now trading, and put it to the option writer, forcing him to pay you $4,000 for stock that is really now worth only $3,750.

People who *write* puts believe the stock is not going down that much, and they want to earn the extra premium income. In that sense they act the same as call writers. They hope that the stock holds steady at the current price and that they collect the premium from writing the option, which they hope will expire worthless to the buyer in a few months. Or they may write puts on a stock they want to own below its current market price.

INDEX OPTIONS

Before we leave the subject of options, let me introduce you to one other concept. Suppose you have a feeling that the market is going up. You expect most stocks to rise, although you don't feel strongly about any one stock. What you would really like to do is buy "the market"— or at least an option on it.

You can do just that by buying an option called OEX 100, based on the S&P 100 index of leading stocks. It is traded on the floor of the Chicago Board Options Exchange, and the option itself represents the price of 100 of the largest blue-chip companies. It includes most of the major, actively traded companies such as IBM, AT&T, Exxon, General Motors, and General Electric.

This is a *market-weighted* index, which means that the current market price of each stock in the index is multiplied by its number of outstanding shares. A move of about 7 to 8 points in the Dow Jones Industrial Average is equivalent to a move of about one point in the OEX index.

OEX options on the S&P 100 index work just the same as put and call options on individual stocks. If you think the market is going up you'll buy a call option with a strike price fairly near the price the index is trading at. If you want to take a long shot you'll buy a cheap out-of-the-money call option.

If the market rises—which means the S&P 100 index rises—the value of your option increases. If the market falls, then your option will lose value. Just as with individual stock options, the cost of one index option could be as little as a few dollars or as much as several thousand dollars, depending on which strike price and which expiration month is chosen.

The only difference between OEX index options and individual stock options is that you cannot exercise the index option and buy the individual stocks. Instead, these options are *settled* in cash. The cash amount is determined by the index value on the expiration date. Again, most investors do not settle up in cash, but instead sell out their option at a profit or loss before expiration date.

LEAPS

The Chicago Board Options Exchange has introduced a new type of option called LEAPS. That stands for Long-Term Equity Anticipation Securities. These are basically long-term put and call options that give you the right to buy or sell a blue-chip stock at a fixed price for up to two years. LEAPS are an interesting tool for the investor who has a long-term time horizon.

A Final Word

Those are the basics of puts and calls, and you should understand how they work before following any advice from your broker. To get more information, write to either the Chicago Board Options Exchange (400 S. LaSalle, Chicago, IL 60606) or the American, Philadelphia, Pacific Coast, or New York stock exchanges—all of which trade listed options. They will be happy to send you a prospectus describing their options. Each exchange also has several booklets explaining the various aspects of the option business.

Remember, options can limit risk or create risk. It all depends on how you use them. Don't be blinded by stories of potential profit. As in all investments, you should understand the downside first.

Expanding Your Investment Horizons

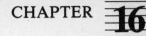

Commodities 101

Commodities futures markets serve an important purpose in determining a fair price for raw materials transactions—whether those transactions take place today or in the future. Aside from their economic justification, the commodities markets also offer speculators an opportunity to profit (or lose) by the assumption of risk.

COMMODITIES AND RISK

There's an inherent risk in being either a grower or user of a raw farm commodity. The farmer who plants corn or soybeans in the spring faces the uncertainty of the summer weather before the crop is harvested. The cereal company knows it must have corn to turn into cornflakes at a specific price per box, but it has no idea what the cost of corn will be after the harvest season. The purpose of the commodities markets is to allow both growers and users to hedge against that inherent price risk—making contracts for future delivery at a specific price, based on all the information available today.

The speculators on the trading floor provide liquidity in this hedging process. They are willing to assume the risk of loss in exchange for the hope of profit. The existence of the speculator who is willing to both buy and sell allows the grower and user to fix their prices and costs, and to plan ahead.

Of course, there are no guarantees that either side will be happy with the price on that future date. A drought could destroy the corn crop. Then the farmer who promised to deliver 5,000 bushels of corn may find he does not have enough harvested. He will be forced to go into the open market and pay a higher price for corn to deliver against his futures sale. Or there could be a bumper crop of corn this year. Then the cornflakes manufacturer would be sorry he committed to pay such a high price in early spring.

Likewise, speculators—whether on the floor or trading through a commodities broker—face the possibility of loss. They must analyze future demand, predict weather conditions, and study other imponderables before committing to buy or sell a commodity in the market.

While some people confuse commodities speculation with gambling, there's quite a difference. Gambling involves the *creation* of a risk—as when a gambler picks up the dice and bets money. Speculation involves the *assumption* of a risk that already exists. There is risk involved in being a grower or user of a product. The speculator is willing to assume that risk.

COMMODITIES MARKETS—HOW THEY WORK

Unlike investing in stocks, commodities speculation is a zero sum game. That means for every winner there is a loser. Or, more accurately, for every dollar in profits on a commodities contract, there is an equal amount in losses. That's because in trading commodities futures a buyer and seller must meet on the trading floor (or through their floor broker) and agree on a price for the contract.

Once that contract is agreed upon, there is one contract of *open interest*. One trader is *long* the commodity contract, and one is *short* the contract. As more buy and sell contracts are agreed upon, the amount of open interest grows. Unlike stocks, where the company issues a specific number of shares outstanding and available for trade, in commodities each new contract adds to the open interest.

Each contract—soybeans, corn, wheat, oats, cattle, pork bellies (unsliced bacon), Japanese yen, U.S. government bonds—trades in specific months—usually four or five delivery months spaced out through the year ahead. The prices of·farther out months may be higher, taking into consideration the interest cost of using your money over the months if you actually own the commodity. In some cases prices of commodities in farther out months may actually be lower, reflecting changing economic perspectives. For example, soybeans may be in tight supply this summer because of a drought last year, but they might be expected to be far more plentiful in November, when the new harvest is in. In that case, soybeans for July delivery would be more expensive than soybeans for November delivery.

It may seem easy to understand why a futures market in grains and livestock would exist. But why a futures market in foreign currencies and interest rates? The answer is the same as for the farm commodities. There is an inherent risk in being a manufacturer buying machinery or components from abroad and having to pay for them in a foreign currency—or selling anything from camera film to pharmaceuticals overseas, and getting paid in foreign currency. After all, currency values change each day. So big companies also hedge their currency or interest rate risks in the futures markets.

One of the greatest attractions—and also the greatest dangers—of the commodities markets is the low margin down payment required to buy a futures contract. In many commodities you can hold a huge dollar value of a contract for as little as 5 percent of the current market value. For example you could control one contract of pork bellies (40,000 pounds of unsliced bacon worth perhaps $20,000) for a margin payment of $1,000. While the money is called "margin," it is not actually a down payment on the value. It is instead considered a "good faith deposit."

The power of margin in commodities resides in the fact that you have tremendous leverage with a small amount of money. If you pay only 5 percent of the value of the contract to buy it, and the price subsequently rises by 5 percent, you have doubled your money. In commodities that can happen overnight. But that leverage is a two-edged sword. If the price falls sharply, your margin account will be wiped out. Your broker will ask for more money, or will be forced to sell you out.

Commodities futures are one place where you can lose *more* than your original investment. Each commodity month has a certain *limit*—a fixed amount, either up or down, that the price is allowed to move daily. (The only exception is the most nearby trading month, in which there are no limits.) If everybody turns bearish and the price of a commodity is falling rapidly, there may be a day on which the offered price falls below the accepted limit and there are still no buyers. No contracts of that commodity will trade that day, although the value of each open contract has dropped dramatically. The market is said to be *limit down*. (The same can happen on the upside; it's called *limit up*.)

If you happen to be on the wrong side of one of these limit markets, your broker will call you when your account is below margin. You will have to put up more money. If the market trades limit up or limit down for several days, you could lose all of your original margin deposit and actually be forced to ante up even more money before your account can finally be sold out.

Now you see the key attraction and key danger of the futures markets. Not only do they move quickly, but your money moves quickly as well. You can build a fortune fast—or lose it fast.

Every novice commodities trader hears stories of pigs or soybeans being delivered to someone's front lawn. But while hundreds or thousands of futures contracts may trade on any commodity, only a very small percentage actually result in the buyer or seller making or taking delivery of the product itself. Most contracts are closed out—at a profit or loss—far before the actual delivery expiration date.

And don't worry about your front lawn. Instead of delivering the product, what actually changes hands is a *warehouse receipt*—a certificate of ownership. Money also changes hands when delivery is made. As we noted, buyers and sellers of futures contracts are required to put down only a small fraction of the value of the commodity—as little as 5 or 10 percent. But when it comes time for the user to actually take delivery of the commodity, the balance must be paid in cash.

All commodities futures markets function in basically the manner we have just described. They are used by speculators and hedgers around the world to establish fair present and future values for raw materials.

Certainly there is a great opportunity for profit in the futures markets. And the futures markets can be a definite tool to reduce risk and exposure inherent in other markets or businesses. The key is to understand how these fast-moving markets operate before you put your money at risk—and to understand the special risks inherent in commodities trading.

TRADING COMMODITIES

You have probably heard stories of ordinary young men and women starting with a small sum of money and making a fortune in the commodities futures markets. One classic example is Chicagoan Richard Dennis, who started out as a young man from one of Chicago's working-class neighborhoods and parlayed $1,600 borrowed from his family into a reputed $200 million fortune in the 1970s and 1980s.

Or there is the legend of Gene Cashman, a Chicago policeman, who gave up walking his beat in the 1950s and went down to the floor of the Chicago Board of Trade. When he left the trading floor in 1980, he had created a dynasty, and his fortune was estimated at $50 to $100 million.

What you often don't hear about is the number of young people who arrive on the floor only to "bust out" a few months later. Many start out as order clerks or "runners" to get a taste of life in the "fast lane." But it's not that easy.

In the commodities business you find out very quickly whether you have the talent and instinct to be successful as a trader. There is a bottom line in your trading account every day. You either make money or you lose. Of course, it is expected that you will take some losses along the way—but you can run out of money very quickly if you are not attuned to the markets.

What does it take to be a successful trader on the floor? Some say it takes brains, but there are many success stories told about traders who didn't know much about the economics of the commodity they were trading; they just had a "feel" for the markets. Others say it takes a mathematical mind, capable of figuring out minute differentials instantaneously. But many successful floor traders have no time to calculate spreads in prices; they trade instinctively.

Very few people will ever consider a career of trading on the floor of the commodities exchanges—even though "seats" (memberships) may be leased for a few thousand dollars a month. But hundreds of thousands of people trade the commodities futures markets every year through their brokers.

The point of the stories above is to illustrate how difficult it is to make consistent money in the commodities markets—*even if you are at the center of the action on the trading floor every day*. Now, how difficult do you think it is to make money if you're on the phone with your broker once or twice a day? And, more important, if your broker has such great ideas, why isn't he or she leasing a seat and trading for his or her own account right on the floor?

There are certainly many successful commodities brokers giving advice and counsel to retail clients. If you decide to trade commodities, you have to find one of them before your money runs out in these fast-moving markets. And remember, today's winning broker may not have the same "hot hand" next season.

Many individual commodities speculators figure they don't have enough risk capital to speculate in several markets. So they invest in commodities *pools*—a sort of commodity mutual fund. These funds have had mixed results. For the year ending in August 1989, out of 126 funds that had been in business for a full 12 months, 65 reported gains, 60 reported losses, and one was unchanged. While the best performing fund gained 49.7 percent, the worst performer *lost* 40.3 percent. The average performance of all those funds for one year: a gain of .2 percent—or almost no change in their net worth. If the money had been invested safely in Treasury bills during the same period with absolutely no risk, it would have grown by 8 percent.

For track records of public commodities pools, contact Managed Account Reports, 5513 Twin Knolls Rd., Suite 213, Columbia, MD 21045 (301-730-5365); $20 for a single copy. They will also consult with individuals to find appropriate fund managers.

COMMODITIES EXCHANGES

Commodities are traded on exchanges around the world, but the most active markets are in the United States. The Chicago Board of Trade is the nation's oldest and largest commodities exchange.

Founded in 1848, it created the concept of futures markets. The Chicago Board of Trade currently has 3,600 members in its several divisions. It is the world futures marketplace for wheat, corn, oats, soybeans, soybean meal, and soybean oil.

The Board of Trade also has a thriving financial futures division with one of the most widely traded commodities in the world—U.S. government bonds. In addition, the Board of Trade has contracts in 5- and 10-year Treasury note futures, mortgage-backed securities, municipal bond futures, 30-day interest rate futures, and a stock index futures contract. There are also options traded on each of these financial futures contracts.

The trading volume at the Chicago Board of Trade reaches more than 150 million contracts a year. When interest rates are active, the U.S. government bond contract may trade more than 80 million contracts; in times of agricultural uncertainty such as a drought, the farm commodities contracts surge in volume.

For more information about the Chicago Board of Trade, contact the exchange at 141 W. Jackson Blvd., Chicago, IL 60604 (312-435-3500).

The Chicago Mercantile Exchange traces its roots to the post-Civil War days. In 1919 it was known as the "butter and egg" exchange—a group of small markets. Today it has grown to trade more than 100 million contracts a year on commodities as diverse as cattle, hogs, pork bellies, lumber, and a whole range of financial futures that are traded on its International Monetary Market and International Options Market divisions.

It was the Chicago Mercantile Exchange that actually created the concept of financial futures back in the early 1970s, when international currency exchange rates were allowed to float freely. Visionaries at the Merc realized that with fluctuating international exchange rates, companies would need some form of hedging against the risk of loss in currency transactions. Today the Merc trades futures on seven foreign currencies as well as interest rate futures in Treasury bills and Eurodollar CDs. The Merc also trades options on many of their futures contracts.

The Chicago Mercantile Exchange's best known financial future is the Standard & Poor's 500 futures contract. It trades 40,000 contracts on an average day—each contract worth roughly $170,000 of stocks (depending on the price level of the stock market). This futures contract is used primarily by big institutions and pension funds to limit the risk on the stock portfolios they own. But an individual speculator can control one S&P index futures contract for a small amount of margin—around $10,000.

Starting in 1991 the Chicago Mercantile Exchange pioneered around-the-clock trading through its Globex system, which provides computerized trade matching around the clock when the actual trading floor is not in session. Not only are Chicago Mercantile Exchange contracts listed on Globex, but it is expected that contracts from exchanges around the world will also be listed for this "after-hours" electronic trading. The Board of Trade has its own competitive computerized trading system, dubbed Aurora, that is also expected to start operations in 1990.

For more information on trading any of the futures contracts listed at the Chicago Mercantile Exchange, contact the exchange at 30 S. Wacker Dr., Chicago, IL 60606 (312-930-1000).

NEW YORK COMMODITIES EXCHANGES

There are several commodities futures exchanges based in New York. The New York Mercantile Exchange has a thriving futures market in crude oil, gasoline, and heating oil, as well as options on those futures. This exchange also is the site of futures trading in platinum and palladium.

The NYMEX, as it is called, was founded in 1872 and today is the premier market in these important industrial and energy commodities. It has 816 members, and trading volume on the exchange totaled more than 34 million contracts in 1988. For more information on the exchange and its contracts, write to: The New York Mercantile Exchange, 4 World Trade Center, New York, NY 10048 (212-938-2222).

The Commodity Exchange, Inc. (COMEX) is also located in the World Trade Center in New York, (212-938-2900). It is best known for its gold and silver futures markets, although it also trades futures in copper and aluminum.

The Coffee, Sugar and Cocoa Exchange is a separate exchange located in the futures trading complex at the World Trade Center (212-938-2800). It trades the "soft" commodities (as compared to "hard" commodities like metals). This exchange makes markets in the three commodities listed in its name and in options on those futures contracts. It also trades futures on the International Market index, which is based on stocks of 50 international firms whose shares are widely traded.

The fourth exchange in this trading complex is the New York Cotton Exchange located in the same building in New York (212-938-2702). It dates back to 1870 and is considered the oldest exchange in New York. It trades not only cotton, but frozen orange juice concentrate futures. Since 1985 the New York Cotton Exchange has had a financial futures market through its FINEX division, which trades futures and options on a U.S. dollar index, five- and two-year Treasury notes, and a European currency unit (ECU). In 1988 more than three million contracts were traded on this exchange.

The New York Futures Exchange (NYFE) was created in 1979 as a subsidiary of the New York Stock Exchange. The NYFE trading floor is now located with other commodities exchanges in the World Trade Center (212-656-4949).

The NYFE trades six contracts. The most prominent is a futures contract based on the New York Stock Exchange composite index, which reflects the movement of all common stocks listed on the NYSE. The NYFE also trades options on the NYSE index, and a futures and options contract based on the Commodity Research Bureau's futures price index—a widely followed indicator of inflation in raw materials. Other stock futures contracts track the performance of institutional stock managers.

There are dozens of other futures markets located around the world, but the United States has the distinction of maintaining leading markets in the world's most widely traded commodities.

STOCK INDEX FUTURES AND PROGRAM TRADING

Money managers of huge institutional funds have found that they do not need to actually buy and sell stocks in their portfolios when they think the market is going to make a move. Instead, they can buy and sell the futures representing the stocks. The commissions are lower, and the effect on the price of the underlying stock is smaller. In the late 1980s, these stock index futures gave birth to two concepts that later shook the marketplace—*program trading* and *portfolio insurance*.

Program trading was merely a way of programming computers to take advantage of differences in prices between the financial index futures and the stocks themselves. Computers could establish valuations instantly—and direct purchases and sales of a group of stocks, or the futures, to try to profit from differing values. For instance, if the index futures were trading at a discount to the computed value of stocks in the index, the computer would issue a buy order for the futures.

Waves of buying and selling swept through the markets, affecting both stocks and futures prices. Program trading had such a dramatic effect during the crash of 1987 that the New York Stock Exchange temporarily shut down its Direct Order System, which allowed the huge orders to be processed by computer and sent directly to the stocks' trading posts. In the "Friday the 13th" October 1989 stock market drop, program trading was once again blamed for accentuating the market's volatility. New programs were instituted to limit the use of computers in directing program trading orders, and many brokerage firms and institutions voluntarily stopped program trading for their own accounts.

Portfolio insurance was a similar concept. Professional managers reasoned they would be protected in a decline if they held their stocks and sold the futures indexes. It was a reasonable concept that proved disastrous in accentuating the stock market crash of 1987. The problem was that too few portfolio managers took out the insurance *before* the crash. They only decided to sell the futures once the stock market started heading down. That's like buying fire insurance after your house catches on fire! The result was to cause a wave of selling in futures, which then activated the computer programs to sell the actual stocks to narrow the differential between the two.

Trading index futures is not for the average speculator. It requires some real study plus the use of some accurate computer and timing techniques. But you should be aware of how these futures can affect the basic underlying markets.

COMMODITIES REGULATION

All commodities trading in the United States are regulated by the Commodity Futures Trading Commission (2033 K Street, NW, Washington, D.C., 20581). However, each exchange has its own self-regulatory procedures.

Firms that are members of the exchange may be *clearing members,* which are the backbone of each exchange, putting their own firm's guarantee behind the trades made by its members or their clients. Other firms doing business with customers may *clear through* these clearing members. That means these smaller firms put up their margin deposits and act as customers of the clearing firm.

While there is no intrinsic difference between doing business with either a clearing or nonclearing member of an exchange if you are an individual customer, there is a subtle sense that the financial strength of a clearing firm might add a greater degree of security to your transactions.

When you are solicited to do business with a commodities firm, ask about their exchange memberships and whether the memberships are clearing or nonclearing. Then check with the clearing firm and the exchange to make sure there are no significant complaints against the firm. You might also check with the Commodity Futures Trading Commission or with the industry's self-regulatory association: The National Futures Association, 200 W. Madison St., Chicago, IL 60606 (800-621-3570 or 312-781-1300).

Gold and Silver

GOLD—WHY IS IT UNIQUE?

For thousands of years, gold has held a special fascination for man. Because of its rarity, it has been considered the ultimate store of wealth that could not be matched by any other form of currency. Gold is so scarce that all the gold ever mined throughout history would fit into a cube measuring just 56 feet on each side!

Not only is gold extremely rare, but it also has properties unmatched by any other metal. Gold is virtually indestructible, yet it is so soft and malleable that one ounce of gold can be stretched into a wire that is five miles long—or hammered into a sheet so thin that it covers 100 square feet. Gold does not rust, tarnish, or corrode. It's no wonder that during the Dark Ages alchemists worked feverishly—but unsuccessfully—to turn base metals into gold.

GOLD—THROUGHOUT HISTORY

Even during more modern times there have been attempts to convince mankind that some other form of currency—usually paper—was "as good as gold." All of those attempts have failed. Even currencies said to have the backing of gold have eventually been repudiated in favor of something more tangible. In times of financial crisis or war, mankind inevitably turns to gold as a safe haven, a store of wealth. Over thousands of years, mankind has learned that while politicians can create paper and promises, even their political alchemy cannot create gold.

The United States, like other countries, has at various times been on a *gold standard*. That meant the currency was considered convertible, or at least backed by actual gold reserves. The amount of gold held in reserve limited the amount of paper currency that could be issued.

The original currency of the revolutionary colonies was called the "continental." So many of them were issued that they gave rise to the old phrase "not worth a continental." Immediately after the Constitution was ratified in 1792, Congress created the National Mint. The 1792 law directed American money to be made of gold, silver, and copper. During the early nineteenth century, individual banks could issue their own currency. But when many of them took advantage and created what the marketplace considered "too much" currency, the populace again demanded "real" money—gold and silver coins. The United States went off the gold standard during the Civil War, and "greenbacks" were issued. A great argument ensued between those who wanted to print more greenbacks as a way of creating inflation and thereby pushing farm prices higher, and those who wanted to go back to the gold standard. A compromise was reached, and the greenbacks, mostly in $10 denominations, remained in circulation. The gold standard was eventually restored in 1879.

Again during the Depression, the United States got off the gold standard, at least domestically. Gold had been priced at $20.67 an ounce. It was revalued to $35 an ounce (devaluing the currency, since it now took more paper money to buy one ounce of gold). Private ownership of gold in any form except for jewelry was prohibited in the United States, and only collectors were allowed to own gold coins.

Still, during the next 40 years the United States considered itself on a partial gold standard, because while U.S. citizens could not own gold, Uncle Sam would still take gold out of Fort Knox and pay out to foreign governments who presented their dollars in exchange for gold at the fixed price of $35 an ounce.

But then the inflationary effects of the Great Society programs of the late 1960s and the Vietnam war took effect. The government had created too many dollars, and many of them were in the hands of foreigners. It was French president Charles de Gaulle who pressed the issue—demanding gold for dollars held by the French Central Bank.

President Nixon realized that the United States gold reserves would be drained, so on August 15, 1971, he closed the gold window to foreign central banks. He also raised the official price of gold to $42.22 an ounce—where it is officially maintained to this date. The United States severed its currency ties to gold, although it holds to this day its gold reserves in Fort Knox. Those gold reserves have not, however, been officially audited since the days of the Eisenhower administration.

Now the dollar is backed only by the "full faith and credit" of the government—that is, the promise to pay. The Federal Reserve System can create new money at will by going out into the huge debt market and buying U.S. Treasury securities, paying for them with newly created dollars or bank credit deposits.

Private ownership of gold was legalized again for U.S. citizens on December 31, 1974. In subsequent years, fears about the buying power or value of the dollar grew. It became apparent that the government (actually the Federal Reserve) was creating huge amounts of new credit—devaluing the savings of millions of Americans. The oil shortages and the Iranian hostage crisis contributed to the general air of uncertainty.

Once again, as in previous eras of currency uncertainty, the smart money switched to precious metals—gold and silver. By spring of 1980 the price of gold had risen to over $875 an ounce, and silver was trading at over $50 an ounce. Of course, in retrospect it is easy to see that prices of the precious metals moved to excessive heights. But it was a real lesson for another generation of Americans who learned that their currency was not "as good as gold" but only as good as the government's promise to keep the country's monetary system sound. Lacking faith in that promise, the public turned to gold and other commodities as a store of wealth.

GOLD—THE STORE OF WEALTH

What does it mean to say that gold is a *store of wealth?* Well, take a look at Figure 7. In 1975 the median home price was $39,242. You

Figure 7:   Gold Retains Its Purchasing Power

Median Home Prices

1975

$39,242
244 ozs

1988

$112,500
256 ozs

could purchase this home with 244 ounces of gold, then officially priced at $35 an ounce. In 1988, the median home price had jumped to $112,500—nearly triple the 1975 price. But you could still purchase this home with about the same amount of gold—256 ozs.—at the free market price.

If you had kept your money in cash or currency, the combination of inflation and taxes would have eaten away your buying power. But even considering that gold pays no interest, it still maintained its buying power over the years. Thirty years ago two silver dimes bought you a gallon of gas. These same coins still do—when you value them at their silver content. A $20 gold piece purchased a good suit of clothes. It still does!

That's the argument for owning some precious metals in any investment portfolio. You might own the bullion itself, or bullion coins, or rare collector's coins. You can own stocks of companies that mine gold or silver, or you can buy options on many of those stocks. You can use maximum leverage and buy futures in the precious metals.

Each of these strategies has a different amount of risk—and reward. Some are long-term, buy-and-hold strategies. Others require instantaneous market timing. Make sure you are using a reputable consultant or broker, no matter which strategy you choose.

The price of gold, like other commodities, is basically set by the balance of supply and demand. Of course, in times of crisis, there are emotional considerations that can push prices beyond reasonable levels that would be determined by supply and demand. Those emotional issues are not a modern phenomenon. Just think back to the Gold Rush of 1849, or even earlier to the Spanish ships that set sail to the New World in search of gold. Throughout history, gold and greed have been closely intertwined!

It has been estimated that only about 2.9 billion troy ounces of gold (a troy ounce is 1.1 avoirdupois ounces, the kind you see on your bathroom scale) have been extracted from the earth from the beginning of recorded history to the present. This stock of gold is growing only about 2 percent each year as a result of new mining. About 10 percent of all the gold ever mined has been lost in one way or another. (Think of all those shipwrecks!) And about half of the balance is owned by various governments and other international organizations.

Although the U.S. government embarked on a program to sell some of its gold in the late 1970s, it is estimated that the U.S. government still owns about 260 million ounces. In recent years the U.S. government has used some of its gold to mint coins in commemoration of events like the Olympics and for investment gold and silver Eagle coins minted only from newly mined U.S. gold and silver. (These are the only coins authorized for investment in IRA accounts.)

The largest share, about 1.4 billion ounces, remains in private hands. It is used for jewelry and decorative purposes, and it is hoarded in the form of gold coin or bullion. Even though numerous companies in countries around the world are involved in the mining of gold, the annual production of gold adds only about 50 million ounces—an increase of about 2 percent in the world's stock of gold. So the real source of supply in the gold market—unlike soybeans which grow a new crop every year—is the gold now owned by individuals and governments.

HOW TO BUY GOLD—COINS AND BULLION

You can buy gold in its purest form by purchasing gold bars or wafers. These are considered *bullion* gold and are available in sizes ranging from one gram to 400 ounces. Each bar will be stamped with numbers designating its quality (fineness), which should be at least

99.5 percent pure gold. Of course, there is a charge for making these bars or wafers, and the cost of buying them becomes a smaller percentage of your purchase price if you buy the larger bars. These bars can be purchased through coin dealers, brokerage firms, and even through some banks.

You can also buy gold bullion in the form of bullion coins. These coins, such as the American Eagle, Canadian Maple Leaf, Australian Nugget, or the Britannia from Great Britain and others are available in sizes from one-twentieth of an ounce to one ounce. Each of these coins may have a different denomination embossed on its face, but the value of the coin is determined by its gold content, not its stated face value.

The gold in each of these coins may have a different degree of fineness, or purity. Gold coins often contain alloys of other metals such as silver and copper in order to make them more resistant to scratches and dents. Make sure you are comparing the amount of actual gold in the coin, not only the total weight of the coin.

For jewelry manufacturing purposes, gold's purity is measured in *karats*—a scale of 1 to 24. Twenty-four-karat gold has at least 999 parts pure gold per thousand; it is considered pure gold. Pure gold is so soft that it can easily be scratched or damaged. Eighteen-karat gold is 18 parts gold and 6 parts other metals, or 75 percent pure gold. Fourteen-karat gold is 14 parts gold and 10 parts other metals, or about 58.3 percent pure gold. If you use the European marking system (also used in Hong Kong and Japan), these karats are equivalent to gold with a fineness of 999, or 750, or 585. (Note these *karats* are not to be confused with *carats* which are a measure of weight for precious stones.)

Since bullion coins are currently being made in relatively unlimited numbers, they have no value as collector's items (except for the proof coins that are minted in limited amounts and to higher-quality specifications). Like the bars, the coins can be purchased from dealers, banks, and sometimes directly from the governments involved in making them. The advantage of bullion coins is that they are small, portable, easily saleable, and they sell for only a modest premium above their gold content to cover costs of minting and distributing them.

Some gold coins are collector's items. They have value far beyond their gold content because they were made a long time ago and are very rare. For example, in 1982 an 1870 $3 gold coin sold for $687,500. In 1988, an 1861 $20 gold coin called a Pacquet Reverse—one of two in existence from that year—sold at auction for $660,000. Coins become more valuable because only a few specimens were minted in any given year—or because they were never released to the public and were melted down by the government.

This is a far different subject than buying gold coins for the sake of bullion. Rare or *numismatic* coins have an impressive performance record for protecting wealth in times of inflation. But they should be purchased only through reputable dealers, and they should be accompanied by a certificate from recognized grading services approved by the American Numismatic Association, 818 N. Cascade Ave., Colorado Springs, CO 80903 (719-632-2646).

Even beyond considerations of quality or grade, you should remember that the market for numismatic coin investments is not as liquid as the market for bullion coin investments. It can be difficult to sell these rare coins. Before getting involved in this market, be prepared to do substantial research, and look for qualified second opinions from experts. In some cases you may ask for a guaranteed buy-back commitment based on the grade given at time of purchase.

If you are buying numismatic coins, bullion coins or bars you should take possession of them and store them in a safe place such as your own safe deposit box. Do *not* leave them to be stored in the dealer's vault. If you are purchasing a large amount of precious metals you can arrange to have them delivered by bonded messenger service directly to your bank, which will pay for them on delivery.

HOW TO BUY GOLD—STOCKS

Many people choose to buy shares in gold mining companies because the stocks not only represent the gold in the ground, but they may also pay dividends. If you are interested in buying gold stocks, you have quite a variety of choices. You can buy shares in South African gold mining companies or avoid them entirely. There are plenty of gold mining companies in North America to choose from. It's wise to avoid penny gold stocks and stocks of mining companies that make wild promises.

Gold mining stocks tend to be evaluated by the amount of gold ore reserves the company owns—and by the cost of extracting that gold from the ore. That cost depends on the gold content of the ore. It may take as much as 17 tons of ore to produce one ounce of pure gold. Obviously, if the price of gold falls below the mining company's cost of production, the stock will be a poor investment.

The *Richard Young International Gold Report* (7811 Montrose Rd., Potomac, MD 20854) is a monthly investment letter that tracks the performance and outlook for dozens of major gold mining stocks, many of them listed on the New York and American stock exchanges.

If you don't want to concentrate on just one or two stocks, you might be interested in a mutual fund that specializes in stocks of gold mining companies. There are many of them. The Fidelity Funds offer Fidelity Select American Gold and Fidelity Select Precious Metals portfolios (800-544-6666). Other diversified gold share funds include: Lexington Gold (800-526-0057), USAA Gold (800-531-8000), United Services Gold Shares (800-873-8637), and Blanchard Precious Metals Fund (800-922-7771). You will find many other funds in the guide to no-load funds mentioned in Chapter 14.

There is one other noteworthy way to invest in gold bullion by buying shares of a company. The stock of Central Fund of Canada trades on the American Stock Exchange. This is a closed-end fund that holds a portfolio of gold and silver bullion. This is bullion held in vaults, already mined from the ground, so buying shares of the fund is a direct investment in the price of the metals.

GOLD FUTURES

For those who want to take the risk of maximum leverage—putting up the least money to make the most—the gold futures market that trades primarily on the COMEX futures exchange in New York offers the most opportunity. However, as we have mentioned before in discussing commodity futures, leverage works both ways. A small amount of money can be turned into big profits—or big losses.

The COMEX gold futures contract covers 100 troy ounces of gold. A good faith margin deposit is required. Depending on the volatility of gold prices at any given time, that may amount to between 5 and 10 percent of the value of the contract. The COMEX also trades listed options on its gold futures contract. (See Chapter 15 for a discussion of how options work.) Use of options can limit total investment risk in trading the gold futures market. However, futures options still expose the options trader to substantial loss because the trader must not only guess right about the price of the metal but must have more precise timing in order to profit.

For more information about trading futures and options on gold or silver, write to COMEX, 4 World Trade Center, New York, NY 10048.

While gold futures markets are the basic mechanism for determining the price of bullion gold at any given moment, there is another important price-setting mechanism in the gold market. Twice every business day in London, representatives of the world's five largest international bullion dealers meet around a table to set or "fix" the price of gold. Bids and offers from their trading rooms around the world are matched up until the group can agree on a set, fixed price for gold for that morning or afternoon. The morning London gold fix takes place at 10:30 A.M. local time, and the afternoon fix is reported at 3:00 P.M. London time.

SILVER

Silver is not only a precious metal; it is an industrial metal. Like gold, it is highly malleable and resistant to corrosion. Those qualities make it excellent not only for jewelry and flatware, but for industrial uses such as wiring in electronics, photography, catalysts, dental and medical supplies, and many other uses.

Silver also has some use in coinage. In 1964, silver was eliminated from our everyday coinage. Remember when your pocket change was called "silver"? It was replaced with other base metals, making pre-1964 coins valuable far beyond their denominations. In recent years silver has found new use in U.S. coinage for commemorative issues and the one-ounce silver Eagle investment coin.

Silver's photosensitivity makes it virtually irreplaceable in the photographic industry, which is the largest single industrial consumer of silver. It has growing use in computer technology. So the price of silver is more vulnerable to an economic slowdown than is the price of gold. The United States annually consumes about 135 to 145 million ounces for all silver uses. In a recession fewer people take vacations, and photographs. Fewer computers will be sold. As demand falls, so will prices.

The price of silver is set in markets traded in world financial centers: London, Zurich, New York, Chicago, and Hong Kong. The most significant silver market in the United States is the COMEX, where futures are traded based on cash prices. The fact that the entire trading world watches these markets around the clock ensures a fair and liquid marketplace and price-setting mechanism. Even the huge resources of the Hunt family could not permanently disrupt the market system, although it certainly pushed silver prices out of line during the spring of 1980.

HOW TO BUY SILVER

If you want to buy silver in its purest form—99.9 pure—you should purchase silver bars or wafers. They come in all sizes, ranging from one troy ounce or smaller up to the 1,000-ounce bar that you see pictured in vaults of silver. Because there is a charge for fabricating these bars, it will be slightly more expensive to buy the smaller sizes.

Silver bars can be bought from brokers, coin dealers, and even some banks. Be sure you deal with a reputable dealer. If possible, ask for delivery to your bank vault, with payment given only upon delivery to the bank. Or else pick up the bars or coins yourself as you present payment. *Do not* store your metals with the dealer. There have been too many instances of consumers believing they had vault receipts and finding only too late that the vaults were empty.

You can also buy what are known as "junk" silver coins. Those are bags or rolls of pre-1964 silver coins. They have no real collector's value other than the silver in the coins. The real disadvantage of this method of owning silver is that the coins are heavy and must be stored securely.

In recent years, several countries have started to mint pure silver coins as collector's items. Among the most popular are the American Eagle one-ounce silver dollar coins. Of course, since they contain almost one full ounce of silver, and since silver is trading for more than $1, these are more valuable than one U.S. paper dollar. Their value depends strictly on the price of silver.

Mexico also mints silver bullion coins—the Onza and the Libertad. Canada and Australia also issue silver bullion coins. You should be aware of the difference between medallions and coins. A bullion coin is an official *coin of the realm,* with a symbolic face value that is guaranteed by the issuing nation. A medallion may look like a coin, but it can be minted by a private company and is not legal tender. That is a moot distinction, since very few people would use a silver dollar at its face value.

Why would modern nations mint coins of precious metals and put a face value on them that is far lower than their current market value based on the silver or gold content? The answer is a very practical reason. Legal tender coins can be imported across international borders without paying any duty. However, medallions are subject to duties.

Many private mints, however, have issued medallions, or bars, or collector's sets of silver bars with designs, and billed them as investments in silver. To the extent that they are made out of silver, they can be considered investments. But many investors have been charged far more than the silver value to acquire these medallions or sets—based on claims that they were part of limited editions. Despite promises of their "collectibility" or rarity, very few of these issues have maintained substantial premiums over their intrinsic silver value.

Some silver coins are indeed collector's items and have value far in excess of their silver content. They date back to early in this century or even to ancient times and have value because of their rarity. Check with a reputable dealer and be sure your coins have been accurately graded (as indicated in the section on gold coins).

You can buy stocks in silver mining companies. Some of the largest silver producers in North America are Hecla Mines, Callahan Mining, and Homestake. Many of these companies are listed on the major exchanges. As we noted with gold, beware of stocks listed on the Vancouver Stock Exchange, or penny stocks. There are more than enough good producing mines to go into your precious metals investment portfolio, without stepping into the "minefield" of penny stocks.

Many banks and brokerage firms offer *silver certificates,* or storage accounts, which allow you to purchase your metal a little bit at a time. You do not have actual possession of the metal. If you use a large, reputable bank or brokerage firm, you can avoid most problems with this type of purchase. But some of the largest, best advertised silver and gold storage programs were exposed as complete frauds in the 1980s. When their vaults were opened, investigators found only blocks of wood painted to look like gold or silver! It's best to take possession of your coins or bars—and then keep them locked safely in your own safe-deposit box at the bank.

Silver futures contracts can be purchased through a commodities broker. The most widely traded contract is listed on the COMEX. The big appeal is the leverage of these contracts. You can control a huge amount of silver for a small fraction of its value, and you don't have to worry about storage or insurance. The downside of buying or trading silver through the futures markets is the unlimited potential for loss.

As with gold, futures options in silver can limit your risk of loss, but recent experience has shown that prices for these options can be very expensive. The broker may take a huge commission, so silver prices have to move up—or down—a substantial amount before you begin to make a profit.

THE GOLD/SILVER RATIO

Many people wonder if there is a basic relationship between the price of gold and the price of silver. The answer is that historically there is a ratio, or range of value, between the two metals. The gold/silver ratio shows how many ounces of silver it will take to buy one ounce of gold. To get the ratio, you simply divide the price of gold by the price of silver.

Setting a ratio between gold and silver is not a new phenomenon. The first record of a gold/silver ratio is 5,000 years old—created when the Egyptian Pharoah Menes fixed the ratio at 2.5 to 1. In ancient Rome the ratio was fixed at 15 to 1.

In 1896, when the United States went on a bimetallic monetary standard, the government created an artificial ratio of 16 ounces of silver to equal one ounce of gold. But at that time the free market was setting the ratio at 32 to 1—since there had been recent huge discoveries of silver that had dropped the metal's value in relation to gold.

During the twentieth century, the average free-market ratio of silver to gold has balanced out at about 32 to 1. Of course that doesn't always hold true. Back in 1979-80, when the Hunt family was trying to corner the silver market and driving silver prices up, the ratio dropped to nearly 15 to 1 (meaning it took only 15 ounces of silver to buy one ounce of gold)—even though both were trading at very high prices. At that ratio, silver was way overpriced compared to gold. When the Hunts received their huge margin call, they were forced to sell silver. The price collapsed, and the ratio moved back to 45 to 1.

In recent years silver has fallen out of favor. In 1987, the silver/gold ratio reached an all-time high of 73 to 1. To many traders, that signalled that silver was undervalued and should perform better than gold. Since then, the ratio has narrowed slightly but has not dropped back to the 32-to-1 level. Perhaps that indicates that the next time gold rises it will be because of fears of financial instability in a recession. A recession would keep the price of silver down as industrial usage slows. You can check the ratio by looking in the financial tables of your newspaper and dividing the price of gold by the price of silver.

OTHER PRECIOUS METALS

Gold and silver are not the only precious metals that are traded on the commodities futures markets in the form of bullion and coins. Platinum has become a widely traded metal in recent years. In 1972, platinum became a significant industrial metal because of its use in catalytic converters used to reduce auto emissions. Since then, platinum, palladium, and other metals have taken on an importance in the world's trading markets.

In fact, Australia has created a platinum coin called the Koala, and Canada has a platinum Maple Leaf. The Isle of Man, a small island nation in the Irish Sea, also mints a platinum coin called the Noble.

Platinum bars and wafers are readily available from coin dealers and private mints. The stock of Rustenburg Platinum Mines of South Africa is viewed as the most significant mining stock engaged in the platinum market. All told, only about three million ounces of platinum are mined in total each year; more than half the total goes for industrial uses.

Investors in platinum should realize it is a relatively thinly traded market, with the most significant futures contract trading on the New York Mercantile Exchange. A large majority (83 percent) of the world's platinum is mined in South Africa, with the Soviet Union the world's second largest exporter. The political uncertainties surrounding those two countries add to the difficulties involved in investing in platinum. Trading platinum is a market best left to the professionals—although many commodities futures firms may be anxious to proclaim the profit potential of this metal.

There are other "strategic," or critical metals that are sometimes promoted as "investments" for those concerned about world financial stability. These metals include rhodium, vanadium, titanium, and chromium. Most are mined primarily in South Africa and the Soviet Union. While all have significant industrial uses and many are critical in our defense industry, it is next to impossible for the individual investor to have an even chance at making money on these commodities. They are mentioned here because every few years a commodities scam takes place with late-night telephone calls urging unsophisticated people to buy immediately. If you get one of these calls, just hang up!

CHAPTER 18

Investment Real Estate

Your family home may be your biggest real estate investment—but strictly speaking it's not investment real estate. The world of real estate investments *outside* the family home can include everything from individual apartments, condos, and apartment buildings to shopping centers, office and industrial properties, or even farmland. You may own these properties directly with your name on the title, or indirectly through a partnership, or even more indirectly through shares in a corporation that owns the property.

Each type of property and each form of ownership has advantages and disadvantages. But all share one thing in common—a belief that for economic reasons the value of the underlying property is bound to increase. In the meantime, while you own the property you expect to get certain benefits such as a stream of income or tax credits that can offset some of your other income.

There's no reason to buy investment real estate if you do not think it will improve in value. The value may rise because of general economic conditions or because of improvements you make in the property, but you should be buying at a price that offers you a chance to make a profit in the long run.

That may seem like a very obvious statement, but it's a fact that got lost along the way in the 1970s, when investors rushed to buy real estate and real estate partnerships solely for the then-current tax benefits.

Along came 1986 Tax Reform and wiped out many of the tax benefits—leaving investors with highly overvalued properties.

The first thing that the various tax reform acts of the 1980s did to make real estate less attractive as a tax-sheltered investment was to lower overall tax brackets. That made deductions for mortgage interest and property taxes less valuable because the top marginal tax bracket dropped from 50 percent to 28 percent (or 33 percent for some investors).

The 1986 round of tax reform changed the depreciation laws. Depreciation is an accounting technique for *writing down* the value of a property. The amount of depreciation becomes an income tax deduction. But the new tax law changed the depreciation schedules. Instead of depreciating the property over 19 years, the depreciation time for residential property was lengthened to 27.5 years. That meant less of a deduction every year for those in the real estate investment business.

The lower capital gains tax was eliminated, which meant that any profit on the sale of a property would be taxed as ordinary income, no matter how long the property was held.

Perhaps the most important tax change for real estate investors was the change in the amount of tax losses and deductions that could be claimed on rental property. Under the current law, an individual can only deduct up to $25,000 of the property's annual losses against salary and investment income—and only if you meet three qualifications:

- You are active in managing the property.
- You have at least ten percent equity in the property.
- You had adjusted gross income of less than $100,000.

Those changes really limited the tax benefits that had been associated with some investment real estate. Active management was defined to mean that you had to justify the time spent managing the property, choosing tenants and supervising maintenance.

If your adjusted gross income moves above $100,000, you can use only 50 cents of deductions for every dollar of income—until your income tops $150,000. At that point passive losses from real estate ownership can no longer be deducted from ordinary income and can only be used to offset similar passive income—i.e., rentals and partnership income.

The changes in the tax laws do not mean that residential real estate is not a good deal. It just means that there must be more economic justification for purchasing the property. You must be sure the rental income is sufficient to offset your costs. That is, you must be sure you have a *positive cash flow.*

A word of warning: If you watch those Saturday morning TV shows you'll see real estate pitchmen selling you on the benefits of a career investing in real estate. They're not trying to sell you property; instead they're selling training courses that show you how to buy a property "for no money down" and then sell it for a profit, reinvest the gains, and buy more property. And they make it look simple.

There's no question that one of the great money-making advantages of investing in real estate is leverage. Where else (except in the commodities futures markets) can you put 5 or 10 percent down, borrow the rest of the money, and then have the potential to double your equity investment in a quick resale? There has to be a catch somewhere—and there are indeed several catches.

First, unlike the commodities markets, where you also have the leverage to turn a quick profit, the real estate market is relatively illiquid. That means you can't just put in a sell order and get out. It could take weeks, months, or longer to unload a property. In the meantime, you are stuck with the carrying costs, which could include a mortgage, property taxes, and maintenance.

There's another catch. Many of those real estate success stories hinge on buying property for no money down. Or getting a desperate seller to take back financing or a second mortgage. There may be legitimate cases for a seller to be desperate—a pending foreclosure, divorce, or other reasons. But why are you the "lucky" potential buyer who gets this bargain property? If it were such a bargain, you'd think there would be a long line of buyers.

All of those Saturday morning television shows introduce you to people who purchased a property and then turned around and sold it at a profit just days after closing. Or they easily made back the money they spent fixing it up. Certainly there are success stories, but there are plenty of disastrous real estate stories, too.

All it takes is a recession or high interest rates to slow the resale market for real estate. That's not to mention the other complications that

can arise when you are trying to sell property. Think back to a time
when you were trying to sell your own home.

Real estate investors will tell you that the secret to investment success
is "location, location, location." I would add another secret that's not
so easy to pin down: "timing, timing, timing."

Great fortunes have been built in real estate—by people who treat it
as a business. Buying distressed property, or having a vision of future
development areas, can have tremendous profit potential. But there is
also great risk in real estate. And anyone who tells you there isn't a risk
is probably trying to sell you something!

The best basic book I have seen written for would-be real estate investors is the personal story of successful real estate developer Demp-
sey Travis, entitled *Real Estate Is the Gold in Your Future* (Urban
Research Press, 1988). Travis makes it clear that any individual can
start with a small amount of money and a great attention to detail—
and wind up making money in real estate. But Travis is also a conservative man who does not advise wild speculation or pyramiding.

If you are going to buy property to manage yourself, I recommend
The Landlord's Handbook by Daniel Goodwin (Longman, 1989). It
will give you information necessary to make that rental property profitable, including chapters on how to choose tenants, structure leases,
and market the property for best results. This book will also show you
how to hire a professional manager (at a cost, of course) if you don't
want to take on the management headaches yourself.

INVESTING IN REAL ESTATE PARTNERSHIPS

In the past, many investors used investments in limited partnerships
as a way to get involved in real estate and take advantage of current deductions and future gains—without worrying if the roof leaks.

The problem with these partnerships was tied right into the well-
promoted "advantages." In addition to the tax law change that destroyed some of the shelter benefits of these deals, the limited partners
had no input into the purchase or management of the properties. That
was taken care of by the general partners—many of whom are now be-

ing sued for breach of fiduciary duty in choosing and pricing the investments of the partnership.

A real estate limited partnership is still an excellent structure for making real estate investments. The real caveats are in the choice of partners and the choice of properties.

HOW A LIMITED PARTNERSHIP WORKS

A partnership is simply a way of associating two or more people to do business. In a general partnership, each partner is equal and each shares equally in the right to conduct business. One partner can commit the entire partnership to an obligation or debt or purchase. And all general partners are equally liable for the business activities of any one partner.

One of the great advantages of partnerships is the way they are taxed. The partnership itself is not a taxpayer. Instead, any earnings or losses taken by the partnership are passed on to the partners. The individual partners then report that income or loss on their personal tax returns and pay taxes at their individual income tax rate.

This special method of taxation of partnerships has some interesting advantages for business. It avoids the double taxation of income faced by shareholders in a corporation. When an investor owns shares in a corporation, first the company pays income taxes on the profits. Then, when the profits are paid out as dividends, the individual shareholders pay income taxes again on their dividend income.

Using a corporation to structure a business has some advantages. The primary one is that corporations limit the liability of shareholders. Even though a shareholder is an "owner" of a portion of the corporation, unlike in a partnership, the shareholder has no personal liability for the corporation's activities. A general partner in a partnership does not have that protection of limited liability.

To create that kind of limited liability, a new sort of partnership structure was created—the *limited partnership*. In a limited partnership there is at least one *general partner* who manages the business and retains personal liability for the activities of the business. The limited partners have no personal liability for any of the actions of the partnership, nor do they have a say in running the business. But they can still take advantage of the favorable tax treatment accorded to partnerships.

Limited Partnership Tax "Deals"

In the 1970s, a number of financial firms realized that limited partnerships could be a very interesting way to pass on tax losses to investors—tax losses that could be used to offset the very high income taxes then being paid on other income. The partnerships would load up on debt and take various tax deductions and credits that could be passed on to the individual partners.

In the 1970s and 1980s more than $100 billion worth of limited partnership interests was sold to investors—much of it tax-motivated. There were limited partnerships in oil and gas, real estate, equipment leasing, cattle and livestock, entertainment, and research and development. Many of these limited partnerships offered immediate tax deductions while holding out the promise that the units of the partnership would be liquidated in the future and taxed at the then-lower capital gains tax rate.

There was nothing inherently wrong with the concept of limited partnerships, nor in many cases with the activities being carried on inside the partnerships. Many had real economic reasons for existence and some did realize the gains that had been predicted.

But other limited partnerships loaded up on real estate or oil and gas properties at highly inflated prices. Salespeople were paid commissions of 8 percent to sell the units as tax shelters, and very high management fees were paid to the managing general partners.

Then along came economic problems and tax changes. First the price of oil plunged, leaving many oil and gas deals with no income to pass on to partners. Many wells simply became uneconomical to drill. The collapse of oil prices brought with it a real estate slump of major proportions in the Southwest—where many of the real estate limited partnerships had invested money in shopping centers, office buildings, and apartments. As the economy slowed there, the real estate remained vacant—throwing off no income to pay down the mortgages carried by the partnerships.

Perhaps the biggest blow to the limited partnership industry was the Tax Reform Act of 1986, which placed major restrictions on the use of losses from limited partnerships to offset income from other activities—including ordinary income such as wages. The law said that losses from passive activities could only be used to offset income from other passive activities. Limited partnerships that were created only to pass on tax benefits were suddenly forced to stand on their own economic benefits. Could they generate income and eventually sell their investments at a profit? Clearly, many could not.

Even worse, many investors had obligated themselves to make further capital contributions to the limited partnerships over the years. It now appeared to be a case of throwing good money after bad. But the investors could be sued if they did not come up with the additional cash.

Investors faced another taxing problem. Most limited partnerships had taken on a great deal of debt—the better to pass on deductions to the partners. Now if the partner sold the partnership unit—even at a loss—he had another tax liability. If the unit's share of the debt amounted to $5,000, then sale of the unit was equivalent to getting off the hook for the debt. The IRS decided that amount was taxable income to the partner.

Suddenly the limited partnerships that had looked like such a good idea in the 1970s and early 1980s began looking like a very bad investment indeed, so investors began looking for a way to get out. But there is no real marketplace for resales of limited partnership units.

What investors in limited partnerships forgot to do is check the way out—the first rule of the claustrophobic investor! The lack of "exits" is the real problem for investors in limited partnerships. The general partners have problems of their own and as a rule will not buy back units.

Selling Your Partnership Unit

Many clients are understandably peeved at the original broker who sold them the deal. But that is the first place to check if you want to sell a limited partnership unit. Those brokerage firms often have an internal bid and offer system for partnership units. The unfortunate thing about dealing with the firm that originally sold the partnership is that it tends to have an over-optimistic view of what the units are worth. Few people in the system are willing to pay that price, and so the firm may say it is "listing" the units, although it could take months to get a firm offer. That leaves a very limited secondary market for the sale of these partnerships. There are other specialty firms that have been created just to buy and sell limited partnership units in the secondary market.

The Liquidity Fund, based outside San Francisco (800-227-4688), will give you a bid on your limited partnership unit. It is considered a *principal* in that the firm may buy these units for its own account or for funds it manages. Sometimes it acts as a *broker,* selling the units directly to other customers. The firm's profit is built into the purchase price. In other words, its objective is to pay a low price, make a profit, and resell the unit at a higher price. Who would buy these units? Liquidity Fund works with a number of brokers who are "scavenging" for bargains among units being sold by desperate investors. It is a growing market.

Liquidity Fund charges a flat fee of $300 per order, which is subtracted from the price you are quoted. If you accept the bid, the firm will send you a purchase contract to sign, so it can transfer your units on the books of the general partner. Unlike stocks, there is rarely a certificate associated with a limited partnership unit; instead, transfers of ownership are made in book entry form with the general partner. It may take as much as two weeks for the paperwork to go back and forth, before you receive a check.

This firm does leave itself an "out," although it is rarely used. If for some reason it decides not to buy your units after you send in your contract, Liquidity Fund guarantees to pay you $100.

You should check at least two different marketplaces before you accept a bid for your unit. Another company that works in a similar fashion, buying and selling units, is Partnership Securities Exchange (415-763-5555). Its standard fee is $250 plus any charges made by the general partner to transfer the unit.

Partnership Securities says it is the only one that will make a firm and binding commitment over the phone. It will send you a one-page contract with a limited power of attorney so your units can be transferred. It will also send you a check immediately on receipt of that signed contract and power of attorney. Partnership Securities buys the units for the firm's own account, although it does not transfer them out of your name until they are ultimately sold to someone else.

You might want to consider a third limited partnership sales firm, which works in a different manner. The National Partnership Exchange (NAPEX), based in Tampa, Florida (800-356-2739), serves as an auction house for limited partnership units. There is no charge to list your unit for sale on its computer bulletin board.

NAPEX will give you information about recent sales of your specific unit and the amount of units that have traded recently. Then you can list your unit with a specific offer price. The listing stays on its computer system for seven days. During that time, brokers from around the country enter bids anonymously. If someone meets your offer price, a transaction is done. If no one volunteers to pay your price, they will notify you of the highest bid for your unit.

National Partnership Exchange charges a fee of $1^1/_2$ percent of the value of the transaction to the buyer and to the seller. For transactions of less than $10,000 there is a minimum $150 fee to each side. This is in addition to any general partner transfer fees—usually from $25 to $75. If you call the National Partnership Exchange directly, you will be sent through its brokerage unit, which will collect another three percent fee from the seller and 7 percent from the buyer. NAPEX sends out the paperwork to both sides and collects the signed agreements. It holds the buyer's funds in escrow for the seller until the general partner acknowledges making the book entry transfer of ownership. The process can take several weeks.

We mention these specific names because the market for resale of limited partnership units is fragmented and therefore has a great potential for fraud. Even the firms listed above may quote widely different prices depending on their evaluation of the sophistication of the seller of the unit.

Many of the major brokerage firms actually use these partnership exchange firms to get rid of their clients' units. Still, you should check prices at several firms—and be sure to get a complete listing of all fees. Find out when you can expect to have a check in your hands. Get the promises in writing!

Unless you're really hard-pressed to raise cash, you may be better off not selling your limited partnership unit at all. Some real estate markets may recover; some deals may work out. But if you do need the cash, check around for the best price before you sell out at a low price and create a bargain for someone else.

REITs

Real estate investment trusts take advantage of a tax rule that allows them to earn income and take profits and yet remain untaxed as an entity as long as they pass on 95 percent of that income to shareholders in the trust.

In the early 1970s, dozens of REITs were set up to lend construction money to developers building everything from office buildings to shopping centers to apartments. But during the 1974 real estate crunch interest rates soared (at that time to an unheard of 11 percent), and many developers could not find long-term, affordable mortgage financing. Some developers went broke, and the REITs got stuck foreclosing on property—much of it half-finished. They suffered substantial losses and gave the entire REIT industry a black eye.

The rebirth of the REIT industry began in the late 1970s. Sharp investors bought out the REITs at bargain prices and found a market to sell those repossessed and unfinished properties. With cash on hand, these REITs, and new ones that were subsequently created, went back to the investment business. Only this time, instead of lending money, they began buying investment properties.

The shares of many of these real estate investment trusts are listed on the New York and American Stock Exchanges. There are about 168 of them that are publicly traded. They work as a sort of closed-end fund containing investment properties. The value of the shares depends not only on the perceived value of the property they invest in, but on the demand for the shares in the trading marketplace. Their value is also affected by the amount and percentage of their dividend payout to shareholders.

Investors can study the properties owned by the trusts and check their track record for paying mortgage interest to the trust. If the properties are fully rented and paying mortgages on time, these trusts can be a good income investment—especially in a time of falling interest rates.

Of course, like any other investment, you have to listen to a broker or else do your homework in investigating the properties within the REIT. The National Association of Real Estate Investment Trusts, a trade association, can provide you with more information about the industry and specific REITs. You can write to them at NAREIT, 1129 Twentieth St., N.W., Suite 705, Washington, D.C. 20036.

There is a way of spreading the potential risk of investing in only one REIT. Several open-end mutual funds have been created to buy the shares of REITs and other real estate-related companies. United Services Mutual Funds (800-873-8637) created the U.S. Real Estate Fund in July 1987 just for this purpose. It owns shares in about 25 different REITs, plus shares in development companies and other real estate-related companies. There are a number of other open-end mutual funds that specialize in investing in the shares of REITs: The Real Estate Investment Portfolio is sponsored by the Fidelity Funds (800-544-6666). The National Real Estate Stock Fund and National Real Estate Income Fund are both sponsored by National Securities and Research Corporation (800-356-5535).

When you choose this way to invest in real estate, you are removed from the day-to-day investment and management decisions. You will not be able to take advantage of some tax benefits, but you do have the advantage of "owning" a share in real estate for income and appreciation possibilities. And you have the even greater advantage of liquidity. You can sell your shares and take your profit or loss whenever you choose.

CHAPTER 19

Art and Collectibles...and a Word of Warning

If you decide to purchase art or collectibles, you should make that decision out of a desire to own the object—not out of a desire to make a profit. That said, huge profits have been made in the world of art and collectibles.

Every year the investment banking firm Salomon Brothers reports on its study of best performing assets. Throughout the 1970s tangible assets such as gold, coins, Chinese ceramics, old masters, and diamonds were among the best performers. The 1980s saw a return to financial assets such as stocks, bonds, and even Treasury bills, which outperformed many tangible assets, as shown in Figure 8.

However, Robert Salomon, the author of the annual study, notes that while tangible assets such as gold, silver, and diamonds did not perform outstandingly well in the eighties, a subset of this category—collectibles—continues to outperform other tangible assets. He notes that collectibles benefit from "the investor's desire to consume conspicuously." And he comments that owning a barrel of oil or a thousand acres of farmland "just does not fit the bill the way owning an Old Master does."

It is entirely possible that the decade of the nineties will become the era of collectibles—in the sense that they are items that are individual, irreplaceable, and memorable. Not all will be expensive to collect, but they will share the quality of conferring some sense of "specialness" upon the owner.

Figure 8:   Financial Assets vs. Tangible Assets (1970–1990)

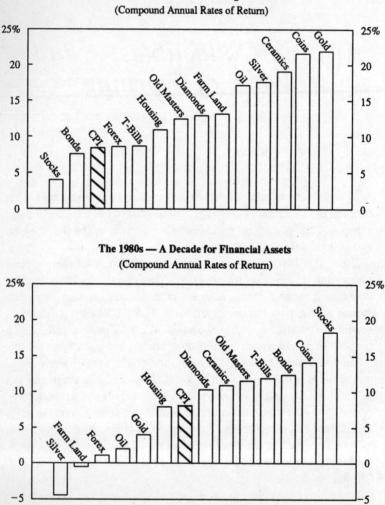

Source: Salomon Brothers Inc.

If you decide to take up collecting, the same basic rules apply whether you are collecting old masters, impressionists, or modern art. The rules apply if you are collecting coins and stamps, vintage cars, oriental rugs, art glass, antique radios, or even baseball cards! If you are spending your money to buy these items, always strive to buy the best in its category. The mere accumulation of objects or the size of a collection rarely makes it a good investment.

A primary rule of collecting is to deal with a reputable source. Of course, there are widely reported instances of amateurs driving out into the country and buying a valuable antique or oil painting for only a few dollars. But those instances are as rare as golfers shooting a hole in one. Serious collecting of rare objects should involve intelligent study on the part of the investor and the use of experts who can locate sources of authentic material. Reputable dealers stand behind their offerings and allow you to have them examined by other experts before completing a purchase. This process of authentication can keep you from wasting your financial resources.

Finally, remember both before and after purchasing your collectible item that this purchase was not based solely on its investment potential. There is *no liquid market* for the sale of collectibles. Unlike a stock, you cannot simply tell your broker to sell at the market.

Auction houses may have a sale for your particular type of collectible only once or twice a year, and they take a cut of 10 to 15 percent out of your sale price. The buyer will also pay an additional 10 percent of the "hammer" price to the auction house. That will limit the net proceeds you will receive from the sale of your item.

Check the want ads under "For Sale—art and collectibles" in any big city newspapers. That's where you will find the prices that may be accepted by a seller who needs cash. In times of economic slowdown, these columns are filled with people trying to unload their assets— once their collectibles—at bargain prices just to raise cash.

When it comes to collecting, beauty is truly in the eye of the beholder. The pleasure in the act of collecting itself, or the enjoyment in beholding a well-organized collection, are beyond financial calculation. But since you are spending your hard-earned money to purchase these items, you should certainly consider the financial risks before you buy.

SCAMS

Before leaving the subject of risk investments, here's a warning about risks far beyond the possibility of losing money in a legitimate investment. It's the risk of being taken in by an investment "scam." Swindles are by no means limited to the world of investments. Every day there are stories about people being taken by furnace repairmen or used car dealers. But the North American Securities Administration Association estimates that investors lose $40 billion a year to investment swindles!

Sometimes an investment con is the result of one of those late night calls from a salesperson urging you to "get in on this investment before it's too late." It's estimated that telemarketing schemes cost consumers $10 billion a year. Other money losing investment deals are advertised through the mail, in the newspapers, and on television and radio. They seem so legitimate that the media allow the advertisements, unaware of the scurrilous nature of the promotions.

All investment con games play upon the greed of the potential sucker. They dangle promises of profits and returns that should be a warning to any serious investor. But greed and gullibility combine to encourage otherwise sensible people to hand over their life savings to these con artists. The simple rule to avoid being conned: "If it sounds too good to be true, it is probably *not* true."

Although investment swindles have soared in the 1980s, they are by no means a modern phenomenon. The father of the modern investment swindle was a man called Charles Ponzi. In 1919, Ponzi set up an "investment company" in Boston to take advantage of the trade in international postal coupons. He promised investors a very high rate of interest.

The secret to his game: Ponzi paid off the original investors with money that came in from subsequent investors. As the original investors received an incredible return on their money, they bragged about their winnings and urged others to get in on the deal. The more people who came in, the more original investors got paid off and the more Ponzi syphoned off to maintain his extravagant lifestyle. Ponzi spent more than seven years in jail for his scheme.

Today the term "Ponzi" is used to refer to any swindle in which the first suckers are paid off with the money of the second group. Eventually, of course, any such game collapses of its own weight. There simply aren't enough potential suckers to keep the game going, so most Ponzi con men (and con women) skim enough of the money to skip town and start over elsewhere. If they aren't caught.

It should be noted that these kind of con games don't have to promise incredible riches. In the 1980s, thousands of Chicago-area savers were fleeced by two companies—A.J. Obie and Diamond Mortgage. Obie promised investors long-term, fixed rates of interest that were two or three percentage points higher than banks were offering at the time. Diamond Mortgage offered mortgage financing to less-than-creditworthy borrowers who could not get a mortgage elsewhere.

The two companies simply matched the investors who wanted the high returns with the borrowers who needed mortgages. Not only was this a bad investment on the face of it—never lend money to a stranger, even with a house as security—but it eventually came out that many of the "mortgages" were fraudulent, with no security at all for investors' money.

The principals of the firms had skimmed off millions of dollars before the companies filed for bankruptcy—leaving thousands of elderly savers bilked of life savings totaling $24 million. Not only will those people not get the investment returns they had expected, but it is unlikely that they will ever see more than 25 cents on the dollar of their original investments. And that money will be paid out over a period of years, after the lawyers and accountants in bankruptcy have received their cut.

We should stress that the television commercials and advertisements for this scam did not promise to double investors' money. They just promised higher returns in a time of falling interest rates. The swindlers knew that if they could appeal to enough suckers, they didn't need to promise the moon.

Thousands of other investors across the nation are fleeced every year in scams involving gold coins (send us the money, we'll hold the coins in our vaults for you!), gold mines (put up some money, we've got a revolutionary new way to extract gold from dirt!), and commodities (buy cotton futures before word of a new kind of boll weevil hits the markets!).

Never, never send money to a stranger who calls on the phone offering a "hot" investment idea. Always check with the regulatory agency that is supposed to register those dealers. Ask if they are members of an exchange or what firm they clear their trades through. Check with the exchange itself as to a firm's membership and any actions taken against it.

For commodities: The Commodity Futures Trading Commission
2033 K St. N.W.
Washington, D.C. 20581
202-254-6387

or the National Futures Association
200 W. Madison St.
Chicago, IL 60606
312-781-1300 or 800-621-3570.

For stock The Securities and Exchange Commission
investments: (SEC)
450 Fifth St. N.W.
Washington, D.C. 20549
202-272-7450.

The SEC is usually reluctant to comment on ongoing investigations, but it might advise you to refrain from dealing with an individual or company.

Also contact: New York Stock Exchange
11 Wall St.,
New York, NY 10005
212-656-3000

American Stock Exchange
86 Trinity Place
New York, NY 10006
212-306-1000

National Association of Securities Dealers
1735 K St. N.W.,
Washington, D.C. 20006
202-728-8000

You may also want to contact the attorney general of your state and your local state's attorney to see if they are collecting complaints about a particular company or individual. They are good sources of information about investment swindles and other scams. Those other scams include vacation clubs, some time-share resorts, and those postcards announcing that you have won a fabulous prize (which usually turns out to be a toy car or boat), which you can redeem by sending cash. Since attorneys general of various states are now actively sharing information on scams, it pays to investigate first.

There's another con game that periodically sweeps the country and eventually costs the gullible a lot of money. But since it appears to be organized by "friends," many people get caught up in the hysteria of getting something for nothing. It's a type of "pyramid" game, variously called the "airplane" game or the "travel" game. The first players put up a fixed amount of money—perhaps $1,000—to buy "seats" on a mythical airplane. The money is paid to the "captain" of the plane. If they can recruit two more players to buy seats, they move up to become the "crew" of the plane. After several rounds, they have moved up enough to become captains of their own planes—collecting $1,000 from each new passenger—or as much as $14,000 (which is usually not reported for income taxes!).

The obvious flaw in this game is that it takes an incredible number of new suckers joining as passengers and paying the entrance fee. In fact, it is mathematically impossible to maintain one of these games for a month. Starting with one game that "split" 30 days in a row, you would need more than 250 million people people to join to keep it going! That's why under laws in most states and Federal Trade Commission regulations, pyramid games are illegal.

Still, people are intensely loyal to these pyramid games because it is often their friends or members of their social or religious groups that enlist them. But the original "captain" who collected the first pot of money is long gone and hard to trace while the last "passengers" are simply out of luck—and out their hard-earned money. Some of the "friends" who get in early do walk away with some money, only to find themselves being sued by people who got in later and lost out. And they find themselves targets of the IRS as well. Once again, you can't get something for nothing. These pyramid games prove it dozens of times a year.

Insuring the Present Values in Your Life

CHAPTER 20

Life Insurance for Protection and Profit

So much unnecessary mystery surrounds the concept of life insurance. Life insurance is simply a benefit paid at death. If the amount paid to survivors is more than the buyer of the policy paid in to the insurance company, then the insured "wins" a bet against the insurance company! Unfortunately, the only way to win this bet is to die.

The simple fact is that if you buy life insurance—or pure death insurance—you will never be around to enjoy the benefits. You are buying money that will go to your heirs. On the other hand, many life insurance products have tax advantages that make them excellent investment vehicles for your excess cash. The key is to sort out the death benefits of life insurance from the investment benefits—and pay only for those benefits you really need.

WHY BUY LIFE INSURANCE?

Not everyone needs life insurance. If you don't have dependents who will need your future earning power in case of your unexpected death, then you may not need to spend money on life insurance. Many people have a small amount of life insurance along with their medical benefits at work. That may be enough to take care of funeral expenses and the cost of disposing of your assets. You may want to have life insurance to pay off debts, such as a mortgage, for your heirs. If you have a large amount of assets, then you might want to buy some life insurance to pay the estate taxes so your heirs don't have to sell those assets to raise cash.

If you *do* have a family or dependents who count on your income, consider what would happen to them if you died suddenly. That idea is the basis for all those insurance company commercials. They create an aura that is almost superstitious: Buy a life insurance policy and have the peace of mind that comes from knowing your family will be provided for. The subtle message is: *Don't tempt fate; if you have life insurance the chance of unexpected events is reduced!* Superstition, yes—but it sells life insurance!

How much life insurance should you have? That depends on how much income you will need to replace—and for how long. If you have young children and your earnings are contributing a substantial portion of family income, then you have to consider how much it would cost to replace a working mother or father's income and for how long this would be necessary. Even parents who do not work outside the home make a substantial economic contribution to a family. Consider what it would cost to replace a homemaker—with a maid, cook, and chauffeur.

As a family grows older, insurance needs change. Once children are out of college and on their own, it may be time to cut back the amount of pure death benefit insurance. Still, a widow may need the protection that life insurance affords before she can start collecting Social Security benefits on her deceased spouse's account at age 60. As children mature and family savings grow, insurance premium money may be better spent investing in assets that will grow to provide a larger estate. In fact, some of that investing can be done inside your insurance policy itself.

People always think they have "enough" life insurance—until they face the real prospect of death. Then it's never enough. The sensible thing to do is sit down and figure out your annual expenses and the amount of income you would like your survivors to be able to count on over the years. Take into account your current debts and future obligations such as educating children. Then you can make some reasonable estimates of how much life insurance you should have—and how you can structure your life insurance to be able to afford it.

THE COST OF LIFE INSURANCE

The truth is that life insurance is strictly a numbers game. The insurance companies keep statistics on how long people live. If you give them your age, sex, and certain risk characteristics such as whether you smoke (or whether you're in a risky occupation), they can predict with reasonable accuracy how long you are statistically likely to live. And they can figure out how much to charge you for pure death benefit insurance.

Over the years, the concept of life insurance has gotten caught up with the concepts of saving and investing. And to the extent that you pay more money to the insurance company than is really needed to buy the death benefit, there may be an extra amount of your premium that accumulates in an investment account. But the amount you pay for the death benefit is, strictly speaking, the amount you are paying for life insurance.

Term Insurance

The cheapest and simplest form of life insurance is pure *term insurance.* You pay for it every year by paying a premium. The cost of the insurance will rise every year because as you grow older the insurance company figures there is a greater risk you will die. The price of the insurance every year is determined by the insurance company's mortality table.

The cheapest form of term insurance limits the period of time that you can keep the policy to perhaps one year and does not allow you to automatically renew or convert the policy. That allows the insurance company to turn you down or change your risk category and charge you higher rates if your health is failing or for other reasons. It's called *nonguaranteed* or *reentry* term insurance. Some nonguaranteed policies are sold for a three-year period. The insurance company will cancel after three years, and you will have to reapply to continue the coverage.

Very few people want to risk being without any insurance at all, so they purchase *annual renewable* term insurance. That simply means that the insurance company guarantees to renew your policy every year as long as you keep paying the premiums. In return for this guarantee you will pay a higher annual premium. Many young families choose annual renewable term as the least expensive way to fund their insurance needs. You are paying for nothing but death benefits—no frills, no additional investments. Because term insurance requires less cash outlay, you can afford to buy a larger death benefit. You can cancel whenever you choose, but after you survive the year you paid for, you will get no money back from the life insurance company.

The main disadvantage of term insurance is that the policy cost keeps rising every year. So you may be faced with the choice of dropping some of the insurance (hopefully after the children are out of college) or switching to a less-expensive policy. Statistics show that only 1 percent of retail term insurance policies stay in force long enough to pay death benefits; almost all term insurance is dropped without value.

Term insurance is also sold as annual renewable and *convertible,* which gives the policyholder the right to switch to a different kind of policy offered by the insurance company at some time in the future. Having the option to convert your policy will cost you a little more in annual premiums, but it could be worthwhile because as the price of your term policy rises over the years, you might want to switch into a policy with more level premiums.

In fact, some term policies are sold with a guarantee of the same premiums over a five, ten, or fifteen-year period. It's called *level term* insurance. You're not beating insurance companies out of any money on these deals. They simply add up what they would have charged you over five or ten years and divide by the number of years, creating an average payment. Then they include a calculation to allow for the fact that they are getting extra money in premiums in the early years, which can reduce your overall cost. In the early years you pay slightly more than necessary for your insurance; in the later years your annual payment is slightly less than pure term would have been. When you buy a level term policy, make sure the premiums are guaranteed for the entire 15 years.

Term insurance is really the easiest form of insurance to understand. There are few complicated concepts to master and no investment choices to make. But this simplicity does not necessarily make term insurance *easy* to buy. It is sold by hundreds of different insurance companies—and each will quote a different rate. Some offer very low rates the first few years and then escalate them sharply in subsequent years. To figure out which is the best term insurance for your situation, you have to decide how long you are going to keep the policy and then compare average total premiums over a period of five, ten, or fifteen years. Overall costs could vary as much as 50 to 100 percent for the same term insurance coverage with different companies.

You don't have to take an insurance agent's word for what's best for you. InsuranceQuote Services, Inc., a subsidiary of David T. Phillips & Company, one of the largest insurance brokers, will match your personal data (age, sex, insurance needs, etc.) with the most competitively priced policies from dozens of major top-rated insurance companies. At no charge, they will send you a computerized printout of the term insurance policies they recommend for your personal situation—at the lowest prices. And they compare term insurance prices not only for the first few years but over five, ten, fifteen, and twenty years. Of course, they'd like to sell you a policy, but there is no pressure, and you can compare these figures with the ones your insurance agent is presenting (InsuranceQuote Services, Inc., 800-972-1104).

Whole Life Insurance

Whole life insurance is simply a term insurance policy that has level premiums for the policyholder's entire life. When a whole life insurance policy is purchased, the insurance company sets a fixed annual premium based on age, sex, and your risk characteristics. The amount of the premium cannot increase over the years for any reason. Obviously, over that long period of your lifetime, the insurance company will collect a lot of money up front—far more than is actually required to buy the basic death insurance while you are young. The extra dollars in your whole life policy are invested in the general fund, or portfolio, of the insurance company. Over the years you will have built up an investment in your policy—beyond the amount needed to pay for the annual charge for death benefits.

Those general investment portfolios are invested in long-term bonds and mortgages. To the extent that the investments are successful in generating gains or interest, some gains may be funneled back to the policyholder. If you buy a *participating policy,* which most whole life policies are these days, then when the company's investment fund makes extra money it may be paid out to the policyholder in the form of a *dividend.* (This dividend is treated as a return of the premium you paid during the year, not as a taxable dividend which you might get on a stock.)

Some whole life policies illustrate that they will be fully paid up within a short period of time—perhaps seven to ten years. These are often called "vanishing premium" plans. The dividends and interest earned on the investments are left in the policy to pay future premiums so that the policy will be fully funded. But the assumption that the insurance will be fully paid for in a short time also depends on the performance of the investment fund that generates the earnings.

While the policyholder hopes the insurance company will have a good performance in its investment fund, there is no guarantee of any dividends. You may look at the track record of the company in paying dividends, but the past is no guarantee of the future. And as a policyholder of one of these whole life policies, you have absolutely no say about how the insurance company's general fund is invested.

In the last decade insurance companies came to realize that they could sell a lot more life insurance policies if they offered policyholders competitive returns or the chance to decide how their excess premiums should be invested. Over the years investors began looking at some of the real advantages of putting additional money—beyond what was needed to pay the death benefits—into a life insurance policy. The key advantage is a tax-free buildup of cash within the policy, which makes the investment grow even faster. But potential policy buyers wanted to make sure their investment money would earn top returns—and they wanted some control over choosing those investments.

That's how simple death benefit life insurance policies turned into some of the most exciting and tax-advantaged investment vehicles of the 1980s and 1990s.

INSURANCE AS AN INVESTMENT

Until the late 1970s, many people looked upon their whole life insurance policies as a sort of "forced savings" plan and as a reasonable investment. Then two changes occurred that caused rebellion among insurance purchasers and big changes in the insurance industry.

During the late 1970s, interest rates skyrocketed in response to soaring inflation. Money market funds were created to allow savers to get the benefits of those higher interest rates. Savers quickly became sophisticated enough to chase the highest yields available—either in Treasury bills or in money market funds.

At just about the same time, a shocking report was made public. In 1979, the Federal Trade Commission announced results of a multi-year study showing that returns on whole life insurance policies held over 20 years averaged out to only between 2 percent and 4.5 percent. Policies held for shorter periods of time actually earned *negative* rates of return.

Consumers were outraged. They quickly decided to borrow against the cash value of their life insurance policies at the then very low rates of 4.5 percent or 5 percent, and to reinvest the money in money market funds earning 10 percent or higher. The huge sums being withdrawn quickly convinced the insurance companies that they had to offer a better deal to their policyholders.

For the last ten years, insurance companies have been racing to create and offer some of the most creative and, from an investment point of view, attractive policies that could be developed.

Universal Life

It all started in the early eighties with *universal* life. These new policies sorted out the money that was to be paid to provide death benefits and the money that was being set aside by the insurance company to earn a rate of return. Then universal life did what no other policy had before: It disclosed all of the insurance company's expenses and charges—and promised a fixed, competitive rate of return to be paid for one year on the investment portion. At the end of the year, a new rate would be set for the next 12 months. The insurance companies also set a minimum guaranteed rate that would be paid, usually about 4 to 5½ percent, bettering the rate shown in the FTC study.

The insurance company would invest policyholders' premiums in a separate fund, which would seek the highest short-term returns. Since the returns would compound each year tax-deferred inside the policy, policyholders no longer had to borrow from their policies and invest elsewhere. In fact, the high tax-sheltered returns became an incentive to invest more money than was really necessary for insurance purposes into these new universal life policies.

So many people were pouring so much money into these policies that Congress passed legislation in 1984 that created specific guidelines as to how much "excess" money could be invested in a policy for it to retain the tax-sheltered characteristics of life insurance. This is called the *maximum funding level* of the policy. You could actually invest more money, but only if you increase the death benefits that are part of the policy. But it really does not make sense to pay for unneeded increased death benefits just to get the tax deferrability. There are other vehicles in the insurance industry, such as *annuities,* that can do that same job without the insurance cost. Annuities will be explained later in this chapter.

There are some things to watch out for when considering the purchase of universal life. First, every year the insurance company can change the amount it charges for the actual insurance (death benefits) up to a certain maximum. Second, the insurance company's administrative expenses, which are deducted from the earnings, could also increase.

On the other side of the ledger, many universal life policies are sold with illustrations of a continuing high level of interest rates. But if rates were to fall substantially for a few years, the earnings of the policy might not be enough to generate the promised return at the end of ten or twenty years. In fact, if interest rates fall, the earnings of the policy might not be enough to pay the ever-increasing cost of just the death benefits. (Remember, the annual death benefit cost will increase just like it will with term insurance.) If the assumptions go wrong, owners of universal life policies not only forfeit the pot of gold at the end of the rainbow, they could wind up having to fork over a hefty amount of cash just to keep their life insurance in force.

When purchasing a universal life policy, ask the agent to illustrate the potential return not only at the current rate of interest, but at an interest rate 1 or 2 percent below the current rate. Even a relatively small decline in interest rates can make a substantial difference in the policy's earnings over the years—and in the ability of the policy to generate enough cash to pay the actual death benefit premiums in the future.

Variable Whole Life Insurance

The creation of variable life insurance policies allowed a new freedom to policyholders: They could choose the type of investments they wanted the insurance company to use for their premiums. A portion of their premium payments still went to fund the death benefits, but with the balance there was now more of a choice than with universal life, which only offered a short-term interest rate guarantee or whole life, which offered primarily bonds and mortgages as investments.

Variable life policies offer a number of different investment alternatives. If the investments are successful, then the face value of the policy is increased upward on the anniversary date of the policy. No matter what the results of the investment, the face value cannot fall *below* the original face value.

Variable whole life policies charge fixed premiums. In return for those fixed premiums they guarantee that the face value of the policy will remain intact, no matter what the performance of the investments. But the fixed premiums may be offset by the fact that, if invested successfully, the investment portion of the premium will grow tax deferred.

Many companies offering variable life policies now give policyholders a choice among a series of mutual funds, usually run by well-known mutual fund management firms. There are money market funds, common stock funds, income-oriented funds, and bond funds to choose from. The insurance company may offer unlimited opportunities to switch between funds, or limit the number per year or quarter. They may charge a small fee everytime you switch between funds.

Before you invest in a variable life or annuity policy, you might want to consider the performance of the funds they are offering as investment vehicles. It might be worthwhile to pay a higher management fee or commission to the insurance company, if past performance of its funds leads you to believe you can make up those fees with superior investment performance.

Remember that when you make these mutual fund investments *inside* a tax-sheltered life insurance product, any gains realized at the time you switch between funds are not taxed. They contribute to building your investment.

Universal Variable Life Insurance

This performance can be particularly important if you choose a new hybrid form of both universal and variable life insurance—*universal variable life insurance.*

This combination of universal life and variable life allows you, the policyholder, to set most of the terms and conditions of your insurance policy as long as the basic minimum payments for death benefits continue to be paid. Instead of being required to pay fixed, level premiums at a specific time (as with variable life) you can now tell the insurance company exactly how much you would like to pay and when. (Again, the basic insurance requirements must be met.) You can also decide how the money will be invested. And if you choose, you can alter the face value amount of the insurance to meet your needs or your ability to pay the premiums.

Single-Premium Whole Life Insurance

From universal life insurance it was only a small jump to *single-premium whole life insurance,* which has become very popular. The premise was simple: Why spread things out? Take one lump sum of money, buy fully paid-up insurance, and put the rest in a fixed or variable investment within an insurance company so it can grow and compound tax-deferred.

Most fixed, single-premium policies guarantee a rate for one year or more. That rate guarantee is net of any expenses, fees, commissions, and charges for death benefits. So the policyholders know what rate of return they are going to get. Every year the insurance company will set a new rate of return that is guaranteed to be competitive, because if it is not, policyholders would switch out.

Single-premium *variable* life policies offer the same investment alternatives described above for universal variable life. The attraction is that policyholders can make their own investment decisions and have tax-free switches between alternatives. That has the potential to make the investment fund grow even faster.

Not only do the policyholders get an attractive, tax-free rate of return, but their beneficiaries get the face value of the insurance if they die—income tax free. In policies issued before June 21, 1988, policyholders could take a loan against the contract without paying income taxes or penalties—even if they were younger than age 59½.

Uncle Sam considered this too much of a good thing. The ability to compound your money tax-free *and* to spend the compound earnings tax-free was too much. So the law was changed as of June 21, 1988. Policies issued after that date now restrict your access to the tax-deferred earnings. You can still get at your money—but Uncle Sam will tax your loan or withdrawal to the extent of the gain in your policy, *and* impose a 10 percent penalty tax on the withdrawal if you are under age 59½.

This change made the older (pre-June 21, 1988) policies more valuable because they still allow withdrawals of the interest earnings, via policy loans, without current taxation or penalties. If you have an old single-premium policy and do not like the current interest rate the company is paying, do not abandon it! You can do a *1035 tax-free exchange* (named after the tax law that allows it) into another policy and not forfeit your tax-free withdrawal privilege. If there is a surrender charge on your old policy, some companies will absorb most of that cost for you.

Some newer (post-June 1988) single-premium whole life policies still allow tax-free withdrawals—but only if the policies meet strict tests regarding the amount invested. Uncle Sam defines the amount that can be put into a single-premium policy to purchase the life insurance based on your age and sex. It's called the "seven pay" threshold, and your insurance agent can tell you the exact amount you will be allowed to invest in one of these policies and still retain the tax-free withdrawal privilege.

Beware, though, because on many of these plans that still qualify for the tax-free borrowing privilege, the commission loads in the early years can be very high. That reduces the amount of your money that goes into the investment fund and lowers the return. Check the surrender charge, a portion of which represents the commission, before you purchase one of these policies. There are some no-load single-premium life policies that allow 100 percent of your money to go to work for you.

If you invest more than the allowed amount, then your policy is considered "too investment-oriented" and is defined as a *modified endowment contract*. It still gets the same benefits of tax-deferred compounding, but any withdrawals will be subject to the restrictions and penalties established on June 21, 1988. That means you would have to pay ordinary income tax and the ten percent surtax if you are under age $59\frac{1}{2}$ and decide to withdraw some money.

Some policyholders decide to borrow regularly from their single-premium whole life policy in their later years, depleting the investment account. The loan does not have to be repaid, but the amount of the loan will eventually be deducted from the death benefits. If you purchased the single-premium whole life policy after June 1988, any borrowings are taxed as ordinary income.

When the holder of one of these single-premium whole life contracts dies, the proceeds pass to the beneficiary with no income tax liability and free of probate. There may be estate tax consequences, depending on how the policy was owned.

Costs and Expenses

With all of these investment-type insurance policies, the costs are going to be higher than the costs of buying straight term insurance. After all, the insurance company has expenses involved in setting up these policies and keeping track of the paperwork. So, if you just need term insurance and do not have extra money to put into the policy for investment purposes, then you should not be buying these products.

Before you get in, ask about *all* the costs associated with the policy. The first cost is the agent's commission. It is usually taken out of the first year's premiums. So if you were to invest a sum of money in one of these policies, you can be sure the insurance company is going to want to make up its commissions and costs before letting you out.

There will either be a front-end commission deducted from the amount going to work in your chosen insurance investment, or there will be a *back-end load,* or *surrender charge* if you decide to get out of your policy within the first few years.

Even if you do not surrender your policy early, you will still be hit with taxes when you take the money out. Any gain will be subject to ordinary income tax (at your current tax rate) when the investment profits are distributed to you. And don't forget that if you buy one of those post–June 21, 1988, investment-oriented policies, you could get socked with an additional 10 percent penalty if you surrender your policy before you reach age 59^{1}/$_{2}$.

Be sure to check the amount the insurance company is taking out of your investment to pay for the actual death benefits. It is worth comparing the charges because different insurance companies may use different bases for calculating these rates. They will be the largest ongoing charge against your insurance assets.

There may also be initial policy charges, administration fees, and state premium fees—all of which will be deducted from the money going toward your investment. Ask for a list of every expense that will be deducted from your insurance investment—both in the first year and in succeeding years.

Finally, and it bears repeating, carefully check the reputation and rating of the insurance company itself. Even if the actual investment account is to be held in other mutual funds, the insurance company is the holder and custodian of your funds. You want to make sure it will be around to pay them out when needed.

Most insurance companies are rated by A.M. Best, the oldest of the insurance company rating bureaus. You would be wise to deal only with companies rated A or A +. There is no national insurance fund for insurance companies, as there is for banks and savings and loans.

In spite of the fact that many states have *guarantee funds,* most of them are not funded with actual cash. The guarantee funds rely on the willingness and ability of insurance companies doing business in the state to bail out any potential defaults.

When one large insurance company, Baldwin-United, failed in 1983, holders of its annuities and other insurance products had to wait years before settlements were made. They eventually got their original investment back, but not the very high interest rates they had been promised. Only pressure from the insurance companies on the brokerage firms that sold the products, and the willingness of some large insurance companies to assist in the bailout, brought relief to the insureds and annuitants who had been promised by salespeople that the state-guarantee funds would save their clients.

In 1991 insurance regulators took over the nation's twenty-seventh largest life and health insurance company—Executive Life of California and Executive Life of New York. These companies had invested in junk bonds in order to promise high rates to those who bought its life insurance policies, annuities, and guaranteed investment contracts for pension funds. When the value of the bonds in their portfolios collapsed, the two firms were shut down and more than 250,000 policyholders were left in doubt as to the eventual repayment of their investments. Many were surprised that A. M. Best had given the company an A+ rating just eighteen months before the collapse. That's why you should check several different rating services—including the Weiss Research Insurance Safety Ratings (See page 302 for toll-free number).

Suddenly, it looks like purchasing insurance has gotten complicated! That's when most people just give up and blindly follow the advice of an insurance broker or agent. Indeed, if you just want basic life insurance, you do not have to get involved in these insurance investment products. But if you are looking for one of the best tax-sheltered opportunities to make your money grow, you absolutely must understand these new insurance investment products.

The chart in Figure 9 on pages 296 an 297, provided by insurance expert Ben Baldwin, should help you sort out what is available in life insurance products—and which products are best suited to your insurance and investment needs.

ANNUITIES

Annuities are a way to create your own retirement plan—or build a pool of savings for any future need. The very word annuity scares many people away from this interesting, tax-deferred financial planning product. So let's start with some definitions.

An *annuity* is simply a contract between you and an insurance company—a contract that promises a stream of payments over a period of time—starting now or sometime in the future. You put in an initial amount of money—either in one payment or in a series of payments. The insurance company invests that money, and promises to pay you a specified amount each month for either a set period of time, or for your lifetime (or the combined life of you and your spouse). You can choose to have the insurance company start paying a regular monthly check immediately. That's called *annuitizing*. Or you can allow the insurance company to invest your funds and then start receiving your monthly checks at some point in the future.

You have another choice. Instead of choosing the lifetime stream of payments (annuitizing), you can take out only the interest earnings every year to live on. You will have to pay ordinary income taxes on the money you take out and a 10 percent surtax if you take money out before age $59^1/2$, but your capital stays intact and can be left to your children.

If you choose an *immediate annuity* the idea is that you will never run out of cash in your lifetime. If you give an insurance company a specific amount of cash, it will tell you how much it can pay you monthly. The monthly payment amount will depend on your age and the amount you are depositing, plus the insurance company's estimate of the amount it will earn on the money.

If you give the insurance company your lump sum of money in return for a promise of monthly payments, you have only one risk—that you will die next month and the insurance company will get to keep the balance of the money. Many people do not like taking that risk, so they structure the annuity to refund the balance to a beneficiary.

One way to do this is to buy a ten-year *period certain and life annuity,* which guarantees to pay you a certain amount over your lifetime—no matter how long you live. But if, for example, you die in six years,

Figure 9:   Life Insurance Product Analyzer

	General Description	Investment Vehicle	Investment Flexibility	Premium Flexibility	Face Amount Flexibility	Appropriate For
	TERM—Mortality & Expenses ONLY					
Non-Guaranteed Term	Lowest Cost *Poor Quality*	NONE	N/A	NONE *Increases Yearly*	NONE	*Very limited situations*
Yearly Renewable and Convertible Term	Quality Term *After Tax Life Insurance*	NONE	N/A	NONE *Increases Yearly*	NONE	*Limited Cash Flow Temporary Needs Protection NOW*
	TERM "PLUS"—Mortality & Expenses "PLUS" ADDITIONAL DOLLARS FOR INVESTMENT					
Whole Life	Tried and True *Basic Coverage Dividends make it great.*	Insurance Co. selected *Long-term bonds and mortgages*	NONE *To change investment of capital, borrowing from the policy and reinvesting is required.*	NONE *Billed premium remains level. Dividends can provide reduction or elimination. Loans Available*	NONE *If you want more, you buy new, IF you can pass a physical.*	*The Conservative Older Insureds* *Substandard Insureds*

Universal Life	"How much would you like to pay... When?"	Annual Interest Sensitive Investments	NONE To change Investment of capital requires WITHDRAWAL of capital.	MAXIMUM Just enough for Mortality and expenses, or AS MUCH AS LAW ALLOWS	Increase it or decrease it as it suits your life setting... Stay Healthy for major increases.	Younger Insureds Variable Needs Like short-term interest rate investments.
Variable Life	We will put it where You want it.	Common Stock Bond Funds Guaranteed Interest Rates Zero Coupons Money Markets etc., etc....	You Name It. You Split It. You Move It. You Borrow It. Both fixed and variable rates.	NONE Billed premium remains level. Loans available	NONE If you want more, you buy new, IF you can pass a physical.	The Investor. An alternative to ...Buy Term, Invest Difference.
Universal Variable Life	"**You Decide!**" How much... Where... When?	Common Stock Bond Funds Guaranteed Interest Rates Zero Coupons Money Markets etc, etc....	You Name It. You Split It. You Move It. You Withdraw It.	MAXIMUM Just enough for Mortality and expenses, or AS MUCH AS LAW ALLOWS	Increase it or decrease it as it suits your life setting... Stay Healthy for major increases.	The Investor. An alternative to ...Buy Term, Invest Difference. I want it MY WAY!

the annuity will continue to pay the same amount monthly to your beneficiary for another four years—until payments have continued for a total of ten years. (You may be surprised to know that the ten-year payout practically guarantees that you will receive your total initial investment, plus interest, back from the insurance company.)

The insurance company can be instructed to continue paying the monthly payments to a spouse. This is called a *joint and survivor life annuity*. It will keep making those fixed monthly payments until the death of the second person. Obviously, with a commitment that covers the lives of two people and therefore is a greater risk to the insurance company, the fixed monthly benefit from that lump sum will be smaller. To see how those options would affect your monthly payment, let's take the case of a 65-year-old male (with a 65-year-old spouse) who makes a deposit of $100,000 to an immediate annuity.

- If he takes the simple life annuity that pays only until his death, he could expect to receive about $931 a month.
- If he takes the ten-year period certain and life policy (which guarantees payments for ten years to him or his beneficiary), he would get a monthly check for about $883.
- If he opts for the joint and survivor policy (which pays his survivor the same amount monthly for the survivor's lifetime), he would get a monthly check of about $784.

These are realistic examples, but different insurance companies will offer different payouts depending not only on the age and sex of the annuitant, but on the current interest rate climate.

One concern with buying an annuity is the purchasing power of the dollars you will get back in the future. People who purchased annuity contracts in the early 1970s felt that $400 or $500 would be an adequate sum to supplement their Social Security benefits in their old age. But then prices doubled in the next decade, and their fixed payments looked insignificant when compared to the cost of living.

If you are willing to give up the certainty of a fixed annuity check every month, you could purchase an *immediate variable annuity*. In these annuities, the insurance company does not promise a fixed rate of return, but instead invests your money in a riskier underlying investment vehicle—perhaps in common stocks in a mutual fund. Your monthly annuity check might increase with the investment performance of the mutual fund, but it could also decline if the investment fund performs poorly.

When you receive income from an immediate annuity, it is partially taxable but not all subject to current income tax. The IRS recognizes that a portion of the money you are receiving every month is a return of your invested principal. The insurance company will let you know which portion of your monthly payment is considered taxable and which portion is a nontaxable return of investment. This is figured out through a formula based on your life expectancy. If you happen to live longer than expected, eventually your investment will be considered as fully returned to you, and future annuity payments will be considered fully taxable.

There are a number of ways to structure annuity payouts. The more risk you ask the insurance company to take, the smaller the fixed monthly payment will be. Before handing over your lump sum to an insurance company, carefully compare the amounts each company will promise you. Once you make the decision to hand over the money and annuitize, that is start taking out those lifetime payments, you cannot change your mind. You cannot get your lump sum of money back, nor can you switch into another annuity. So do your investigating first, before you buy an immediate annuity.

By using annuities correctly you can create an immediate stream of income that will last a lifetime. But there's another great advantage to annuity contracts. Because of the way the tax laws are written, you can use an annuity to build up tax-deferred money and not pay taxes on the interest until you take the money out.

To purchase one of these *deferred annuities* you can make one initial payment or a series of payments. Your money can be put into a fixed-rate investment or a variable investment program that will let you choose between stocks, money market, and longer-term bond investments. Check carefully on the investment vehicles being offered by the insurance company before purchasing a variable annuity. The same investment opportunities described in the discussion of variable insurance apply to variable annuity contracts. You are simply getting the tax-free buildup of your investment funds without purchasing any life insurance.

Naturally, there are some restrictions on an attractive investment such as this. If you take money out of an annuity before age 59½, you will pay a 10 percent penalty plus ordinary income taxes on the amount that is an interest withdrawal. That penalty is waived if benefits are *annuitized*—paid out in equal payments scheduled to last over the life of the annuitant.

If you purchased your annuity after August 1982, the first withdrawals are always considered to be the interest earnings, and are therefore taxable. Only after you have withdrawn all the accrued interest will the withdrawals be treated as a tax-free return of your principal. (If you purchased an annuity before August 1982, you can take your entire original investment out first without paying any taxes.)

You must also take into account the possibility that you will have to pay surrender charges if you take a substantial amount of your money out of the annuity in the first few years after purchasing it. While it may appear that you are not paying a commission to buy an annuity, the insurance company will probably impose a surrender charge for early withdrawals. The charge may range from 6 percent to 10 percent of your initial deposit, although the penalty may decline by about 1 percent a year and be eliminated entirely after the fifth or sixth year. Most companies will allow you to make penalty-free withdrawals of up to 10 percent of your account balance each year.

Some annuities actually charge a front-end load, or commission, which reduces the amount of your investment that is working for you. Since you are probably planning to leave the money working inside the annuity for a number of years, you are better off with the contracts that have back-end, or surrender, charges. At least those will gradually disappear over the years, and meanwhile all of your money is working for you.

There are some other important facts to consider before buying an annuity. First, you are giving your money to an insurance company, so you must check its track record. The company should be rated A+ by Best.

Second, if you are buying a fixed-rate annuity, check the guarantees carefully. Some companies guarantee only the first year's rate and may drop the rate in later years. A few good annuities will guarantee their current rate for as long as ten years. Also be sure to ask if there is a *bailout provision*. That is, make sure you can get out of your annuity with no penalty if the rate falls below a certain reasonable level.

If you choose a variable annuity, you will be given a choice of investments. Check the investment options carefully. How well have their available mutual funds done in recent years? Also note how often you are allowed to switch between investments. Variable annuities using mutual fund types of accounts will also charge you the mutual fund management fee every year. They may also charge small fees known as *mortality fees* to guarantee the value of your annuity at your death.

What happens to your annuity money when you die? You will be expected to name a beneficiary. The tax rules relating to annuities depend on whether you had already started receiving a stream of income from the annuity and also on who is designated as the beneficiary.

If the beneficiary is the annuity owner's spouse, and if the stream of income payments has not yet started, then the surviving spouse can elect to continue to let the annuity money grow and compound tax-deferred. If the stream of income payments has already started, then the spouse has no choice but to continue receiving the payments on the same schedule as originally planned.

If the beneficiary is not the spouse, and regular income payments have not yet started, then the beneficiary has a choice. He or she can take a one-time lump sum distribution. Even if the beneficiary is under the age of 59¹/₂, there will be no income surtax penalty, but all income buildup beyond the original annuity investment will be taxed at the beneficiary's ordinary income tax rate.

The beneficiary can also elect to *annuitize*—that is, to receive a planned stream of payments from the annuity. To the extent that they reflect earnings on the original investment, they will be taxable in the year the benefits are received. If the stream of annuity payments had started before the death of the original owner, then the beneficiary has to continue receiving the monthly payments on the original schedule—and paying taxes on the amount that is considered investment income.

At death, the value of the annuity will depend on the earnings of the investments within the fund. Guaranteed-rate annuities will have a certain designated buildup. Variable annuities could show gains or losses. Some variable annuities will guarantee that no matter what the performance of your investments within the annuity, your beneficiary will receive at least as much money as you originally put into the annuity—which is the reason for the mortality charges mentioned earlier.

As you can see, putting your money into a well-chosen annuity has definite tax advantages that can allow you to take a sum of money that you are willing to set aside until retirement and make it grow dramatically. But like all other investments, it still leaves you with several responsibilities. First you must choose the proper insurance company and annuity product. Then you must decide whether you want to make your own investment choices or settle for the fixed-rate guarantees.

Comparing annuity contracts can be difficult because you generally have to deal with insurance salespeople and trust that they are presenting the annuity with the best features and returns. However, the David T. Phillips Company has a toll-free telephone service (800-223-9610) that you can call for a monthly analysis of the ten best single-premium deferred annuities and single-premium life insurance plans. Independent Advantage Financial Services, Inc. (1-800-TAX-CUTS) will also send you a listing of its "honor roll" annuities with high safety ratings.

Finally, you should always check the financial status of the insurance company from which you are buying any life insurance product. As we mentioned earlier, insurance companies are rated by A.M. Best and should display this rating prominently in their literature. The Best rating services are also available at your public library. But the Best ratings often are based on the size or dollar amount of the company's assets—and not necessarily on an in-depth analysis of the assets themselves.

In an era when many insurance companies are promising high yields on annuities and other products, it makes sense to investigate how the company is earning enough interest to pay out high yields and still make a profit. Weiss Research, Inc. of West Palm Beach, Florida has published the *Insurance Safety Directory*, which costs $189 and examines the investments of 2,000 life and health insurance companies. But if you don't want to buy the entire book, Weiss Research will prepare a seven-page report on any insurance company for $45 or will give you the company's rating over the phone for a $15 fee, which can be charged to your bankcard (1-800-289-8100). The book also should be available in public libraries.

Insuring Your Wealth

We spend much of our lives working to obtain possessions. We save, and sometimes go into debt, to be able to purchase important material things such as a home or car. We collect objects of art or spend money on more frivolous items such as furs and jewelry. Then suddenly we realize that the purchase price is not the only cost of owning these possessions: If we value them, we must insure them against loss, theft, or damage. Thus begins an ongoing additional cost—insuring your wealth.

HOMEOWNER'S INSURANCE

Your home is your most important investment. Before you even close on the property, your mortgage lender will demand that you have basic insurance coverage for at least 80 percent of the home's current replacement cost, or 100 percent of the mortgage, whichever is higher. But it's up to you as the homeowner to make sure that the coverage is adequate, not only for the structure, but for your personal property within the home.

It's only when you start to study homeowner's insurance that you realize how much could go wrong—and cost you money. Fire is the obvious problem, but insurance companies have categories of "perils" that could affect your property.

The eleven basic perils covered by most standard (HO-1) insurance policies include:

- fire or lightning
- smoke damage
- windstorm or hail
- explosion
- riot or civil disorder
- damage caused by vehicles
- damage caused by aircraft
- theft
- loss of property when removed from a house in case of fire or other dangerous situation
- vandalism
- breakage of glass that is part of a building

It sounds like a list of plagues from the Old Testament, yet this is only the most basic coverage offered. In fact, most homeowners buy a *broad form* (HO-2) policy, which offers additional coverage for things like:

- damage caused by falling objects
- roof collapse under the weight of ice, snow, sleet
- collapse of any part of the building
- damage caused by hot water pipes or heater exploding
- damage caused by frozen pipes or air conditioning system
- damage as a result of electrical surges to appliances (except TVs)

A third type of policy called *special form* (HO-3) provides even broader coverage by insuring the structure of your home for everything except certain exclusions. (Although the list of exclusions is not long, it is a good idea to read them through.) Contents coverage remains the same as in the HO-2 policy. Generally speaking, insurance companies would rather sell you the HO-3 policy, so the pricing is attractive when compared to the HO-1 and HO-2 policies.

There is an even more complete policy called *comprehensive* (HO-5), which covers both the structure and contents for all 18 listed perils and just about anything else *except* flood, earthquake, war, and nuclear accidents!

Apartment dwellers need a special form of coverage tailored to their needs—HO-4. In the case of an apartment dweller, this standard renter's insurance policy will cover not only furnishings in the apartment, but property away from home (such as in your car), for all the perils included in the broad form (HO-2). It will also provide coverage for additional living expenses. The building is responsible for coverage of the structure itself.

Condo and co-op owners need a special policy (HO-6) designed to cover not only their personal property, but additions and alterations they have made to their apartment that are not covered by the building's insurance. The coverage is similar to the HO-4 policy.

When you buy coverage on a home, you are insuring the structure and contents, *not* the land on which the home sits. After all, even if the house is destroyed completely, you will still own the land. Keep that in mind when determining how much coverage you need. Most insurance companies will not allow you to overinsure your property. On the other hand, if you are underinsured (insured for less than 80 percent of the value of the home), many companies will place a limit on the amount they will reimburse for a loss.

The amount of your insurance should be refigured every year as the policy is renewed. Inflation may make the value of the home and contents increase. Many policies have an automatic inflation guard endorsement that increases the amount of coverage to keep up with inflation. But perhaps you modernized a kitchen or added a recreation room. Those kinds of additions will boost the value of your home and should be covered by additional insurance.

Generally speaking, the contents of the house will be insured for about half of the amount for which you insure the house itself. If, however, your contents represent more than 50 percent of the value of the home's structure, you can purchase additional contents coverage. But the way the policy is written can have a major impact on the amount of money you will collect in case of damage or loss.

Replacement Cost or Cash Value

Most policies specify that the insurance company will pay you the actual cash value for any losses. That means if your living room furniture is eight years old and destroyed by fire, the insurance company will pay you what they estimate is the value of an eight-year-old couch and chairs. Not very much. The alternative is to make sure your policy is written to cover *replacement cost* of any damaged property. That means the insurance company would give you enough money to completely replace your old living room furniture with brand new items of similar quality. Obviously, replacement cost insurance is going to be more expensive, but it is also going to save you a lot of headaches in case you have to collect.

Proving Your Loss

Another thing that could save you agony in the future is making a complete inventory and record of the contents of your home. If you have a video camera or can borrow one, that is the simplest way to do the job. Just go from room to room photographing the contents and describing them on the tape. Then be sure to store the tapes in a place where they wouldn't be destroyed along with everything else in case of a fire. An alternative is to keep a listing or log book of the items in each room, perhaps in a folder with bills showing the costs of more expensive items.

Bringing Down the Cost of Homeowner's Insurance

The cost of your policy will depend on a number of factors rated by the insurance company. If you are in an area that has a high burglary rate, then the insurance will cost more. You may be able to bring down the cost of your insurance by installing a burglar alarm system. Retired people often trade quality for lower homeowner's insurance rates because they are home during the day acting as a deterrent to burglars. Nonsmokers often get lower rates because they lower the risk of fire damage.

One way to lower the cost of homeowner's (or renter's) insurance is to accept a higher deductible. The deductible is the amount you will have to pay before the insurance comes in to pay for any losses. Raising the deductible amount from $100 to $500 can substantially lower the premiums on your insurance.

Floaters

Your standard homeowner's or renter's policy will cover your basic personal property with several important exceptions. The insurance company will limit its coverage of things like jewelry, furs, silverware, and artwork to a flat figure—perhaps $1,000. The only way to cover these items for their true replacement value is to buy a *floater* policy— a sort of mini-insurance policy on each individual item. You'll need a current appraisal of the value of each item listed, or *scheduled,* separately on the floater. The cost of this insurance can really add up, but it's the only way to protect valuable personal items. Be sure to check with your insurance agent to find out which items should be covered by the floater.

Flood Insurance

Standard homeowner's policies *do not* cover flood insurance. However, most states belong to the federally subsidized flood insurance program. Communities that follow federal guidelines for building in areas with flood potential qualify to join the program. This type of federally subsidized flood insurance is then purchased at a low cost through private insurers from the National Flood Insurance Program.

Be warned that even with this federal flood insurance program there are severe limitations about what can be covered. Excluded items include anything stored below ground level in a basement, except for major appliances such as a water heater or washer and dryer. Check carefully to see what your flood insurance covers and what is excluded.

Other Natural Disasters

If you live in an area that is prone to earthquakes, insurance coverage must be written as a special addition to your basic coverage. Not surprisingly, more than half of all earthquake policies are purchased in California.

Ever since May 18, 1980, when Washington state's Mount St. Helens volcano erupted, there has been increased interest in insurance against volcanic eruptions. Even though most homeowner's policies in that area had specific exclusions for volcanic eruptions, the vast majority of insurers covered the damage under the section calling for coverage against explosions. Volcanic eruptions are now covered as part of most standard peril policies.

Additional Coverages

All forms of homeowner's policies include liability coverages that apply not only to the policyholder, but to all family members who live in the home. These coverages include liability, medical payments to others, and physical damage to the property of others.

The basic personal liability on a homeowner's policy is $100,000— although higher amounts can be purchased, usually for just a few more dollars. This section is designed to protect the policyholder against a claim that is not business- or auto-related. It protects against lawsuits from those who may be injured on one's property—or if the policyholder or family member is involved in an incident away from home. This section even covers damages caused by the family pet.

The medical payments section of the homeowner's policy usually will pay out $1,000 of medical bills—without regard to fault—to someone injured in the insured home, or if you or a family member injures somebody away from the home. This coverage does not pay for injuries to the policyholder or family members.

Your policy should have coverage for "additional living expenses"— just in case your home is so badly damaged by the kind of losses covered in the policy that you and your family have to live in a hotel or eat in restaurants while the home is repaired. The insurance company will reimburse you for the difference between these expenses and your standard living expenses.

In addition, most insurance policies will provide coverage for "reasonable repairs" such as board-up service in case of broken windows. Some insurers will reimburse property owners for fire department services in areas where those charges are billed separately.

Many policies will reimburse policyholders up to $500 should they lose their credit cards and others charge purchases to their accounts. (This is in addition to the immunity given by federal law for fraudulent charges above $50 on lost or stolen credit cards.) The same limit applies when a policyholder happens to accept counterfeit money in good faith, or in the case of check forgery.

Read Your Insurance Policy

In the last few years, the insurance industry has developed new, easy-to-read language for most homeowner's policies. Take out your insurance policy right now and check to make sure that your coverage is adequate to cover the cost of replacing your valuable items. If you have any questions, call your agent.

AUTO INSURANCE

There are more than 30 million auto accidents a year, and in 1990 they will cost an estimated $100 billion in damages, not to mention deaths and casualties, according to the Insurance Information Institute. Of every $10 that Americans spend for property and casualty coverage, more than $4 goes to pay the premiums for insuring motor vehicles.

Most states require car owners to have some form of auto insurance or demonstrate proof of financial responsibility up to certain limits. As with your homeowner's policy, the best advice is to read your current policy (or any proposed policy) carefully and ask questions about coverages you do not understand.

There are six basic types of auto insurance coverage.

> *Bodily injury liability* is insurance to pay claims against the policyholder as a result of injuries to pedestrians, people riding in other cars, or people riding in the insured's car. It covers the policyholder and family members when they are driving someone else's car with permission, and it

usually applies to anyone driving the policyholder's car with permission.

If the policyholder needs a legal defense, this section of the auto insurance will pay for it. And if a court decides that the policyholder is liable for injuring someone else, then the insurer will pay the judgment—up to the limits stated in the policy.

Medical payments insurance covers medical and funeral expenses resulting from injuries related to use of the car. This portion of the insurance pays regardless of who is at fault in an accident. The medical payments portion of the policy covers the policyholder, resident family members, and guests in the policyholder's car.

Uninsured motorist coverage pays for the policyholder's injuries (not property damage) if he or she is hit by another motorist who does not have insurance. The policy may also include underinsured motorist coverage, which will pay off excess medical bills in case the other motorist does not have enough bodily injury liability insurance.

Property damage liability insurance pays claims if the policyholder's car damages the property of others. That includes damage to cars, buildings, and telephone poles. If another person files a claim for this type of damage done by the policyholder or a family member driving the car, the insurance company will defend the claim and pay off if necessary.

Collision insurance pays for damage to the policyholder's car if it rolls over or collides with another vehicle or object. It does not matter who is at fault; the insurer will pay your repair costs—less the deductible. The insurance company may then try to get that money back from the other driver's insurer.

In collision insurance, the deductible amount—the amount you pay before insurance takes over—is a key ingredient in determining cost. You can lower the cost of your auto insurance by accepting a higher deductible—perhaps $500 instead of $200. Some companies will sell policies with deductibles as high as $1,000.

Comprehensive insurance covers losses from theft or damage such as fire, glass breakage, falling objects, explosion, vandalism, malicious mischief, contact with a bird or animal—as well as earthquake, windstorm, hail, and flood. It, too, is sold with a deductible.

The price, or premium, you will pay for car insurance depends on a number of factors. Where you live will determine the rate you pay, no matter what your driving record. If you live in an area that has a high theft or accident rate, then you will pay higher rates. The National Safety Council says that roughly three of every four accidents occur within 25 miles of drivers' homes, so where you live has an impact on what you pay for insurance.

All drivers are classified by age and sex to determine insurance rates. Based on accident statistics, young unmarried men pay the highest auto insurance premiums. Women over 30 who are the only drivers in their household and drivers over 50 are most likely to get premium discounts.

Your driving record also affects the amount you will pay for insurance. Speeding tickets and previous accidents will increase your premiums. If you use your car for business, that might increase your premium, but if you insure more than one car, you could be eligible for a discount. The value of your car can also have an impact on the amount you will pay for insurance.

If you have a teenager who arrives at that magic age and gets a driver's license, you can expect to see a sharp increase in your auto insurance premiums. There are, however, discounts granted for driver's training programs and for students who maintain at least a B average in school. Also, if your child is in school at least 100 miles from home, a discount is available.

It is possible to lower the amount you pay for auto insurance if you decide not to take the collision and comprehensive coverage. That means you will be responsible for any damage to your car in case of an accident. If your car is older or not worth repairing, you might forgo collision coverage.

Insurance for High-Risk Drivers

It may be difficult to get *any* auto insurance if you have a bad driving record. A company will be understandably reluctant to grant or renew insurance to someone it considers a bad risk. For those people, every state has an *assigned risk pool* in which every insurer in the state agrees to take on some of these poor risks in proportion to the amount of business the company does in the state. If this is your problem, check with your state insurance commissioner to see what provisions have been made to get auto insurance at reasonable rates for people in your situation.

Some companies will write auto insurance no matter what the driving record—if you're willing to pay the price. This is called the nonstandard market. These companies, usually advertised on late night television, will offer more liability insurance than the assigned risk companies will write. The problem is making sure the company will be around to pay off in case you have an accident. Again, check with your state insurance commissioner before sending a check to one of these companies.

No-Fault Auto Insurance

Many states have adopted *no-fault* insurance plans. This simply means that your own insurance company pays off if you are in an accident—no matter who was at fault. No-fault came into being because many state courts were jammed with auto accident cases in which parties were arguing not over who was at fault, but over how much the injuries were worth in settlement of a lawsuit. With no-fault insurance, policyholders receive their benefits immediately—no questions asked. Other issues such as pain and suffering can be adjudicated in the court system.

Not all state no-fault laws are the same. All allow people to sue if the damages or injuries reach a certain "threshold" level. Others specify just how much money must be paid in certain instances such as lost income of a wage earner. Most do not include no-fault provisions for property damage, only for medical liabilities. If you are moving to a no-fault state, check the provisions of the insurance laws carefully to make sure you have any excess coverage that might be required in addition to the basic no-fault policy.

Car Rental Insurance

When you take out your auto insurance, check to see what is covered when you are renting a car. When you are standing at the car rental counter and are asked to accept or decline various rental insurance provisions, it's good to know whether you really need to pay extra for all this daily insurance—at a very expensive rate.

The most common option is the CDW—collision damage waiver. About 26 percent of people renting cars from major companies purchase CDW. This guarantees that the renter will not be held financially responsible for damage to the rented car as long as he or she follows the terms of the contract. The car rental company has its own insurance which will cover the cost of the repair. But at a cost of $9 or $10 a day for CDW, the car rental company is making a lot of money at the renter's expense. Additional charges for theft and accident liability insurance drive up the price of a car rental even higher.

The fact is, most major auto insurance policies usually cover people for those potential liabilities when they drive rented cars. Under your car insurance policy you still may have the obligation to pay a deductible, and file a claim. Most homeowner's policies will cover the theft of your luggage from a rented car, subject to its own deductible.

The real advantage to taking the CDW waiver is that many car companies now make you liable for the entire cost of the rented car in case of an accident. And they have the credit card charge slip that you signed in blank when you rented the car. If you declined the CDW waiver and have an accident that you want your insurance company to pay for, they may just charge you for the damages and force you to file a claim with your insurance company in order to get your money back.

It is wise to check your insurance coverage before you set out on a trip. You might also want to rent your car with one of the premium credit cards that automatically cover the CDW, allowing you to decline that waiver when you rent the car. (See Chapter 6.)

DISABILITY INSURANCE

Disability insurance is probably the most overlooked type of insurance. It is insurance against loss of income. Your earning power is probably your most valuable asset. So while you spend time and money insuring your house, car, and life, it is even more worthwhile to insure your ability to work.

While some employers and many unions offer some sort of limited monthly payments if a worker is disabled on the job, many highly paid professional people never give a thought to what would happen if they were suddenly unable to perform the work that provides their income. According to one study, people in their forties are three times more likely to become disabled than they are to die before age 65. There is a one in two chance of a 30-year-old being laid up for more than three months before age 65.

Social Security does provide a disability income, but only after lengthy reviews of medical claims and evaluations of your ability to work at any occupation. The Social Security disability claims process is so arduous that many disabled people never receive benefits.

The answer is privately purchased disability insurance, which can be structured to provide payments based on your inability to do your own particular occupation, even if you are able to perform another less-demanding and lower-paying job. You will probably need enough disability insurance to replace between 50 and 70 percent of your gross earned income. You don't need coverage for your entire income, because if you pay for the disability insurance with after-tax dollars, the money you may eventually collect will be tax-free. Companies that provide disability insurance will require proof of income and a complete physical exam before they write coverage.

The cost of disability income is based on several factors. Your occupation is one key determinant. If you are in a high-risk occupation involving physical labor, you might find it hard to get disability insurance. Similarly, if you are in a specialized profession, such as a surgeon, disability insurance may be more expensive. Remember, you want a policy that will pay a full benefit when you can no longer perform your *own* occupation. That would cover the surgeon who lost the use of his hands but could still perform other medical duties such as diagnosing patients.

As a less expensive alternative, you might want to choose a policy that will pay full benefits for five years if you cannot perform your own occupation, and then pay a reduced benefit in subsequent years to compensate you if you return to work at a reduced pay level. This is called a residual benefit.

The length of time you want to receive disability benefits will also affect the cost. Some policies will pay only for five years, while others are structured to pay until you reach age 65 and qualify for Social Security. Others may pay benefits over your lifetime. Some pay a flat amount, and others will escalate payments in line with the cost of living.

You can lower the cost of disability insurance by agreeing to a longer waiting period before benefits kick in. You might have enough savings to cover you for a six-month period, or you can time the disability benefits to kick in when your employer's sick leave policy runs out.

The wording in a disability policy is often quite complex. The main thing to be sure of is the actual definition of disability and any exclusions in the definition. Be sure the policy will make up a difference in income if you can only perform a lower-paying job or can only work part-time. The best policies will pay a residual benefit without ever having required that you be *totally* disabled.

You will definitely want a policy that is noncancellable and has a guaranteed annual premium. That means your premium can't be raised and your policy can't be cancelled unless you stop paying premiums. Be sure the policy doesn't force you to keep paying premiums once you are disabled.

About one-third of the disability policies sold by major companies these days are sold to women. The insurance companies say women have a higher disability rate (their studies, not mine!), so women may be charged slightly higher rates. Women seeking disability insurance should look for a company that has "unisex" rates.

Prices on disability policies are competitive and subject to change, reflecting insurance companies' experience with these claims. The trend in prices is up. That's another good reason not to postpone locking in a fixed premium. You can always switch policies later if a better deal comes along. Use an independent insurance agent with some experience in disability to bring you several policies and help you compare prices and terms.

For a 40-year-old salesman in good health, an annual disability policy with a six-month waiting period that pays $2,000 a month until age 65 should cost about $635 a year. But if our 40-year-old were a surgeon, he could expect to pay as much as $883 a year. Nonetheless, that might be a small price to pay for the guarantee of a stream of income in spite of a future disability.

UMBRELLA LIABILITY

If you carry an umbrella for a rainy day, "just in case," then you might want to think about carrying an umbrella liability insurance policy to protect your assets—just in case.

In a sense, all insurance purchases are a bet against some unexpected event happening in the future. Obviously, some events are less likely to occur than others. For instance, we insure for eventual death; that is an inevitability—only the date is uncertain. We insure our homes against fire and theft, even though these may be remote possibilities. But if you have substantial assets you might want to insure against a real catastrophe—a lawsuit that claims more than your basic insurance coverage will pay.

Generally, a typical auto insurance policy will pay $100,000 per person for bodily injury sustained in an accident. That can cover passengers in your car or in another vehicle in the accident. There is usually a total coverage of $300,000 in bodily injury per accident. And typical policies pay out only $50,000 in property damage liability related to an auto accident.

Your homeowner's coverage probably has similar liability limits—about $300,000 to $500,000 in comprehensive personal liability. That sounds like enough to cover most foreseeable incidents, but in this day of huge judgments in accident cases you might want to take a second look.

If you have substantial personal assets, you might become a target of one of those huge lawsuits. What if your teenager is involved in an auto accident causing multiple injuries? What if your dog bites the neighbor's child? What if your golf ball hits someone? A court could decide that your liability in any of these cases is far greater than your basic auto and homeowner's policies will cover.

A 1989 study by Jury Verdict Research, Inc. and the Insurance Information Institute shows that the average payment by insurance companies in vehicle lawsuit settlements has risen over 40 percent since 1973. Three of every 100 auto liability settlements exceed $1 million!

That's where an umbrella liability policy comes in. These policies are sold in $1 million chunks. They are sold by your regular insurance agent, although many companies will demand they write your underlying home and auto insurance before they write an umbrella liability policy. The insurer will probably also require a $500,000 minimum coverage on the underlying policies. Then, if someone wins a huge claim against you, your basic policy will cover the first half million dollars of any judgment and the umbrella pays the balance.

These are relatively inexpensive insurance policies that cost between $100 and $150 per million dollars of coverage. Considering your potential liability, it might be worth the extra insurance dollars each year—even if you are insuring against a longshot.

CHAPTER 22

Insuring Your Health

Nearly 180 million Americans have health insurance, and 80 percent of them have group health insurance through their employer. But for millions of others—especially the poor, the self-employed, and the retired—finding and affording adequate health insurance is a real problem.

If you do have health insurance through work, you should understand its provisions, benefits, and costs. Many employee benefits plans give options for care and other programs that must be evaluated. If you do not qualify for an employer-sponsored plan, be aware of different health insurance programs that may cover you and your family. And if for some reason you must leave your job, your first consideration should be continued coverage of your health insurance needs.

EMPLOYER-SPONSORED PLANS

Employer health care costs have been one of the fastest growing areas of the corporate budget, with annual increases for medical costs rising about 20 percent in recent years—far above inflation. That's why so many businesses are changing their employee health plans and asking employees to share costs and responsibilities for keeping medical costs down.

Most companies will offer three basic types of coverage to all full-time employees: regular medical/surgical insurance, hospitalization insurance, and major medical insurance. In addition, the company may offer dental insurance coverage and disability coverage.

The basic medical/surgical insurance covers your visits to a doctor (usually for treatment of an illness, *not* a regular checkup). It will pay for doctors visits if you are in the hospital, and it will pay for prescription medicines and specialized tests done outside of a hospital.

But the basic medical/surgical program of most companies will not pay *all* these expenses. According to a Hewitt Associates survey, 70 percent of medical plans require employees to pay the initial medical expenses incurred every year by paying a front-end deductible. That amount is generally about $100, but some plans require employees to pick up the first $250 of medical expenses every year.

The second part of most health plans is the hospitalization benefits. This part of the plan will pay all or part of the costs of hospitalization and in-hospital procedures, testing, and surgery. Again, most plans do not pay all hospital expenses. Most plans have a *coinsurance* provision requiring the employee to pay between 10 and 20 percent of the costs. These plans may also have a very desirable *stop-loss* feature that limits an employee's out-of-pocket costs to a maximum of perhaps $2,000.

The major medical portion of the insurance starts paying *after* the regular hospitalization benefits run out. That's why you should check to see the top limit that your plan will pay under each category. The major medical may have limits of $100,000 or more—an amount that seems huge but could easily be exceeded in the case of a family tragedy or a lingering illness like cancer.

Most major medical plans require the payment of an additional deductible (even after you paid one on your original hospitalization benefits) and will also require you to pay a percentage of the costs as a form of coinsurance—perhaps another 20 percent.

It is easy to see how a family's financial situation could be entirely wiped out by a major illness. There are, in fact, some relatively inexpensive *excess major medical* policies offered through fraternal organizations, which can cover expenses far higher than those on most major medical policies.

While most employee health plans offer the three basic types of coverage, the companies are so concerned with costs that they are creating additional incentives to keep medical costs down. Those may include charging employees a portion of the medical premiums for themselves or for their dependents. If you are taking a new job, be sure to find out if you will have to pay a portion of the premiums, and if your dependents are covered. Also check to see if your dependents are covered for dental insurance or orthodontia.

As part of the new cost-control consciousness, many employee plans now require a second opinion for most surgical procedures (except genuine emergencies) or the plan will not fully cover the procedure. There are new requirements that preadmission testing be done on an outpatient basis. And nearly half of employers say they will pay higher benefits if surgery is done on an outpatient basis.

Usually the health plan benefits are not going to make the final difference in your decision to join a company—with one exception. You must make sure the plan will cover any preexisting condition that you or one of your family members may have. If you or a dependent are being treated for an ongoing illness, the new plan may require you be treatment-free for a period of months before it will cover that condition. It is also important to see if the new company's plan will cover expenses if you change jobs during pregnancy. You may be able to convert the policy from your previous employer to an individual policy in order to cover these conditions. That may not be possible, however, if you are going to join the new company's group plan.

Conversion Coverage

Most major corporate health plans are required by law to provide continued coverage in case you should lose your job, or for family members if the covered spouse dies. The employee, or the surviving family, has to pay for those benefits, but the rate will be relatively low because it will be done as part of the group plan. And there will be no restrictions on coverage for preexisting conditions. The employer must provide continued health coverage for a period of one and a half to three years.

The employee must have another alternative—conversion to a less-expensive group plan that may offer less coverage. This conversion must be initiated within 60 days of termination or loss of job. Needless to say, the employer will rarely go to great lengths to make this offer to a discharged employee, but the benefit is required by law and will be made available on request. If you know someone who has recently lost his or her job, after commiserating, your first question should be about continuing health insurance benefits.

INDIVIDUAL HEALTH COVERAGE

If you are a part-time worker, an independent contractor, or own your own business, you may have a difficult time finding a health insurance plan for yourself and your family. Private insurance packages are costly, and many companies no longer offer individual health insurance plans.

The first thing you should do in seeking health insurance is check to see if you belong to a group that may offer these benefits to its members. Perhaps a business organization, a fraternal organization, or even a church affiliation will provide you with a group plan you can join. Contact the Small Business Administration to find out if there are business associations in your area that offer health plan benefits to members. Some insurance providers still offer *small-business-group-of-one* insurance plans. Only by checking around will you uncover the possibility of belonging to a group that can offer health insurance benefits.

Some private insurers still offer individual medical and hospitalization insurance, although at very expensive rates. Many private insurers have been dropping individual coverage. You should also check with your state Blue Cross/Blue Shield organization to find out about the cost and availability of their programs for individual coverage.

MEDICAID

For those unable to find any other health insurance coverage, Section XIX of the Social Security Act provides a program of medical assistance for low-income individuals and families. The program, known as Medicaid, is administered by each state following certain federal guidelines and limits.

It is usually available to those meeting the standards of other federal assistance programs such as Aid to Families with Dependent Children and Supplemental Social Security Income. In cases where an elderly citizen is eligible for both Medicare and Medicaid, most state Medicaid programs will pay the deductibles and copayments.

HMOs (HEALTH MAINTENANCE ORGANIZATIONS)

As part of the trend toward containing health-care costs, many businesses that offer employee health care benefits are turning toward HMOs—health maintenance organizations. For many people who are not covered by employer plans, HMOs are the most practical way of obtaining complete health care coverage. Today, more than 30 million Americans are covered by HMOs. There are tremendous cost advantages—and a few potential drawbacks—to joining an HMO. Here's how they work.

When you join an HMO, you pay a monthly premium. For a family of four it may cost about $2,500 a year—far less than the roughly $4,000 per year cost of a standard medical/surgical policy for the same family. If the HMO is offered as part of a company benefit plan, the company will usually pay for all or almost all of the cost of the HMO, relieving the family of the burden of paying the deductible amount on standard company health policies.

For that premium, you get comprehensive medical care that includes not only doctors charges, hospitalization costs, and surgical expenses, but also coverage for routine examinations, tests, and preventive care. The HMO may also give you complete coverage for dental care and eyeglasses. (Some HMOs do charge about $5 for a routine office visit.)

In addition to coverage for all medical visits—with no deductible payment required—HMOs have some other advantages. There are no claim forms to be filled out, and no wait for reimbursement of money spent. HMOs do not place a limit on how long you can be hospitalized or on the total size of your medical bills. Most HMOs cover emergency treatment when you are out of town. The facility simply bills the HMO, or you pay the expenses and are reimbursed.

Medicare recipients pay about $30 a month to join an HMO. That means the retiree does not have to pay the first $560 a year in hospital stays and the first 20 percent in doctor bills, as is required under the standard Medicare program. Joining an HMO may also give coverage for eyeglasses, prescription drugs, and dental care, which are not covered under the ordinary Medicare program.

In spite of all those advantages in cost and efficiency, there are some drawbacks to joining an HMO. The biggest one is the fact that once you join an HMO, you must see an HMO doctor and use a hospital designated by the HMO. If you already have a long-standing relationship with a family doctor or specialist, you may not want to switch.

With a large HMO there may be no problem choosing a new doctor who suits your needs. Some HMOs have doctors on staff who receive a salary, and other plans use independent doctors who are on contract to the HMO and see their other private patients as well. However, you are restricted in choosing specialists to meet any future emergency needs. You will be referred to another HMO doctor. If you go outside the HMO, then you are responsible for paying the bills.

Some people complain that they do not have access to the same doctor when they come in for ordinary checkups. Before joining an HMO, you should study its policy to find out whether you will have one regular doctor or will just see the physician then on duty in the clinic. Some HMOs keep their costs down by limiting the number of physicians on duty at any one time, resulting in lengthy waits or in seeing a nurse for routine treatment.

You should carefully evaluate the HMO before joining. The facilities should be convenient, and the list of doctors should be extensive. Do you have a choice of doctors? In an emergency, does the affiliated hospital have a large staff? How are after-hours emergencies handled? How easy is it to get prescriptions filled? These are all questions to consider *before* joining an HMO. The best answers may come from others who are already members.

There is one more difficult consideration to examine before joining an HMO—its financial solvency. In recent months a number of HMOs have expanded too fast, resulting in cutbacks in service and some outright failures. If you are paying your own money for this type of health insurance, you want to make sure the doctors and hospitals will accept you in an emergency without questioning the solvency of your HMO. Check with your state insurance director or with other hospitals in the area to get a financial opinion or reference on an HMO.

PPOs (PREFERRED PROVIDER ORGANIZATIONS)

PPOs—preferred provider organizations—are one of the fastest growing trends in health care. It is a sort of hybrid between standard company health insurance plans and health maintenance organizations. A PPO allows patients to choose their own doctors and hospitals while negotiating with physicians and hospitals for group rates on their services. The result is the traditional fee-for-service medicine at lower cost.

From the point of view of the physician or hospital, joining a PPO creates a large potential market of clients. From the point of view of the insurance company, which often acts as the intermediary, there are several advantages. The insurance company negotiates lower rates to be passed on to the businesses that join the PPO. And the insurance company can review the medical practices and require second opinions. The business that provides the PPO to its employees as a benefit has the advantage of lower medical costs while giving employees what they want most: a chance to choose their own doctors.

Unlike an HMO, a PPO definitely offers patients freedom of choice when it comes to hospitals and doctors. There is, however, a strong financial incentive to use the services of the PPO: Those services may be covered for up to 90 or 100 percent of the cost. If a patient goes to a physician or hospital outside the PPO, only 80 percent of the costs may be covered, leaving them to pay more of the cost out of their own pockets.

The providers of this service do not negotiate a set fee for all services for each patient, as they would with an HMO. Instead, they still charge for each service performed, in the traditional manner. They have, however, prenegotiated certain discounted rates for each service. And they have agreed that there may be a review of the procedures they recommend for each patient. There is nothing to preclude doctors or hospitals from joining as many PPOs in their area as they choose.

PPOs may be sponsored by groups of physicians or by a hospital on behalf of its own services and staff physicians. They may be marketed directly to a business or use an insurance company as an intermediary. A PPO may be limited to just physician services, hospital services, or a combination of both. Many PPOs are broadening their services to include dental, psychiatric care, and pharmacy services.

PPOs are the fastest-growing segment of the health care management business. It is expected that there will be model Medicare PPOs in operation in an attempt to control the rising costs of Medicare Part B (physician and ambulatory services).

If your employer does not offer a PPO as an alternative health care plan, you might ask the company human resources executive to contact the American Association of Preferred Provider Organizations, 111 E. Wacker Dr., Suite 600, Chicago, IL 60601.

MEDICARE

Medicare is a federal health insurance program for people age 65 or older and for certain disabled people. It is paid for in part out of the Social Security tax and in part by contributions from the people who are covered.

Medicare has two parts: hospital insurance (Part A) and medical insurance (Part B). The hospital insurance portion helps pay for inpatient hospital services and some follow-up care. The medical insurance helps pay doctor bills and some other medical services and expenses.

Anyone who is 65 or older can enroll for Medicare medical insurance. There is no requirement that you have Social Security credits to get the medical insurance. The basic monthly premium in 1991 is $29.90 a month, which is ordinarily deducted from the monthly Social Security check. If this medical insurance is being purchased by someone not covered by Social Security, it will be billed quarterly.

You must actually sign up to receive your Medicare medical benefits by filling out an application at your local Social Security office just before you reach age 65. You will need to show proof of age and, if you are retiring, your most recent W-2 form as well. About a month after you apply for Medicare, you will receive a Medicare enrollment card and a handbook with details about your coverage.

In 1991, the annual deductible for Medicare Part B (medical care) is $100. That is the amount the patient must pay before Medicare covers any charges. Each year, after the deductible is met, Medicare will pay 80 percent of the approved charges for covered services incurred during the year. Medicare does not cover the cost of outpatient prescription drugs, eyeglasses, dental care, hearing aids, or routine physical examinations.

When choosing a physician it is easier for the patient if the doctor accepts Medicare assignment—that is, the doctor agrees to the Medicare fee schedule and agrees that what Medicare pays will be 80 percent of his or her total charges. That way, the patient is not left to pay excess charges above the medicare-approved payments. The other advantage is that the doctor takes care of the paperwork, billing Medicare directly and billing the patient only for the 20 percent coinsurance.

Once you start receiving Social Security checks, your Medicare hospital insurance protection (Part A) automatically begins at age 65. There is no cost for this part of the coverage, which is financed through payroll taxes and general tax revenues.

Even if you are not automatically eligible for Social Security benefits (because you did not work long enough to earn the required credits), when you reach age 65 you can still purchase the hospital portion of Medicare. The basic premium for purchased hospitalization coverage in 1991 is $177 a month. But to buy hospital insurance, you must also enroll to purchase medical insurance at a cost of $29.90 a month for 1991.

In 1991, Medicare hospital insurance pays for all but the first $628 of covered services for the first 60 days of hospitalization. For longer hospital stays—from 61 to 90 days—the patient must pay $157 for each of those additional days. There is no coverage for hospitalization longer than 90 days, with one exception. The Medicare recipient has 60 *lifetime reserve days* for hospitalization, which are nonrenewable once used. These reserve days should be saved to cover a period of hospitalization that lasts more than 90 days. There is a coinsurance payment of $314 a day in 1991 when those reserve days are used.

If the patient leaves the hospital and returns within 60 days, there is no new deductible to pay. However, if the patient returns to the hospital later in the year, after 60 days have elapsed, then a new $628 deductible must be paid. If a hospital stay extends over year-end, there is no new deductible to be paid in the new year.

There are strict limitations about inpatient skilled nursing care repayments under Medicare. Before being eligible for this skilled nursing care benefit, the patient must have been hospitalized for at least three days. The doctor must certify the need for skilled inpatient nursing care, and Medicare will check closely that this is skilled care, and not custodial care. If payment is authorized by Medicare, it will cover 100 percent of the cost for the first 20 days. For an additional 80 days the patient pays $78.50 a day and Medicare pays the balance. Medicare does *not* pay for a private duty nurse in the hospital.

In 1989, Congress passed the Medicare Catastrophic Health Insurance Act—a short-lived program that was repealed by the end of that year. The program was designed to provide additional Medicare coverage—at an additional cost of $4 per month added on to the Part B monthly premium, along with a surtax on the income tax liability of those eligible to receive Medicare.

Because the program was repealed late in 1989, the government continued to collect the additional monthly premium well into 1990—before its computer programs could be changed. All of the premiums paid in after January 1, 1990, were repaid. Those who had made quarterly payments to the IRS including a portion of the surtax received a credit or refund from the IRS.

The whole controversy over the Catastrophic Health Insurance Act served to make people aware of the gaps in Medicare insurance, especially for long-term and expensive illnesses and for medicines. That has created a large—and complicated—market for Medicare supplemental insurance policies.

MEDICARE GAP POLICIES

While Medicare provides basic coverage for medical and hospital expenses, there are huge gaps in coverage that must be paid by the individual. Medicare recipients are responsible for paying the annual medical and hospital deductibles, which keep rising every year. In fact, the Part A hospital deductible amount has risen from $160 in 1979 to $628 in 1991. The individual is also responsible for the 20 percent coinsurance payment for each of these bills.

Medicare has other serious gaps. Hospital coverage can run out after a fixed number of days, leaving the patient exposed to a huge financial liability in cases of serious illnesses. If physicians charge more than the approved level of Medicare charges for various procedures, the patient must pay not only the coinsurance, but the amount above the approved reimbursed level. And Medicare does not pay for any prescription medicine for outpatients.

For all of these reasons, many people supplement their Medicare coverage with additional policies that offer to pay all or a portion of the additional costs. Medicare supplements are often advertised on late night television. "We'll pay everything that Medicare doesn't cover—forever!" say the commercials. You can send away for the information, but you need to compare the coverage and study the small print.

One of the most comprehensive Medicare gap policies is offered by the American Association for Retired Persons (AARP) (800-523-5800). They offer several different levels of coverage at increasingly expensive prices. The most comprehensive—and expensive—plan is called M-7 or "AARP Comprehensive." It covers not only all deductibles and copayments, but "reasonable and usual" doctors charges *above* the Medicare approved levels. This policy also covers prescription drug charges.

Each AARP supplement policy is based on the general cost of medical care in each state, so prices of the policies will vary from region to region. You can expect to pay more than $100 a month for the top coverage, but their less expensive policies certainly provide adequate supplements.

You should also check with your state Blue Cross/Blue Shield organization to see which Medicare supplements they are offering. In most states they also offer a range of policies that are usually priced based on age and sex. Most of their policies cover the Part A deductible of $628 per hospitalization stay and the copayment for in-hospital care. The more expensive policies pick up more of the uncovered costs.

Hundreds of other insurance companies offer Medicare supplement insurance with varying costs and coverage. Ever since the repeal of the Catastrophic Coverage Act there has been more public awareness of what Medicare *doesn't* cover. Choosing between the policies can be confusing because the coverages and prices are different. There is some concern that policies may be offered with initial low prices that are subsequently increased dramatically.

Not all policies cover preexisting conditions. Some require a 90-day waiting period or longer before an existing condition can be covered. That could limit your ability to switch from one gap policy to another if prices rise. So check the reputation of the company carefully before being lured by ads offering low prices. Ask for how long the monthly price of the policy is guaranteed.

Even with basic Medicare and a good Medicare supplement policy, you will notice that one expensive medical burden is not covered at all. That is the cost of long-term custodial nursing care. For that you'll need either a huge pool of savings or a policy designed to pay for custodial nursing home care.

NURSING HOME INSURANCE

The biggest potential expense risk in the area of medical care is the expense associated with long-term custodial care. The costs of nursing home care today run about $3,000 to $4,000 a month, and those costs are rising at a rate faster than inflation. Yes, Medicaid will take over long-term custodial care, but only after all other assets have been exhausted.

That's why a growing number of life and health insurers are offering policies to cushion the cost of nursing home care. The problem is that these policies are very expensive, and may not provide adequate coverage to keep other family assets intact. Current policies offered to a 65-year-old person range in cost from $325 a year to $1,750 a year— offering benefits that range from a two-year plan with a $60-a-day benefit, to a lifetime paying plan with a $100 daily benefit that is adjusted for inflation.

A wide range of benefits is available, but the real question is whether there is any economic justification for buying this insurance, as opposed to simply investing the money in an interest-earning account in anticipation of future need.

When considering the purchase of long-term care insurance, be sure the policy is guaranteed renewable for life. The only reason the insurer should be able to cancel the policy is nonpayment of premiums. Also check to see if a longer deductible period before the insurer starts paying will lower the cost of your policy. And the policy should have at least a 31-day grace period offering some protection against the consequences of forgetting to make a payment on time.

Many of the companies marketing these programs recognize they need a huge pool of insureds to make money on the program. If they only market to those already advanced in age, the annual cost will be prohibitive. A 70-year-old seeking $100 a day lifetime nursing home benefits would pay a premium of about $1,800 a year. So the plans are marketed to those just entering the senior stage—at age 65, or even earlier.

Given that a 55-year-old may make premium payments for about 20 years before even reaching the stage where there is a 20 percent probability of needing nursing home care, there is real doubt that the investment of premium in these policies can be justified.

If you are going to buy a nursing home policy, check the fine print carefully. Many have exclusions for preexisting conditions, and those conditions could be so broadly defined that you will have trouble getting coverage for a nursing home stay. Other policies promise to pay for custodial care only *after* a period of skilled nursing care. But many patients with Alzheimer's disease do not require skilled care before they are admitted to a nursing home. If you buy a policy with a limited period of care, it could only delay, not alleviate, the problem of impoverishment of the elderly.

Some policies offer a rider that covers long-term care in the individual's home instead of a nursing facility. Some policies do provide coverage in the event of Alzheimer's disease. Usually this coverage is described as "organically based mental conditions." Make sure it is specifically mentioned in the policy language.

Current headlines make the scare of elderly impoverishment through the costs of nursing home care a real incentive to purchase these insurance policies. But it is entirely possible that the government may extend its coverage to alleviate the problem. Then, premiums paid over the years for this type of insurance would be wasted. The better long-run solution may be the purchase of an annuity against which funds could be borrowed out or paid out to cover the cost of eventual nursing home care if it is needed.

LIFE INSURANCE—EARLY WITHDRAWAL

There is one other possible solution to the expensive costs of long-term nursing care. Several insurance companies are now allowing access to some portion of death benefits while policyholders are still alive. Early in 1990 Prudential Insurance Company introduced a revolutionary new life insurance plan that would allow living policyholders to collect about 98 percent of their death benefits—*if* a doctor says they will die within six months. The policyholder could collect the money in a lump sum to be used for any purposes while he or she is alive, or in monthly payments that would continue being paid to beneficiaries after the policyholder's death. The big drawback to this program is that it defeats the purpose of life insurance—which may have originally been purchased to provide support for survivors. However, in cases where survivors do not need the funds and there are huge medical bills, this new plan could provide dramatic financial relief.

Planning for
the Future

CHAPTER 23

$uccess Takes Planning

Success in money matters takes planning. Money just doesn't magically appear when it comes time for your child to attend college. Children don't automatically grow up knowing the meaning of money. And marriages—or for that matter, divorces—are not harmonious financial situations unless both parties have done some unemotional financial thinking. Remember that old sign: PLAN AHEAd That kind of thinking can be disastrous when it comes to money!

FINANCIAL PLANNING FOR MARRIAGE...
AND DIVORCE

Most people go into marriage thinking they're going to live happily ever after, but all too many marriages break up over issues related to money. There are two types of people in this world—the savers and the spenders. For better or worse, those two types tend to marry each other. And right there you've got a conflict.

The time to discuss money is *before* marriage. When you decide to spend a lifetime together, you should have a pretty good idea of how each of you manages money and credit. If this is a first marriage and there are no children from previous marriages to support, the situation is not terribly complicated.

If both are earning about the same income, there are some basic decisions to be made. Is each person going to contribute a specific amount to a joint checking account? What will be paid out of that account? Will each individual retain some money in a personal savings or investment program? Or will all the money be pooled so that all financial decisions are mutual?

These may not be easy decisions. Few people who have lived independently, worked, and made financial decisions are willing to give up *all* independence. And what fun is it to buy your spouse a birthday present and then have him or her see the amount deducted from the joint checking account? Frank discussions are in order—before the marriage ceremony.

A couple should also discuss things like health and life insurance. Will each be covered under the employer's health plan? Do they plan to contribute to individual IRAs? Are they planning to set aside money in a special account to purchase a home? Will the husband and wife continue to use their separate names, or will one take the name of the other?

Are they going to make a budget? Set up a saving plan? Does each have to account to the other for money spent on personal items such as clothes? Does one have an expensive hobby or sport that will have an impact on the budget?

Perhaps the easiest way to start this discussion is to sit down over a budget book (see Chapter 2) and work out the specifics. When things get down to black and white, the discussion tends to become much more focused.

Prenuptial Agreements

Planning for a second marriage, or a marriage in which one party arrives with substantial assets, can complicate financial discussions. If there are children involved, it is understandable that issues like their college education and inheritance will be discussed and provided for before marriage.

In this case, it would be wise for each to have the advice of an attorney who can draw up a prenuptial agreement that will legally take care of all these issues. In order for this type of agreement to be valid, each partner must fully disclose in writing all of his or her assets. Then provisions can be made in case of death or divorce to distribute those assets. The separate assets can be placed in a revocable intervivos (living) trust, or provided for by a will. (See Chapter 25.)

Once the couple is married they will accumulate joint marital assets. Those must also be provided for according to state law in case of death or divorce. In these cases, it is sometimes advisable to use life insurance to "liquify" an estate so that each partner can be taken care of financially in case the spouse dies, while leaving agreed upon assets to children or other relatives.

Again, the time to discuss these things is well before the marriage ceremony. Each party must have separate legal advice in structuring an arrangement. The old Hollywood stereotype of prenuptial agreements between the young bride and wealthy older husband is way out of date. Today couples of all ages come into marriage with both assets and liabilities. It's wise to plan in advance, so that each is equally satisfied and protected. That kind of planning prevents problems from arising later.

Money and Divorce

While we're on the subject of marriage, it's also important to consider some of the financial implications of *divorce*. Each state has its own divorce laws regarding property acquired during a marriage. That's why it's important to seek competent legal help when you consider a divorce. But attorneys have also been known to prolong divorce negotiations, increasing the size of their fees. So you should immediately ask the attorney what services he will provide in exchange for the original retainer fee—and what the additional charges will be for court appearances and hourly consultations both with you and your spouse's attorney.

Since the attorney's fee is directly proportional to the amount of time spent on the negotiations and settlement, it will save money if you know exactly what your legal property rights are in your state. Find out what the court usually grants for child support and maintenance or alimony in your state. Once you have the parameters of what you are likely to receive, you can save a fortune in legal fees if you and your spouse can agree on a settlement that is fair to both. That doesn't mean you should ignore the advice of your lawyer; it does mean that each attorney has a vested interest in telling his client that "I could have gotten you more" or "I could have gotten you off the hook, paying less."

Sometimes it pays to have an accountant or financial advisor assist in structuring a deal. For example, a spouse may agree to pay maintenance for a period of five or ten years, plus giving the wife a one-time lump sum settlement. That settlement could be invested in an annuity to grow tax-deferred for five or ten years until the period of monthly maintenance runs out. Then the wife could start to receive a check from the annuity every month. Remember the "Rule of 72"? (See Chapter 1.) If you invest $50,000 at 8 percent tax-deferred, it will double to $100,000 in about nine years.

An accountant can tell you if a one-time lump sum payment makes sense where taxes are concerned. A financial advisor can help you purchase the annuity. And you may solve a support problem without paying a huge portion of your marital assets to the attorneys. Often a couple is in perfect agreement about getting a divorce—and miles apart about appropriate financial arrangements. Some divorces must be litigated in court. That's an expensive process, and it's well worth your time to investigate mutually beneficial financial solutions.

TEACHING YOUR CHILD ABOUT MONEY

It strikes me that one of the great problems with our school system is the lack of practical economic education for young students. Very few school systems teach business basics or money fundamentals at the primary level. Yet that is the perfect age to start encouraging children to understand and take responsibility for money.

The first step in teaching children responsibility for money is to allow them to have some money of their own so they can make spending and saving decisions. My own child had a savings account at a bank before he could quite see over the counter. Age six or seven is the right time to explain that "banks pay you money—called interest—if you let them use your money." All it takes is a few trips to the bank to see interest posted to a passbook savings account to give a child an understanding of how money makes money.

If you are a parent or grandparent thinking of gifts for a child, you might want to introduce a fourth or fifth grader to the stock market. Many brokers will charge only a minimal commission to purchase and register a few shares of stock in the child's name. Try to choose a company that will attract the child's interest—Disney or Ralston Purina (the food you feed your dog!).

Explain that the price of the shares will change every day depending on how good business is. Show the child where to check the price of the stock in the daily newspaper. Some children are not interested— and that's perfectly OK—but you may be creating the next Warren Buffett.

Children who aren't interested in the abstract concept of stocks might be interested in collecting stamps or coins. That could be the start of a lifetime interest that is not only monetary, but leads to a real understanding of world history and geography. It's best to start with a limited collector's book created for children and specializing in one area such as U.S. coins of one particular type—perhaps silver dollars.

An invaluable resource for a child starting a coin collection is the annual *Guide Book of U.S. Coins* (called "the redbook"). It is available at department stores or coin dealers. Similar guides are available for stamp collections. The U.S. Post Office offers a wide range of starter kits for stamp collectors, and traveling grandparents can add to the collection whenever they send postcards from their trips! These books and kits will also teach children how to handle the stamps or coins so they will not be damaged. You're teaching more than money here; you're teaching responsibility, too.

If you want to make a lasting gift to an infant or small child who is too young to understand money, consider opening up a mutual fund account in the child's name. Of course, the gains will be taxed to the parents until the child reaches age 14, but you can still build up a substantial amount of money in the child's name. And you have a ready idea for future birthday or holiday giving. By the time a child is old enough to understand, he or she can contribute earnings from jobs like babysitting. Many mutual funds will let you start an account with as little as $100.

The Twentieth Century Fund group (800-345-2021) has some of the best-performing mutual funds of those that allow accounts to be opened with as little as $100. Among their funds, the Twentieth Century Giftrust Investors Fund boasts an average gain of 18.61 percent from 1986 through 1989. Their Twentieth Century Ultra Fund and Twentieth Century Growth Fund each has no minimum investment and each boasts an average annual return of more than 16 percent for the same three-year period. For more funds that allow you to open accounts with $100 minimum investments, see Chapter 14 for information on obtaining the *Guide to No-Load Mutual Funds*.

When you teach a child that money doesn't grow on trees you teach an invaluable lesson. While some would consider this topic too materialistic for a young person, just the opposite is true. Once you teach the child the value of money, material possessions take on new meaning. They reflect the ethic of work and intelligence—two characteristics that should benefit the child in the long run.

Recommended reading for parents who want to teach their children about money: *Teach Your Child the Value of Money,* by Harold and Sandy Moe, Harsand Financial Press, P.O. Box 515, Holmen, WI 54636, $5.95 plus $1 postage.

If the subject of economic education in the schools interests you, you might contact the national headquarters of an organization called Junior Achievement (45 E. Club House Drive, Colorado Springs, CO 80906, 719-540-8000). Many parents remember this as the after-school activity club that formed a business and sold a product. But now Junior Achievement has in-school economic education programs for children from the fifth grade through high school. Its Business Basics and Applied Economics courses have been made available to more than one million children each year with the support of local corporations and businesses who not only volunteer financial resources, but also make their executives available to contribute to the classroom experience.

PLANNING FOR COLLEGE

Without question, a college education is one of the best investments a family can make. Studies have shown that a college education can add $1 million in earning power over a lifetime. There are few investments of $40,000 to $50,000 that can promise a $1 million payoff!

Still, the rising cost of a college education is somewhat shocking. According to one study (*Money* magazine, September 1989), college tuition during the 1980s increased 52 percent in constant dollars at private universities and 31 percent at public universities. During the same period, mean family income grew just 6 percent. This is not a new phenomenon.

The chart in Figure 10 shows that college costs have far outrun the average measures of inflation, not just recently, but for the last 50 years. In fact, since 1980 college cost inflation has averaged 10 percent per year—double the overall rate of inflation. So your savings have to generate an after-tax return far above the inflation rate to meet your college savings goals.

A child seven years old in 1990 would need an estimated $54,000 to complete a four-year program at a public college—assuming 6 percent annual increases in college costs. That study, prepared by the mutual fund management firm T. Rowe Price, says that to meet this expense the parents would have to put away $250 a month and get a pre-tax annual return of 8 percent. If they delay starting the investment program for five years, then they would need to invest $580 per month.

The potential cost of college is staggering. But that shouldn't paralyze you into ignoring the future need. After all, the earlier you start, the more time is on your side. A number of banks, brokerage firms, and mutual fund companies are competing to give you information about future college costs. They want to attract your college savings dollars into their investment programs.

T. Rowe Price, the mutual fund management company (800-638-5660), has created a free College Planning Kit to help parents estimate the projected cost of sending their children to college and develop a savings and investment program that will provide the funds.

Financial Trust Company of Denver keeps track of college costs and predicts future costs at some 3,000 colleges in the country, providing

Figure 10:   College Inflation vs. General Inflation Averages (1980–1989)

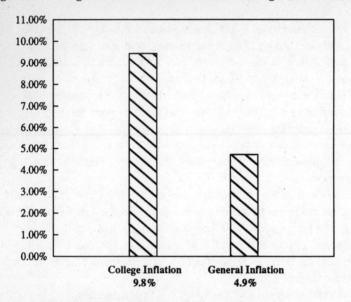

Source: College Savings Bank, Princeton, NJ.

this service as an inducement to use its mutual funds to start a savings and investment plan for college. You pick the college you're interested in and they'll run the program to figure out future costs. There is a charge of $15 per child per school for each estimate (800-328-1222). They calculate the annual increase in college costs and make projections based on the College Board's annual cost book. Then they will advise you just how much money you have to set aside annually (assuming an 8 percent compounded growth rate in your investments) in order to meet your goals in saving for a child's college education.

The real problem for most parents is starting to do something about saving for college while there's time to get the benefits of compound growth working for you. You can plan to set aside a fixed amount of money every year, and that's a good start. But that's not really enough. If you put your college savings in a money market account, you probably are not beating inflation by very much, especially when you consider your after-tax return.

The temptation is to take investment risk to make your money grow. And it may make sense to invest a portion of longer-term college savings in a balanced stock mutual fund. However, the closer you come to the time when you will actually pay out the funds for college tuition and expenses, the more conservative your investments should be.

There are several interesting solutions to the problem of saving for future college costs. The College Savings Bank was set up in Princeton, New Jersey (800-888-2723), in 1987 as an FDIC-insured institution with the specific purpose of offering an insured CD especially created for parents saving for a college education. You can open a CollegeSure Account with as little as $1,000 and add to it in $250 minimum amounts at any time.

What's special about the CollegeSure CD is that it pays an annual interest rate linked to the rate of college cost inflation less 1.5 percent. As average costs of college rise each year, so does the rate paid on your CD. There is no ceiling on the annual rate. And if college costs continue to outpace inflation, you may be earning more than you would on an ordinary CD. However, if college costs should drop, the CD guarantees to pay an annual minimum rate of 4 percent. Each CD is fully insured by the FDIC up to $100,000 per depositor. The interest rate on the CollegeSure CD through July 31, 1991, is 8.25 percent.

These CDs are sold in maturities of one to twenty-five years, and all mature on July 31. You would want to purchase a CD timed to mature in July each year of your child's attendance at college. If you already have an idea which school your child will attend, the College Savings Bank will help you figure out projected costs and returns to decide how much to deposit to the CD every year. According to Peter Roberts, president of the College Savings Bank, more than 60 percent of its depositors make regular additions to the CDs—something like a Christmas Club account.

There are no sales charges or commissions for purchasing a CollegeSure CD, and you will receive a statement of your account balance twice a year. Be aware that this is a long-term savings plan. There is a substantial penalty for early withdrawal from the CollegeSure CD—10 percent of the total in the account if you withdraw during the first three years, and 5 percent thereafter. At maturity the proceeds can be used for expenses at any college or university, or for any other purpose, without penalty.

You do have to pay regular federal income taxes on the interest earned on this CD, so many savers title their accounts in a custodial form for the benefit of their child. Of course, under age 14 a child's interest income above $1,000 is taxed at the parents' rate. (The first $550 of unearned income for children under 14 is not taxed, and the second $550 is taxed at the child's rate.) After age 14, when the money in the CD has really built up, the child will pay taxes on the interest at his own, lower rate.

Before you invest money in a child's name to take advantage of tax rates, however, you should be aware of certain drawbacks. When the child becomes of legal age, the money is automatically his or hers—whether or not it is spent on a college education. Also, if your child is going to need financial aid to pay for college, monies held in his or her name will lower the potential amount of aid far more than if the money is held in the parents' names.

There are other tax-advantaged ways to save for college. Series EE savings bonds pay a market rate of interest and avoid tax liability until they are cashed in. Starting in 1990, if Series EE bonds are purchased and used for college tuition, they will not be subject to any federal income taxes, depending on the parents' income level.

In 1991, interest on Series EE bonds will be tax-free for married couples with adjusted gross incomes of $62,900 or less—or for single parents with an adjusted gross income of $41,950 or less. The tax break phases out above these levels and completely disappears when incomes hit $94,350 for couples or $57,700 for singles. (These amounts will adjust upward for inflation.) To use Series EE bonds for this purpose they must be registered in the *parents'* names—not the child's.

In the last few years a number of states have started offering municipal, tax-exempt college savings bonds—a form of zero coupon bond designed to be used to pay college expenses at maturity. Like other municipal bonds, the interest earned is exempt from federal taxes and in most states from state and local taxes as well.

These college savings bonds are purchased at a discount and mature at face value on a designated date in the future. The amount of the discount reflects a market rate of interest. (See Chapter 10 on zero coupon bonds.) Purchase of these zero coupon college savings bonds should be timed so they mature in time to pay that year's college tuition.

Actually, these zero coupon college savings bonds could be purchased by any investor. But as an incentive, most states offer a bonus of from $100 to $400 if the proceeds are used to pay tuition at an in-state school.

A number of private banks are offering their own version of a zero coupon—a discount certificate of deposit, timed to mature and pay college costs. The certificates pay market rates of interest, and, of course, on these certificates the interest is fully taxable. The advantage is that you start by depositing a relatively small amount of money, knowing it will grow to a fixed sum in the future when you need to pay college costs. The disadvantage is that you are locking yourself into a long-term fixed-rate investment that may not provide a high enough yield to keep up with rising college costs.

Some states are helping parents plan for future college costs by creating a sort of tuition prepayment plan. In Michigan, for example, parents of a six-year-old put up $7,500, which is 82 percent of the current average tuition cost at in-state schools. In 12 years, when the child is ready for college, full tuition is guaranteed at any state college or university.

When the student enrolls in school, he or she will have to pay income tax on the difference between the parents' original deposit and the amount of current tuition. Assuming tuition rises 6 percent a year, the average cost of college at a Michigan school will rise to $18,512. If the child is in the 15 percent tax bracket then, the tax bill will total $1,652.

It's not a bad deal for both parent and child—but some people worry that these tuition guarantee plans will be big money losers for the state. The state must invest the funds to beat education price inflation—or else subsidize the cost of the child's tuition. If that's done by raising tuition for other students, then the program will only contribute to the rising spiral of tuition prices.

Still, if you live in one of the states that offer these programs, it's worth investigating. Different states have different refund programs if your child decides not to attend college, or wants to attend an out-of-state school. In most cases, if your child opts not to use the prepaid tuition, you will lose a significant amount of money that could have been earned if you had saved for college outside the state program.

STUDENT FINANCIAL AID

About half of the students attending college receive some type of financial aid. Nearly $30 billion in assistance is given out to college students each year. So if you need help putting a child through college, it pays to go through the maze of rules and regulations to find out if your family qualifies for some form of aid.

There are three kinds of programs that will give financial assistance to college students. *Grants* are awards that do not have to be repaid. *Scholarships* are usually based on academic or athletic ability; financial need sometimes plays a role in granting scholarships. *Loans* are sums of money lent strictly for educational purposes with repayment required in a fixed number of years, usually after graduation.

The first place to start seeking financial aid is in the high school counseling office. There you will generally find information about federal grants and loans, state-sponsored programs, and funding available directly from individual universities and colleges. This should be done at the same time a student starts looking at colleges—usually during the junior year of high school.

The best source of comprehensive information is the *Peterson's College Money Handbook*. It is updated every year and is available in most bookstores or directly from the publisher (P.O. Box 2123, Princeton, NJ 08540, $11.20 including postage). It gives the cost and aid profiles of the 1,700 four-year colleges in the United States. It also explains the process of applying for different aid programs and helps you compute how much aid your family might receive based upon your income and assets.

Applying for Financial Aid

When a student applies for financial aid based on need, there are generally two forms to be completed. The first is the college's own aid application and the second is one of two forms created by nationwide analysis firms. The Financial Aid Form (FAF) is created by the College Scholarship Service. The Family Financial Statement (FFS) is produced by the American College Testing Program. Some states such as California and Pennsylvania have their own financial aid forms.

Since each college will expect you to apply for any possible federal grants or loans, the FAF or FFS, which can be obtained through your high school guidance office, should be completed and sent with the processing fee to the service's central office. From there they will be sent directly to any scholarship or aid-granting service you designate.

A copy of the parents' tax return from the previous year will be needed to complete these forms. In some cases it will be necessary to submit a copy of the return so the information can be verified. The completed forms should be sent to the processing center in January of the year *before* the student is applying for aid, in order to meet all federal and college deadlines.

A student who is going to apply for federal aid will have to complete the U.S. Department of Education's Application for Federal Student Aid (AFSA) and submit it directly to the government. The deadline for all student aid applications is May 1 of the year before the fall term when aid is requested, but applications should be made early in the calendar year so verification can be completed before the deadline. For questions about any federal student aid program, call 800-333-INFO between 9:00 AM and 5:30 PM EST, Monday through Friday.

Once the AFSA form has been completed, the student will receive a Student Aid Report (SAR) within four to six weeks. The SAR gives two numbers: the Student Aid Index (SAI), which determines eligibility for a Pell Grant, (see page 349) and a number for the expected Family Contribution (FC), which determines the amount the family will be expected to contribute before any other loan programs kick in to help.

Financial Aid Formulas

Each college will make its own determination of the student's need for financial aid. The first step for the school is to determine the parents' expected contribution based on income and assets as displayed on the FAF or FFS. The next step is to integrate any federal programs the student might qualify for. Finally, the college financial aid officer will consider any combination of student loans, campus work programs, or grants that might be available to the student.

Each college will compute the basic amount that the student and his or her family will be expected to pay. Then the school will work to make up the balance of the tuition through various aid programs. The schools use a basic formula to determine the expected parents' contribution: as much as 47 percent of the parents' combined annual income and 5.6 percent of their assets. The aid formula also takes into account assets held in the child's name—and takes an even greater percentage of those assets into consideration. Students are expected to contribute 70 percent of their income and 35 percent of their assets each year.

That formula should make parents think twice about accumulating college funds in the child's name. Although children over age 14 will be in a lower tax bracket, eventually those assets will reduce the amount of aid the student will qualify for. Similarly, a grandparent thinking of gifting $10,000 to a child for college should instead write the check to the parents, where it will count for less when the school determines aid.

In fact, parents themselves might want to reduce assets the year before the financial aid application is due. That doesn't mean giving away the family home. But it could mean replacing consumer loans (which are not considered in the aid formula) with a home equity loan or second mortgage (which will reduce the amount of the family's total assets). Parents might also consider making a large discretionary contribution to a 401(k) plan or a voluntary pension contribution at work. This must be done the year *before* the aid application is filed so that it will not show up as income for the previous year. Assets held in retirement accounts are not considered assets in computing the need for aid.

While the formula for financial aid is strict, most college aid officers will take special considerations into account. A family in the midst of a divorce or with a sudden medical expense might qualify for aid in spite of the formula. Students should check with the college aid office if the family financial situation changes during their years at school.

Government Student Aid Programs

The federal government has five separate financial aid programs for students. Two programs award outright grants: the Pell Grant and the Supplemental Education Opportunity Grant (SEOG). Pell Grants are available to undergraduates who have not earned a bachelor's or first professional degree. The government has created a complex formula to produce a Student Aid Index (SAI), which determines eligibility for these grants. The maximum Pell Grant for the 1988–89 year was $2,200, but the amount received by each student depends on the SAI and the cost of tuition at the school. Applications are due May 1 of the year before the fall term when grants are made.

A Supplemental Education Opportunity Grant (SEOG) is also for undergraduates and is based on need. Unlike a Pell Grant, which is directly financed and administered by the government, SEOG grants are administered by the individual school, using government funds. These funds are more limited, so the SEOG is more difficult to obtain.

Two federal aid programs give loans—the Stafford Student Loan Program (formerly titled Guaranteed Student Loan) and the Perkins Loan Program. The Stafford loans are low-interest loans made by a lender such as a bank, savings and loan, or credit union. The loans are insured by a guarantee agency in each state and reinsured by the federal government. Currently the interest rate is 8 percent.

The maximum loan amount depends on your level of studies. For a first- or second-year undergraduate the maximum loan amount for 1990 is $2,625 a year. In the third and fourth undergraduate years the maximum loan amount is $4,000. The amount rises to $7,500 a year for graduate students. Overall, for both undergraduate and graduate studies, the maximum Stafford loan amount may not exceed $54,750.

The application for a Stafford loan can be obtained from a participating financial institution, the college, or the state guarantee agency. This loan depends on financial need, so the appropriate forms must be filed with the government. There is a 5 percent origination fee for the loan, and repayment begins six months after graduation or after the student leaves school. Repayment is expected to be at least $50 a month or $600 a year.

The Perkins Loan Program works in a similar manner, except that this low-interest (5 percent) loan is made directly from the federal government, and the amount may be as much as $4,500 for an undergraduate in the first two years of study.

The government has two additional loan programs that are administered *without regard to financial need*. The PLUS Loan Program provides low-interest loans to qualified parents of dependent undergraduate and graduate students. The Supplemental Loans for Students (SLS) Program provides similar loans to independent undergraduate and graduate students.

Application for these loans is made at a participating bank or financial institution, and the rate is variable—not to exceed 12 percent. PLUS allows parents to borrow up to $4,000 per year or a total of $20,000 for each dependent child who is enrolled at least half-time as a student. The limitations are the same for students who borrow under the SLS program. With both of these loans, repayment must begin 60 days after the last loan disbursement.

The government also has a College Work-Study Program that allows the student to go to school less than half-time and still receive aid. These programs are administered independently on each campus.

Private Loan Program

In addition to the government loan and grant programs, which are based on need, there are hundreds of scholarships offered each year based on everything from religious affiliation to ethnic heritage to parental membership in local civil groups. These are generally smaller grants, and they may serve to reduce the amount of federal aid that will be offered, but they are definitely worth pursuing.

Every year Prentice-Hall publishes a new edition of *The Scholarship Book: A Complete Guide to Private-Sector Scholarships, Grants and Loans for Undergraduates*. The scholarships listed range from the easily accessible to the merely amazing. There are scholarships available at Harvard University for people named Murphy, Anderson, or Pennoyer. These were endowed back in the 1600s! There are scholarships available for women who are licensed to pilot helicopters, and for male and female ex-caddies! Corporations and labor unions provide scholarships for children of workers. Fraternal and civic organizations provide grants to children of members or area residents. The list goes on and on.

There are several private scholarship search services that will tap into databanks of potential scholarships and grants. Much of this information is available in the Prentice-Hall guide and other library reference materials, but if you want to pay $65, they'll do the work for you.

The largest of these services is the National Scholarship Research Service (122 Alto St., San Rafael, CA 94901, 415-456-1577). It was founded more than ten years ago and has developed an extensive computer database of more than 200,000 available scholarships. Executives of the service say that more than $6 billion in privately funded scholarship money goes unclaimed every year! They point out that 80 percent of the private sector scholarship money does not require the student to show need.

To use the NSRS, a student can write or call requesting information and an application consisting of about 40 questions. The $65 charge covers a computer search of applicable scholarships. If the student checks the service the following year to see if new funding is available, the cost drops to $20.

NSRS also cooperates with Prentice-Hall to publish three books about scholarships: *The Scholarship Book, The Graduate Scholarship Book,* and *The International Scholarship Book.* These should be available in your public library.

National College Services, Ltd. (600 S. Frederick Ave., Gaithersburg, MD 20877, 301-258-0717) is another long-established firm providing assistance to students searching for financial assistance for college. It has its own huge database of more than 200,000 student aid resources. It also tracks federal aid programs and athletic scholarships. Many high schools subscribe to this database service to guide their students. Individual consultations for college financial planning are also available.

National Merit Scholarship Program

Every year the National Merit Scholarship Program awards approximately 6,000 scholarships to high school students. In 1989 the program awarded $24 million worth of scholarships. Selection is based on academic achievement and leadership characteristics, not on need. All students who take the PSAT/NMSQT test in October of the junior year of high school are automatically enrolled in the program. More than 19,000 high schools across the country participate in this program.

The PSAT is the initial screening factor for the one million students who enter the program every year. Those who score in the top one-half of one percent of each state's high school junior class become semifinalists. They are notified of that status in the fall of their senior year. Then they fill out an application and provide information on their activities. The school sends along academic records and recommendations.

Subsequent SAT results on tests taken before December of their senior year must be forwarded to the National Merit Scholarship Corporation. The winners are selected by an outside committee of college admissions officers and high school counselors. They look at the total student—including academic record, extracurricular activities, and leadership contributions to school and community. Finalists are notified in February of their senior year that they are being considered for monetary awards.

There are three types of National Merit scholarships awarded each year.

- The first is a $2,000 nonrenewable grant issued by the Scholarship Foundation itself. Winners of these awards are selected by the corporation's committee.
- There are also Corporate Sponsor awards that are given to finalists who meet criteria specified by various corporations. Many of these awards are renewable, and on average they range from $500 to $2,000 a year, although some are for much more.
- In addition to these scholarships, many colleges and universities sponsor awards for finalists planning to attend their institutions.

If you would like to know more about the National Merit Scholarship Program, consult your high school guidance counselor or write to The National Merit Scholarship Corporation, 1560 Sherman Ave., Evanston, IL 60201.

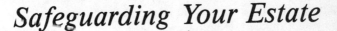

CHAPTER **24**

Safeguarding Your Estate

Your estate consists of all the property you own: a home, bank accounts, vested benefits in pension plans, death benefits payable from life insurance, and investments in stocks or in a family business. Your estate also includes personal property such as clothing, jewelry, cars, and furniture. You may own these things outright or share an ownership interest with a spouse, partner, or associates. When you die, all the assets in your individual name will be distributed. That distribution can be made in accordance with your written wishes, or it can be done by a stranger appointed by the state.

It makes sense to plan the distribution of your estate and to leave official written instructions. By doing so you can save taxes, make sure property is distributed to those of your choice, assure that your children or dependents will be properly taken care of, and eliminate many family arguments. Yet it's estimated that 70 percent of American families don't have a written estate plan.

Many people avoid estate planning because it makes them all too aware of their mortality. It's as if not thinking about death will postpone its inevitability. Yet one spouse often has a difficult time convincing the other to make a will or set up a trust. My answer: a form of reverse superstition. Something tells me that being prepared will ward off the unexpected; having an estate plan prepared in advance will lessen the chances of untimely death. At least it's a more practical superstition!

Some people put off creating a written estate plan because they think they don't have enough assets to worry about the tax collector, or because their property is in joint name with a spouse. It's true that since 1981 all property left to a spouse, regardless of its value, has been exempt from federal estate taxes.

But estate planning involves far more than avoiding taxes. The young couple with their home in joint name and few other assets may have young children. If both parents were to die in an auto accident, one surviving the other by only a few hours, would they want the state to name a guardian for their children? Would they want their relatives squabbling over custody?

If they had no children and the husband survived his wife by a day, then her share of the estate would pass to him. When he died, the entire estate would pass to his family—her in-laws! Is that something you want to see happen in your family?

Some people spend a lifetime mentioning that after their death the heirloom family necklace or oil painting must go to a specific relative. None of those provisions—no matter how often they are verbalized— would have any legal bearing on the distribution of an estate unless it was written into an estate plan.

YOUR WILL

Your will—your last will and testament—simply states whom you wish to receive what part of your estate after you die. It also names an executor to administer your estate and a guardian for your minor children.

Spouses can have a joint will if they designate the same beneficiaries and the same executor for their estates. However, it is recommended that each have a separate will, taking into account the possibility that the other spouse might die first.

You should use a trained attorney to draw up a will, although this is not an absolute necessity. If you follow some of the popular do-it-yourself plans, some flaw in the language could invalidate the entire will. Handwritten wills are valid in most states, but some jurisdictions restrict the type of property that can be distributed in a handwritten will. As of this date, videotaped wills are not admissible in court in any state—although a videotaped statement might be admissible in support of a will to show that the person making the will was of sound mind and not under duress or undue influence.

A legally enforceable will must be witnessed by two people who do not stand to benefit from the provisions of the will. There should be only one signed copy of the will (photocopies are not admissible in court), and it should be kept in a safe place. Do *not* place it in a safe-deposit box if you live in a state that requires safe-deposit boxes to be sealed on the death of the owner.

When you make a will, your lawyer will need a list of your assets, including property, bank accounts, pension interests, and money owed to you. You should also have a list of your obligations—mortgages, installment loans, and business obligations—and your life insurance policies, including ownership and beneficiaries. You will also have to furnish documents that might affect the distribution of your estate, such as any old wills, premarital agreements, or divorce decrees.

Your lawyer will want you to designate an executor and successors, as well as guardians and successor guardians for minor children. You will also have to list special bequests of property to be made to individuals—naming and clearly identifying the individual (and last known address, if possible) and describing the property to be distributed. If you have been married before, there may be special provisions for stepchildren or children from a spouse's previous marriage. Perhaps additional children will be born or adopted. Finally, the attorney will want to know how you would like things handled if both you and your spouse should die together in an accident.

Changing a Will

If you want to change the provisions of your will, you don't need to write a completely new document, but the changes must be made legally and in the proper form. In most cases, all that's necessary is a *codicil* to the will. The codicil must clearly state the existing provision of the will that is being modified. The codicil must be witnessed, just as the will, and the two documents should be kept together.

You might want to change a will if your marital status changes. In fact, in some states, an old will that does not specifically provide for a new spouse will be automatically revoked.

You might also want to change a will if your financial status changes dramatically, or if you no longer own something you left to someone in your will. As children grow up, provisions for their education and for trusts may no longer be needed. And, of course, the federal estate and inheritance tax laws change frequently, requiring new documents. For these reasons, you should review and update your will every few years.

Revoking a Will

Revoking a will should also be done properly according to state laws. In most states, it is not enough to merely tear up the old document. You should create a new will stating that all previous wills are revoked, or prepare a codicil that revokes a portion of the existing will.

Contesting a Will

In most states a will may be contested only by a person affected by the will. A petition must be filed with the court stating the grounds for contesting the will. Some acceptable grounds are fraud, undue influence, or lack of competence by the maker of the will. The court will hold a hearing to see if the objections are enough to deny the validity of the will. If a will is contested, it can delay distribution of the assets for a lengthy period of time. You may want to put a provision into your will to eliminate the bequest of any beneficiary who contests the will.

Naming an Executor

The person named as executor in a will assumes a serious and time-consuming responsibility. He or she will be paid for that job out of the assets of the estate, as determined by the court. But even the substantial payments accorded to executors may not compensate for the time and effort involved.

The executor works with the lawyer in taking the will through probate court. Once the court rules the will is valid, the executor has a series of duties to perform. Specifically, the executor is expected to:

- open a checking account for the estate and receive payments for estate assets and make checks for estate expenses through this account
- inventory the contents of safe-deposit boxes
- file death certificates required in processing life insurance claims and stock transfers
- process claims for medical insurance and apply for benefits such as Social Security or veterans benefits for the estate
- invest funds and sell assets when necessary
- prepare income tax and estate tax returns
- distribute assets

The list of the executor's responsibilities goes on and on. We note them here to make sure that when you choose an executor you choose someone capable of handling all of these responsibilities.

Dying Without a Will

If you die without a will or other written estate plan, you are considered to be *intestate*. That means the state will distribute your estate according to its rules. In most states, the surviving spouse is entitled to one-third to one-half of the estate. The remaining amount is divided among surviving children or their offspring. Each state has a specific law regarding the amount that will be passed to the remaining children and grandchildren. Of course, the state-named executor has no real incentive to complete the process quickly or efficiently.

ESTATE TAXES, PROBATE FEES, AND TRUSTS

Estate taxes are one reason to do some estate planning. Although an entire estate can pass tax-free to a surviving spouse, the subsequent death of the surviving spouse could generate a huge federal estate tax bill. Since January 1, 1987, the government has charged no federal taxes on estates under $600,000. In figuring the value of your estate, the government includes everything you own—even the face value of your life insurance policies. For estates above $600,000, the estate tax rate ranges from 37 to 55 percent!

Those aren't the only fees your estate might have to pay. Probate costs could take another chunk of your assets—perhaps up to 10 percent! Probate has nothing to do with taxes. It's simply the process of shepherding your will through the court system, changing title to your assets, and distributing them to those named in your will.

Probate fees charged by the attorney who performs this service must be approved by a judge in most districts, but they are generally approved as long as the court considers them "reasonable." Some states calculate probate fees as a percentage of the estate size. Under this method, the attorney gets a fixed percentage of all assets owned by the decedent on the date of death. This calculation does not include any liens or mortgages. So if you are leaving a $350,000 home to your heirs but have a $200,000 mortgage on the property, the probate fee would be a fixed percentage of the $350,000, even though the heirs would also inherit a huge mortgage.

The process of probate makes your estate very public. Anyone can check court records to find out not only the amount of your assets, but the names and addresses of your beneficiaries and how much they are going to receive. Probate is also very time-consuming. It could take from nine months to two years to settle your estate—even longer if someone contests the provisions of your will.

Don't let these considerations cause you to give up on the idea of estate planning, but be aware that there are more cost-effective ways to pass on your assets.

Joint Tenancy

Titling assets in joint name is one way of making sure an individual will inherit property without going through complicated probate procedures. However, there will be probate required to transfer the assets on the death of the survivor. Also, many states require that bank accounts held in joint name be held aside until state taxing authorities can verify amounts.

One problem with titling real property in joint tenancy is that you lose control of the property. It cannot be sold without the consent of the other joint tenant, and the property could become liable for that person's debts and taxes. One of the largest disadvantages of joint tenancy is that it can eventually create a huge tax liability for the surviving spouse.

Trusts

When the topic of estate planning arises, you will need to understand two different kinds of trusts.

A *testamentary trust* is a trust created by a will and administered by a trustee named in the will. It does not go into effect until the person who made the will dies. Testamentary trusts are frequently set up to provide income or an educational fund for young children or grandchildren.

An *inter vivos* trust is set up during the lifetime of the person creating the trust. An inter vivos trust can be either *revocable* or *irrevocable*. Assets transferred to an irrevocable trust cannot be transferred out. The creator of the trust forever gives up ownership and control of the property placed in the trust. There are numerous tax and nontax reasons for establishing an irrevocable trust.

For example, an irrevocable trust is often used to purchase and own life insurance policies. When an irrevocable trust owns a life insurance policy, the proceeds are not included in the estate for estate tax purposes. (If the person who dies owns the policy personally, the proceeds will pass to the beneficiary free from income tax, but the value of the proceeds *is* included in the estate for estate tax purposes.) When life insurance is placed in an irrevocable trust, the creator of the trust may gift additional funds to the trust to continue paying for the policy. If there are no funds to pay the premiums, the policy may lapse. That's one way out of an irrevocable trust.

The other kind of trust is a revocable living trust, or *inter vivos* trust. It is so useful in estate planning that we'll devote the next section to explaining why instead of having a will many people are better off creating a living trust.

THE LIVING TRUST

A *revocable living trust* is simply a trust created by a living person to hold title to his or her assets. The person who creates the trust does not lose control over those assets and may dispose of them or replace them at any time. You simply transfer title to all of your assets (such as real estate, stocks, personal property) to the name of your living trust. You still retain control over your assets because you are both the trustee and the beneficiary of the trust. If you like, you and your spouse can be co-trustees.

The provisions of the trust itself can be changed at any time while its creator is alive. When you create the trust, you will name a successor trustee who can automatically carry on your financial tasks after your death or if you become incapacitated. While you are alive, you continue to manage your property just as you did before you created the trust. But the revocable living trust has some incredible advantages for the person who creates one.

First, a revocable living trust avoids probate. Any assets in the trust prior to death go directly to your beneficiaries without attorneys' fees, probate fees, or court costs. There is no delay in distributing your assets.

A revocable living trust is private. Since no papers regarding the living trust are filed in court after your death, any distributions of your assets are completely private. Actor Bing Crosby successfully used this concept of estate planning, and no one ever knew exactly how much he was worth at his death—or how he distributed his assets among his family members.

A revocable living trust can protect you from a guardianship or conservatorship if you become disabled or are unable to manage your assets while you are still living. Instead of having a court step in to designate a guardian, the successor trustee that you have named will simply step in to manage your affairs without government interference and expense.

A revocable living trust allows you to determine how your estate is managed and spent even after your death. You can turn assets over to your children at a specific age. You can protect children of previous marriages by specifying assets to be provided for them.

Most revocable living trusts provide a "no-contest" clause, which prevents any beneficiaries from attacking your estate plan.

When it comes to estate taxes, a revocable living trust may be used to reduce or eliminate federal estate taxes. A single person can pass a $600,000 estate tax-free, but a married couple can pass $1,200,000 tax-free to their heirs.

A revocable living trust does not affect income taxes while you are alive. In fact, you file your income tax returns exactly as you did before you created the trust. There are no new returns to file, and no new liabilities are created. When you transfer title of property into the trust, there is no new basis or tax liability created. You should transfer all real estate into the revocable living trust so that you can avoid probate in every state where you own real property. When property is in the trust, there is no probate anywhere.

If you choose to sell assets from the trust, you sign your name exactly as before, simply adding the word "trustee" after your name. You'll open a bank account, brokerage account, or money market account with your name in the title of the trust. "The John Doe revocable living trust, dated __/ __/ __, John Doe, trustee." You can buy any new assets in the name of the trust.

There are some assets that might be too cumbersome to title in the name of your living trust. For instance, while your money market fund or certificate of deposit would be titled in the name of the trust with yourself as trustee, your everyday checking account would probably be held in your own name. (Then the checkout clerk at the grocery store won't be asking why you signed the check "Mary Smith, trustee.") You might want to hold the title to your car in your own name instead of in the trust. Because there will inevitably be some items left out of the trust, you will still need a *pourover will* to distribute those few assets after your death.

Your lawyer will help you create the provisions of the living trust. In many cases, you will want your assets to be divided after your death. Some may go directly to your spouse in a new trust, while the balance may be placed in another trust. The surviving spouse can draw on the assets of the other trust, subject to certain restrictions. When the surviving spouse dies, both trusts are passed on to the children who are successor trustees—completely free of estate tax.

It is wise to understand the workings of a living trust before you consult an attorney who is an estate specialist. You see, the original cost of drawing up an ordinary will is not the real money-maker for attorneys. They'll offer to keep a copy of your will in their "vaults" so they can be of assistance to the survivors at your death. They'll gladly take the will through probate—a service which nets them substantial fees. When you place all your assets in a living trust there is no probate and no probate fees. Understandably, most lawyers are not lining up to offer their services to set up living trusts.

For more information I suggest you read an excellent book on the subject: *Loving Trust* by Robert Esperti (Viking, $19.95). Another easily understandable publication is *The Living Trust Handbook* (Phillips Publishing, $49.95, 1-800-722-9000). (This company bears no relationship to David T. Phillips Co.)

There is also an easily understandable videotape on the subject put out by a California-based law firm that specializes in creating living trusts. It's the Robert Armstrong Living Trust Seminar video ($21.95 plus shipping and handling, Armstrong, Fisch and Associates, 1-800-327-5922).

David T. Phillips Co., the previously mentioned national insurance brokerage firm, offers a living trust estate planning service through a national network of attorneys specializing in these plans. A complete living trust plan is guaranteed in four weeks after receipt of your financial documents. The cost is $1,050. If you don't want to commit to the purchase of such a plan without more information, they will perform an estate analysis, including tax projections, for $35 (800-223-9610).

If you only want to spend $24.95 on a "do-it-yourself" living trust, the original 1965 book on the subject *How to Avoid Probate* by Norman Dacey has been updated and reissued by Macmillan Publishing. Dacey says the forms included in the book will allow you to create your own estate plan, bypassing attorneys completely. For your safety, though, it's probably worth your while to seek competent legal advice so that your living trust will protect your estate the way you want it to.

SURVIVORSHIP LIFE POLICIES

When planning your estate, you must take your life insurance into consideration. As mentioned previously, you might want to place some of your insurance into an irrevocable trust. Since your estate will not own the life insurance, it will not be considered part of the estate in computing estate taxes. That allows you to pass on more money to your heirs.

But sometimes the estate itself needs to have some life insurance money available to it—in order to pay the estate taxes on assets that are not readily saleable. The insurance industry has designed policies especially to fill this need. They are called *survivorship life,* or *joint and last survivor insurance.* These policies are especially designed to keep your estate from scrambling to find money to pay estate taxes. (A classic example of this type of problem occurred in the estate of chewing gum heir, William Wrigley. The estate was forced to sell the Chicago Cubs baseball team in order to raise cash to pay estate taxes.)

Many couples structure their estate plans to take advantage of the unlimited marital deduction. That is, when the first spouse dies, the entire estate can pass to the surviving spouse with no federal estate taxes due. But when the second spouse dies, everything over $600,000 will be subject to federal estate taxes ranging from 37 percent to 55 percent.

This may seem like a problem only for the very wealthy, but think again. Inflation has pushed up the value of homes and personal property and business interests so that more and more middle-class families may face estate taxes on the death of the second spouse.

Federal estate taxes are due and payable within nine months of death. If there is no liquidity, or cash, in the estate, your heirs may have to sell off valuable assets at bargain prices in order to pay the taxes—an estate sale. Or they will have to borrow the money to pay the taxes, and that can involve substantial interest costs.

There is an alternative. You can purchase life insurance that will pay the estate taxes immediately. This is not life insurance designed to provide money for your heirs; it is designed to protect the value of the assets you leave to them. Of course, it is expensive to purchase this life insurance while you are alive, but it may work out ultimately to be far less expensive than requiring your heirs to sell off properties in order to pay estate taxes.

What kind of insurance policy should you buy? In the past, each spouse purchased an insurance policy on the life of the other. That proved to be a very expensive strategy. But more and more insurance companies are offering policies that pay off on death of the surviving spouse. While not inexpensive, survivorship insurance is far less expensive than the combined cost of policies on both spouses. That's because the insurance company has the use of your money until the second spouse dies.

If you purchase a survivor policy, it should be established in an irrevocable life insurance trust. That way, the proceeds of the insurance policy do not become part of your estate. If the survivorship policy is included in an irrevocable trust, you will want to choose one that does not build up a lot of cash value that must be retained in the trust.

There are several ways to structure the premium payments on a survivorship life policy. You can pay annual premiums for twenty years, or you can pay higher premiums for just six or seven years and get the policy completely paid for. Either way, it means you will be parting with cash now to buy insurance your estate will need later.

The numbers can work to your advantage if you are willing to pay up front. Imagine you will leave your heirs a $1.6 million estate. The first $600,000 will escape federal estate taxes. Your heirs will owe approximately $330,000 in estate taxes on the balance. But for a total premium outlay of perhaps $4,380 per year over the next seven years, a 55-year-old couple could purchase $500,000 worth of survivor insurance. That's a $30,662 current cost to have a half a million dollars on hand to pay your estate taxes.

If that kind of arithmetic makes sense to you, consult with both your attorney and insurance agent to make sure the concept and numbers fit with your estate plan.

DEATH OF A SPOUSE

Finances are not always pleasant to discuss, especially in the context of death. However, sensible and loving people will plan ahead to make the burden of death less weighty on those who are grieving. Setting up a plan of action leaves fewer difficult decisions to make alone. Understanding your spouse's wishes can be a comfort in a troubling time.

But here's a word of warning: While it's helpful to preplan a funeral, there are substantial risks when it comes to *prepaying* a funeral. The American Association of Retired Persons warns that 800,000 Americans have prepaid funeral contracts, but not all will deliver as promised.

Many plans do not provide inflation coverage to increase the value of your funeral package if you live for a number of years. Other plans keep any excess over the ultimate cost of your funeral instead of returning the funds to survivors. And some of these packages are marketed by outright crooks who simply take the money and run. Instead of buying a prepaid plan, it might be cheaper in the long run to have enough money in a jointly held savings or money market account to cover the expected costs of a funeral.

The average cost of a funeral should run around $3,000. That covers items such as a casket, memorial services, and the use of the funeral home. But it does not include the cost of the burial site, limousines, and flowers—which could double the cost of the funeral. The Federal Trade Commission requires funeral directors to provide itemized price lists that can be used for comparison shopping. Even at this difficult time, it might be wise to visit two funeral homes and compare their costs and services. You should not be pushed into purchasing merchandise or services you do not want or cannot afford.

Most of your estate plan will be set forth in a will. It is important that each spouse read and, if possible, participate in the creation of the other's will. Usually a will is not read until after the funeral. So you might want to leave special burial instructions in a separate letter. Many times a spouse will be left as executor of a will. Even if a widow is not named as the executrix, she will be responsible for arranging the funeral and collecting the insurance proceeds.

The funeral director will help the surviving spouse obtain certified copies of the death certificate. These will be needed to collect insurance proceeds or to transfer title to property held in joint name. The surviving spouse should contact the insurance company immediately and ask for the forms required to make a claim. This form might have to be attested to by the deceased's doctor, the undertaker, and one or two witnesses.

The insurance policy may be paid out in a lump sum—a large amount that arrives when the surviving spouse is not in the best state of mind to make investment decisions. The insurance company will usually hold the money and invest it in a money market fund, or it can be placed in a bank account until decisions can be made.

The insurance company will sometimes offer to create an annuity (see Chapter 21) with the money—a guarantee of payments over the lifetime of the surviving spouse. The survivor is in no way obligated to arrange the annuity with this insurance company, and at a later date may want to shop around to find an annuity that offers the best payout. It is best not to make any permanent financial decisions about insurance money for the first few months.

Since a spouse can pass an unlimited amount of money to the surviving spouse without regard to federal estate taxes, the survivor should have immediate access to joint checking or savings accounts. But for stocks, bonds, and other properties held in joint name, it is necessary to transfer title to the survivor—or to the survivor and another joint tenant. In states that tax inheritances, this will require an inheritance tax waiver, which signifies that all appropriate taxes have either been paid or do not apply to this property. A special return must be filed with the state's inheritance tax department to obtain this waiver.

The survivor should then instruct a stockbroker to send all certificates—unsigned—to the transfer agent. Along with the certificates the broker must send a certified copy of the death certificate, the inheritance tax waiver (if necessary), and instructions regarding the transfer. A signed *stock power* should be sent along separately for each certificate being transferred. The brokerage firm should sign and guarantee the signature on the stock power form.

Real estate titles do not have to be transferred immediately. In fact, many times title is not transferred until the property is sold—at which time a death certificate is attached to the deed. However, if a property is changed from joint tenancy, then all insurance policies covering the building or contents should also be changed. That way, if a claim is entered, the check won't be made out to the decedent.

Transferring title to a car can be a bit more difficult because automobiles are rarely titled in joint name. The vehicle will probably become part of the estate, at which time the title will be cleared through the probate process.

From this point on, especially if the estate is complicated, the lawyer or law firm that created the will should probably give instructions for the probate process (unless the deceased's property was automatically transferred through a living trust). It will help if the couple has made their investment and business decisions together, and if each spouse knew the other's legal and investment advisors.

One contact a widow might want to make immediately is the family banker. As noted in Chapter 5, a woman should have independent credit in her own name. That will solve the problem of being left without funds if she is widowed. If those provisions have not already been made, the bank at which most household accounts have been kept should be notified so she can immediately have access to a credit card in her own name.

The key thing is to make no irrevocable financial decisions in the days immediately following a death. That includes decisions about the sale of the family house, the long-term investment of insurance proceeds, or the distribution of family heirlooms.

Numerous con games and scams are perpetrated on grieving widows and widowers. It is all too common for con artists to read obituaries and then call and ask when they should deliver the jewelry or other merchandise allegedly ordered before the spouse's death. Of course, they will want immediate payment for the "gift" that was to have been presented. The fact that this "gift" is worthless will be discovered only after the delivery charges have been paid.

It's wise to leave someone in the home during the funeral. Again, the funeral notice is often a signal to burglars who know the entire surviving family will be attending services. It's almost indelicate to discuss financial matters or security matters under these circumstances, but a little practical advice can go a long way toward avoiding some potential disastrous mistakes.

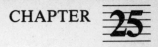

Your Retirement

Planning for retirement is a subject many people avoid far too long. When you're just starting out in a career, retirement seems far away. Then family responsibilities start to pile up, making saving for the distant future difficult, if not impossible. As children reach college age there are even more financial demands on the family budget. And when you can finally see your way clear to saving some money for retirement—retirement is not very far away!

RETIREMENT PLANNING

Many studies say that an adequate annual retirement income should be at least 50 to 60 percent of your final salary. When you retire, many of your work-related expenses will drop. You will no longer have to include commuting and some clothing expenses in your budget. However, medical expenses may be expected to increase. You will get some income tax breaks when you retire, but you may want to spend more money traveling.

Fortune magazine estimated the amount of savings that its median subscriber—age 45 with a household income of $83,000—would need to retire comfortably with no drop in standard of living. First, using an estimate that his or her income would increase 6 percent a year—just beating inflation, which is factored in at a 4.5 percent increase each year—the magazine calculated he will be making $266,192 in 20 years.

Assuming he needs 70 percent of that amount on which to retire, he will need substantial personal savings. Social Security at that time should provide an inflation-adjusted $22,500 a year. If he has a typical pension program, it will provide him with an additional $60,000 a year. In order to cover his living needs, he should have saved an additional $1,146,000 on which he can generate an after-tax return to make up the necessary annual income to keep up his standard of living! To amass that amount of savings, this average worker would have to set aside 17 percent of his pretax income every year.

That's the potential problem—in differing degrees—facing all working people who want to retire without reducing their standard of living. Add in the uncertainties of inflation, and health considerations, and it becomes obvious that it's important to plan ahead for retirement.

It's hard to predict what it will actually cost you to live when you retire. Even if you can structure your lifestyle, you have little control over the value of what your retirement dollar will buy. Those who retired just 20 years ago in 1970 had a dramatic lesson in what inflation can do to the value of a dollar saved for retirement. Today it takes one dollar to buy what 32 cents purchased in 1970!

To the extent that you have control over your retirement dollars, you have to invest them while taking potential inflation into consideration. That means you may not want to tie up your money in long-term, fixed-rate bonds. Some of your retirement assets will not be indexed to inflation. Many pension funds provide fixed dollar benefits that are not geared to offset any fall in purchasing power. Social Security does provide a cost-of-living (COLA) increase annually, but strains on the system may limit future COLA increases.

Many working people figure that Social Security will be enough to carry them through retirement. They see their parents and grandparents living in a fairly comfortable retirement style. But the current generation of retirees is getting one of the best deals that Social Security will ever be able to offer—receiving far more in benefits than they paid in. Even so, Social Security benefits currently average only around $10,000 a year.

The Social Security Administration estimates that Social Security benefits will replace about 57 percent of the earnings of a minimum wage worker, but only about 28 percent of the earnings of a person who had income at the maximum amount subject to Social Security tax during his or her lifetime ($50,400 in 1989). If you earned above that maximum taxable level, then future Social Security benefits will provide an even smaller percentage of replacement income. Of course, the higher your income before retirement was, the more likely you are to have a company pension plan or personal savings to supplement your retirement income.

For those who are now in their thirties, there are some real questions about whether the Social Security trust funds will have enough assets left to pay promised benefits when they retire after the year 2020. It's basically a matter of numbers. When Social Security was started, there were far more people working compared to the number of people aged 65 and over.

In 1960, the ratio of covered workers to beneficiaries was 5.1 workers to each beneficiary. In 1986, there were only 3.3 workers for every beneficiary. And by 2029, when the last of today's baby boomers is ready for retirement, it is expected that there will be fewer than two covered workers for every beneficiary. Not only are Americans living longer, they are expecting a higher standard of living in retirement. Yet there will be fewer workers available to provide that retirement income through their contributions to Social Security.

Will future workers be willing to pay higher Social Security taxes to support their grandparents? Will the growing number of senior citizens have enough political clout to force this burden on their children? Will the Social Security trust funds have enough assets to cover all the politicians' promises? There are no certain responses to these questions, but there is a certainty that you will have to start thinking about retirement sooner or later. The sooner the better.

SOCIAL SECURITY

In 1987, the Social Security Administration studied the sources of retirement income. They found that Social Security provided 38 percent of retirement income on average, saved assets provided another 24 percent, earnings during retirement provided 17 percent, pensions amounted to 15 percent of retirement income, and 6 percent came from other sources. Since most people will depend on Social Security for a large portion of their benefits, it's important to know exactly what Social Security is likely to pay you at retirement and how likely it is that there will be money available to cover your benefits.

In 1988, Social Security paid out $236 *billion* in benefits to 39 million people—much of it tax-free. That sounds like a lot of money, but only *half* was paid to retired workers; the balance went to disabled workers or families of retired or deceased workers. Medicare health insurance claims, which are processed by the Social Security Administration, paid out an additional $86 billion.

There are two main Social Security trust funds. The retiree program is the best known, and the money in it comes from the Old Age and Survivors Insurance (OASI) fund. The Disability Insurance (DI) fund provides benefits to the disabled and to widows, spouses, and dependents of disabled or deceased workers.

Medicare is administered by the Health Care Finance Administration (HCFA), although the Social Security Administration processes applications and claims. There are two separate Medicare trust funds—the Hospital Insurance (HI) fund and the Supplemental Medical Insurance (SMI) fund.

There is also a Supplemental Security Income (SSI) program that is separate from the Social Security trust funds and is paid for out of general tax revenues. SSI helps many elderly or disabled people who have low incomes and limited resources. In 1988, less than half of the 4.5 million people who received these SSI benefits were age 65 or older. Benefits under the SSI program must be applied for through the Social Security Administration.

Congress passed the Social Security Act in 1935, and the retirement benefits program went into effect on January 1, 1937. The program had two main objectives then: to insure against loss of income by replacing a portion of earnings after retirement, and to provide a minimum floor of income support for the aged. Since then, the law has been amended many times to provide more benefits and to increase the taxes that pay for the program.

The most important thing to realize about Social Security is that although payments *into* Social Security made by wage earners and employers are directed to the Social Security trust funds, there are really no huge pools of money sitting around in a special account waiting for you to retire. In fact, the Social Security system is a pay-as-you-go system, with the money being put in by today's workers transferred immediately to today's retirees.

In 1983, the balance in the Social Security trust funds got so low that a series of reforms was enacted to bring more money into the system. Payroll taxes increased to 15.3 percent in 1990, paid on earnings up to $51,300. Compare that to the original Social Security tax when the program was created back in 1935. Then the combined employer-employee tax was only 2 percent levied on the first $3,000 of earnings for a total maximum tax of $60!

The reforms raised the retirement age gradually until retirement at age 67 becomes standard in the year 2027. They required all new federal employees to participate in the system (a short-term benefit that will increase revenues, but a long-term hazard that will increase the number of people collecting benefits). The reforms also delayed cost-of-living increases by six months.

In the 1990s, thanks to the reforms of the previous decade, the Social Security Trust Funds are starting to build up a surplus. But government accounting techniques allow any surpluses in the trust funds to offset deficits in the annual federal budget. The trust fund money cannot be spent for other purposes such as defense or government operations, but it does reduce the amount the government has to borrow to finance its deficit. In fiscal 1989 the budget deficit would have been $204 billion instead of $152 billion if the Social Security surplus had not been counted. It is not hard to imagine that as the surpluses build to await the baby boomers' retirement, the federal government might vote to actually start *using* those funds for other purposes.

Even with the surpluses created by the latest reforms, it's likely that the Medicare fund will become insolvent in the mid-1990s. The Old Age and Survivors Insurance fund should have plenty of money until the year 2026, at which point the balances in the fund will start to decline and be totally depleted in the year 2047. Those estimates are based on moderately optimistic assumptions about the economy. Of course, if the OASI fund is used to bail out Medicare in the mid-1990s, then both funds will have problems.

Either way, by the end of the first quarter of the next century—when today's baby boomers will be retiring—the promises of Social Security will be questionable. But for those currently retired or nearing retirement, Social Security should provide the promised support.

Social Security Taxes

As you earn money in a covered job, both you and your employer (or you alone, if self-employed) pay into the Social Security system. You and your employer will pay an equal share, totaling 15.30 percent of your income (7.65 percent each) up to a maximum covered income of $53,400 in 1991. That makes the maximum Social Security contribution $5,123.20 *each* for both employee and employer in 1991. In 1991, there is a separate taxable wage base of $125,000 on which 1.45% is deducted to pay for Medicare hospital insurance.

It *is* a lot of money; some people pay more in Social Security taxes than they do in income taxes. The Social Security tax is withheld from every paycheck until the maximum taxable amount for the year is reached. You may see it under the heading FICA on your paycheck stub. That stands for Federal Insurance Contributions Act.

Covered earnings include all wages, salaries, bonuses, and commissions, including tips if they total $20 or more a month. If you are self-employed, you will pay Social Security taxes on your net annual income if it's at least $400. Self-employed people pay at a rate of 15.30 percent in 1991, on the first $53,400 of earnings. Half of the taxes can be deducted as a business expense.

Your Social Security Benefits

In order to be eligible to receive a Social Security check based on your own work history at retirement, you must have 40 quarters of coverage or "credits"—approximately ten years of work. The amount of money required to earn one credit changes every year. In 1991 you earn one credit for each $540 of wages or self-employment income. You can earn no more than four credits per year, but credits earned over your entire lifetime count toward making you eligible to receive Social Security benefits.

For those who qualify as auxiliary or survivor beneficiaries—i.e., widows, dependents, and divorced spouses, the qualifications are slightly different, so you should check with your local Social Security office.

The wage earner who retires in 1991 at age 65 can expect to get the average monthly benefit of $685. But the actual amount of your Social Security check is determined by your total lifetime covered earnings. Someone who paid in the maximum amount every year would get a check of $1022 if he or she retired in 1991.

The wife or husband of a retiree who receives a monthly Social Security check will be entitled to a spouse's benefit at age 65. The spouse's benefit is equal to one-half of the retiree's benefit. Or the spouse may elect to take permanently reduced benefits (37.5 percent) starting at age 62. These benefits are not payable until the retiree begins accepting benefits. If the spouse has worked, he or she may be entitled to higher benefits based on individual covered earnings records.

Other members of your family may also become entitled to monthly benefits. A spouse of any age with eligible children under age 16 (or any age, if caring for a disabled adult child) would be entitled to 50 percent of the worker's benefit. Each eligible child under age 18 or disabled would also become eligible for 50 percent of your benefit, up to a family maximum. The total amount of benefits that all the members of one family may receive based on the earnings record of one worker is limited to the maximum family benefit. Check with Social Security to see what the specific limitation would be if you have a large family of dependents.

A divorced spouse, if married to the retiree for at least ten years, may be eligible for reduced benefits as early as age 62, or full spouse benefits at age 65, based on the earnings record of the former spouse. A divorced spouse can receive benefits if the worker is at least age 62—whether or not the worker has started receiving benefits. This benefit is terminated if the divorced spouse remarries.

A widowed spouse can start collecting benefits under the deceased spouse's account at age 60. The benefit at age 60 would be 71.5 percent of what the worker would have received at age 65. If the survivor elects to wait until age 65 to collect benefits on a deceased spouse, then he or

she will receive increased benefits. Check with your Social Security office to find out the exact amount of benefits you would receive as a
surviving spouse.

Every year benefits are increased to reflect changes in the cost of living. The change is based on the increase in the consumer price index
from the third quarter of the previous year to the third quarter of the
current year. In January 1991, benefit recipients received a 5.4 percent
increase in their monthly payments.

The normal retirement age today is 65. That is the age when you can
get full retirement benefits. If you choose to retire early, you can get reduced benefits starting at age 62. These benefits are permanently reduced by 20 percent from what they would have been if you had waited
until 65 to start receiving benefits.

If you postpone retirement until after age 65, your benefits will increase at least 3 percent per year for each year you delay retirement—
until age 70. After you reach age 70 you will not get any increase, and
they will automatically start paying you a monthly benefits check if
you have previously applied for Social Security benefits but were
placed in a "work suspense" status because you had high wages.

Estimating Your Benefits

It is wise to check with Social Security periodically to make sure that
your work and contribution records are complete and accurate. You
can get a free estimate of your retirement benefits by calling 800-234-
5772. Social Security will send you a form to complete with some basic
information, including your Social Security number, last year's earnings, an estimate of your current year's earnings, and the age at which
you plan to retire.

Obviously this is only a current estimate of benefits. If you are close
to retirement age, it will be helpful. If you are younger, it may serve as
a shocking reminder of how much more money you will need beyond
what Social Security will provide you.

Either way, it's good to make sure your records are on file accurately
with the Social Security Administration. Check your Personal Earnings and Benefit Estimate Statement for any incorrect earnings post-

ings or gaps in records. If you find any errors, contact your local Social Security office right away.

Applying for Benefits

You do not automatically start receiving Social Security checks at age 65. You have to apply for your benefit. You should contact your local Social Security office about two or three months ahead of time, bringing with you a certified copy of your birth certificate or other acceptable proofs of age. Phone first, and ask what proof of age is acceptable. They will send you an application to fill out in advance.

Social Security recommends that you apply over the telephone instead of making a trip to one of its offices. If you prefer, you can schedule a specific appointment with your nearest Social Security office by calling 800-234-5772.

If you are applying for benefits based on your spouse's work record, you will need a certified copy of your marriage certificate. Divorced spouses will also need a certified copy of the divorce decree.

If you are unsure of whether to apply for benefits based on your own work record or your spouse's, your local Social Security office will figure your benefits both ways and advise you of how to receive the larger amount.

Social Security checks normally arrive on the third day of the month after the month for which the benefit is paid. If that day is a holiday, then the check should arrive on the previous business day. You may elect to have your check deposited directly to your checking or savings account, which ensures not only safety, but immediate interest earnings on your money. A monthly Medicare medical insurance premium of $29.90 is automatically deducted from your check in 1991 unless you specifically state that you do not want the coverage.

Earnings Limitations and Taxes on Benefits

If you continue to earn income after your Social Security benefits start, those benefits may be reduced because of the "earnings limitation," or "retirement test." This applies until you reach age 70, after which you can earn any amount and still receive full Social Security benefits.

The earnings limitation allows you to earn only up to a certain amount each year without affecting your Social Security benefits. In 1991, that amount is $9,720 for beneficiaries age 65 to 69. It is $7,080 in 1991 for beneficiaries under age 65. (Retirees who continue to have wages are still subject to FICA tax withholding from their paychecks.

If you earn more than the limits for your age bracket, starting in 1990 benefits will be reduced by $1 for every $3 of excess earnings for those who are age 65 to 69. For Social Security recipients under age 65, benefits are reduced by $1 for every $2 earned. This limitation applies until age 70, even if you are self-employed. After age 70 there is no earnings limitation, and all recipients receive full benefits.

Not counted as earnings for this test are things like pensions and re- tirement pay, payments from annuities, dividends and interest from in- vestments, rental income (if you are not in the real estate business), and various worker's compensation and unemployment insurance benefits. Lottery winnings are also excluded from the earnings limitation.

There is a special way of determining your earnings limitation in the first year you begin to receive benefits. That year you can receive your full benefit in any month where you earn less than 1/12th of the earn- ings limitation. That may affect your decision about when to actually retire from your job. If your total earnings for the year are not more than the earnings limitation, you will get benefits for the entire year.

In addition to receiving lower benefits if you continue to work, in some cases your Social Security benefits could be subject to federal in- come taxes. There are two income levels at which part of your benefits become taxable—$25,000 for an individual or $32,000 for a couple fil- ing jointly.

To find out if you might be affected by this rule, you must add to- gether all of your federally taxable income (which includes things like bank interest, dividends, rents, and taxable pension benefits) along with all your nontaxable interest income (such as the income you might receive from municipal bonds). Add to that total one-half of your an- nual Social Security benefits.

If that total is more than the $25,000 or $32,000 limit stated above, then a portion of your Social Security benefit will be subject to federal income taxes. How much? The lesser of one-half of your annual Social Security benefits or one-half of the amount by which the combined total exceeds the $25,000 or $32,000 limitation. Notice that for this calculation, nontaxable interest such as municipal bonds gets thrown into your earnings pool to determine taxable income.

If you are required to pay federal income taxes on a portion of your Social Security benefits, you will pay taxes at your marginal tax rate.

The IRS has a special booklet (No. 554) entitled "Tax Information for Older Americans," which includes all necessary information regarding Social Security benefits and taxes. You can get this booklet from your local IRS office.

Your local Social Security office also has a number of booklets explaining various retirement benefits. One booklet in particular, called "Retirement," (No. 05-10035) is especially helpful and is available free of charge.

If you would like to study the Social Security system itself—its problems and its provisions—I recommend reading *What Will Social Security Mean to You,* published by the American Institute for Economic Research, Great Barrington, MA 01230 ($5 by mail).

IRAs

The biggest advantage on your side when you start planning for retirement is *time*. The longer you have to save, the harder your savings can work for you—especially if you have the money invested in tax-sheltered accounts where it can grow without the burden of annual income tax payments.

Here's an example: Take $2,000 a year and put it away in a bank certificate of deposit paying 8.5 percent. If you use $2,000 in *after-tax* dollars to fund this account each year, and if you pay 28 percent income taxes on the interest, your savings will grow to $118,431 in 25 years. If you are able to make *tax-deductible* contributions to a retirement savings plan and do not have to pay income taxes on the interest every year, then your $2,000 annual contribution would grow to $170,709 in 25 years. That's a difference of $52,278!

Figure 11 illustrates an example of how a $50,000 investment earning 10 percent compounded would grow in a tax-deferred account.

The longer your retirement savings plan has to grow, and as long as you can take advantage of tax-deferred income and growth within your plan, the better off you will be at retirement.

The federal government originally created the Individual Retirement Account in 1975 to help people save for retirement, but only those not covered by other qualified retirement plans were allowed to deduct contributions to IRAs.

Then, in 1982, as part of tax reform, the basic $2,000 individual IRA deduction was extended to anyone who had at least that amount in earned income. Contributions to individual retirement accounts swelled to a total of around $277 billion by year end 1986. The expanded IRA deduction not only created personal savings, but contributed to capital available for economic growth. That's why it was so

Figure 11: The Power of Tax-deferred Investment Growth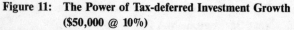
($50,000 @ 10%)

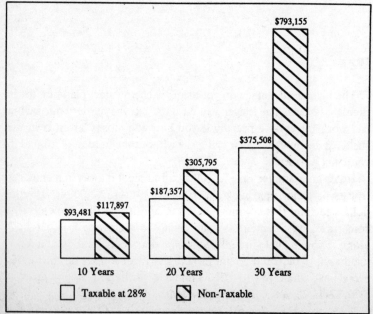

surprising that the Tax Reform Act of 1986 phased out the deduction—and thereby the incentive to save using an IRA.

Here's how they work now. Anyone can contribute to an IRA based on income earned during that year. There is a maximum allowable contribution of $2,000 per year or 100 percent of compensation, whichever is less. You can only contribute money out of earned income such as wages or salaries. So, for example, if you earned only $1,500 in wages, you would be eligible to contribute $1,500 to an IRA. Money received from interest, dividends, Social Security, pensions, rentals, and other such sources does *not* count as earned income for figuring IRA contributions.

While anyone with earned income can contribute to an IRA, even if covered by a pension plan or other retirement program at work, *not everyone can deduct the amount of the IRA contribution on the federal tax return*. The deductibility of an IRA is determined by your level of income and by your coverage in other plans. If you or your spouse are *not* covered by an employer's plan (for example, a defined benefit or defined contribution retirement plan, pension, profit-sharing, SEP, or other retirement plan) then you can make a tax-deductible contribution to an IRA of up to $2,000.

Remember, *no matter what your income, IRAs remain fully deductible if you are not covered by another retirement plan*. If you or your spouse *are* covered by another pension plan, then your IRA contribution may still be deductible, depending on your level of income.

Income Limits for IRA Deductions

The government estimates that two-thirds of IRA holders were still eligible for an IRA tax deduction, even after the 1988 changes in the law, which limited deductions based on income (except for those not covered by other retirement plans).

If you are covered by another retirement plan, your contribution to an IRA will be limited by your level of income. Single people with (tax-adjusted) incomes under $25,000 can still take the full IRA deduction. The deductibility of the contribution phases out with incomes above the $25,000 level and disappears with incomes over $35,000. For married couples filing a joint return, the deduction is phased out for incomes above $40,000 and disappears completely when joint taxable income reaches $50,000.

If both spouses are working, then each can set up a separate IRA and contribute up to $2,000 or total taxable income, whichever is smaller. Whether the contribution is eligible for a full, partial, or no deduction at all is based on the maximums cited here.

One spouse can set up a separate IRA for a nonworking spouse, under certain guidelines. A joint tax return must be filed, and the spouse must have no compensation for the year. Then the total IRA contribution, including that for the spouse, is allowed to be $2,250 or your taxable income for the year, whichever is smaller. The amount can be divided between the two accounts in any proportion, as long as no one IRA receives more than $2,000 in any one year. The deductibility of the contribution is still based on the restrictions listed above for combined joint income.

Nondeductible IRAs

You may still make a contribution to an IRA even if you do not qualify to take that contribution as a tax deduction. The money you contribute will grow and compound inside your IRA account, and none of the earnings will be considered taxable until the money is distributed to you during retirement. That's why many people continue to contribute to their IRAs even though their higher income level or coverage under another retirement plan means the contribution is no longer deductible.

If you do choose to make a nondeductible IRA contribution, you should keep careful documentation and file special form #8606 when you file your income tax return. *Be sure you do not blend nondeductible and deductible contributions in the same IRA account.*

Rules for IRA Contributions

If you are going to contribute to an IRA, you must make that contribution up until the date that year's tax return must be filed—not including extensions. So, if you want to contribute for 1990 based on your income that year, you have until April 15, 1991, when your federal income tax return is due. The contribution must be clearly labeled for the year in which it will be deducted.

You don't have to wait until you file your tax return to add money to your IRA. In fact, the earlier in the year you make your contribution, the longer your money will have to grow and compound tax-deferred. So although you file your return on the 15th of April in the following year, you should make your contribution as early as possible in the previous tax year.

IRA Withdrawals

There are a number of other legal restrictions regarding when and how you can take the money out of an IRA and how the money can be invested. There is a stiff penalty for withdrawing funds from your IRA before the age of 59$^{1}/_{2}$. You will pay ordinary income taxes plus a penalty of 10 percent if you take money out early for any reason. The only exceptions are distributions made because you became disabled or decided to *annuitize*, or start an early program of regular, substantially equal payments to be made over your lifetime.

You *must* start withdrawing money from your IRA by April 1 of the year *after* you reach age 70$^{1}/_{2}$. The amount of withdrawal each year must meet federal guidelines that are based on your life expectancy. If you have several different IRA accounts, at age 70$^{1}/_{2}$, you can total their value and withdraw the required amount from just one account.

When you open an IRA account you will be required to name a beneficiary—the person who will receive the proceeds of your account should you die.

Where To Invest Your IRA

You must set up a clearly labeled and segregated account—or accounts—for your IRA contributions. The trustee or custodian must be a bank, savings and loan, or approved custodian such as a mutual fund or brokerage firm. You cannot combine the money in your IRA with any other account outside the IRA, nor can you pledge the IRA as security for a loan.

Within those guidelines, there is plenty of flexibility to invest your IRA money. You can put it in a CD or money market deposit account at a bank or S&L where it will earn guaranteed insured interest. You can open an account with a mutual fund company and have a choice of riskier investments that could make your money grow faster, or face the potential of loss. You can open a self-directed IRA at a stock brokerage firm and choose investments you feel comfortable with, such as individual stocks or bonds. You may invest in limited partnerships that own real estate, or natural resources, or other long-term investments.

There are two schools of thought about how to invest your IRA. One says "go for it." Invest the money in stocks because you will have a long time to make it grow (assuming you are not near the age of retirement). Personally, I think that IRA funds are best invested conservatively. Any capital losses in your IRA account are not deductible against ordinary income. And over the long run, untaxed interest buildup can create a substantial retirement fund without much risk.

This is the old argument between the tortoise and the hare: Should you take it slow and easy and build up a predictable sum of money to retire on in your IRA, or should you take some big leaps to make profits? A lot depends on your own willingness to take risks.

Here's a helpful hint for investing your IRA funds after you reach $59^{1}/_{2}$—the minimum age at which you can withdraw money from your IRA without penalty. Many banks and S&Ls recognize that depositors might want or need to start withdrawing their IRA funds after reaching this minimum age, so they may waive any penalties for breaking out of an IRA CD before its term expires. That penalty waiver allows you to invest in the longest-term, highest-yielding CD being offered for your IRA. If rates move higher you can just switch to a higher-yielding CD without penalty. Check with your bank or S&L and get their ruling on this in writing before you commit to a long-term CD.

Your decision about where to invest your IRA money can be changed easily. If you think you want to switch frequently from stock investments to money markets, then you should invest in a no-load mutual fund family (see Chapter 14) that will allow you to do so. You are also allowed to transfer your IRA from one custodian to another, so you can take money out of a bank CD and transfer it to a mutual fund company or brokerage firm. Just make sure you follow all the correct procedures for moving money directly from one account to another.

IRA Rollovers

Under some limited circumstances, you can take the money out of your IRA for a short period of time—60 days—before transferring it to another custodial account. You should only take advantage of these IRA rollover rules when you are switching from one IRA custodian to another or when you are receiving a distribution from one retirement plan, such as a company pension plan, and are reinvesting the money into another tax-deferred IRA. You are only allowed *one* IRA-to-IRA rollover a year where the money is available for 60-day spending.

You must make the rollover contribution by the 60th day, or else all of the IRA money will be taxed as ordinary income and subject to penalties if you have not yet reached age 59¹/₂. The only exceptions to this rule arise if a financial institution has become insolvent and the funds are frozen. Then the money must be transferred within ten days of when withdrawal is allowed.

If you change jobs, or if your employer restructures the company pension plan, you might get a retirement distribution long before you are ready to retire. If you take the money out and spend it, you may have to pay ordinary income taxes on it at a time when you are still in a high tax bracket. If you are under age 59¹/₂ you would face a stiff 10 percent penalty, and you would lose the privilege of letting the money grow and compound tax-deferred. You can save those tax benefits by rolling over the contribution into another qualified IRA within the required 60 days.

At some point in the future you might want to take your rollover money from a former employer and roll it into a new employer's plan. Therefore, you should establish a separate IRA rollover account so that you do not combine those funds with an IRA you previously established for yourself. If you need a portion of your money, you might roll over some of your IRA distribution and keep the rest. The portion that is rolled over under the strict rules will continue to grow and compound. The portion that you take out will be subject to ordinary income taxes plus the 10 percent early withdrawal penalty if you have not yet reached age 59$\frac{1}{2}$.

Don't let the complexity of distribution rules and rollovers dissuade you from contributing money to an IRA. The overriding benefits of tax deductions and tax-deferred growth make IRAs an excellent investment. In fact, their only real negative is the limitation on contributions. So later in this chapter we'll show you how to get similar tax benefits for even larger amounts of money.

401(k) PLANS

Another kind of retirement savings plan bears the unlikely name of the tax code section that created it—401(k). In spite of the name, the plan offers one of the most creative ways to build a retirement nest egg. In effect for only about a decade, it is estimated that nine out of ten Fortune 500 companies sponsor 401(k) plans—and that employees have more than $100 billion invested in them.

A 401(k) plan is simply an employer-sponsored plan that allows you to contribute a portion of your salary to a special account set up by the company and defer paying taxes on the contribution and on the investment income in the plan. It's a sort of do-it-yourself retirement program that has many advantages.

The law sets a ceiling of 20 percent of a worker's gross compensation—or a fixed amount indexed to inflation ($8,475 in 1991)—whichever is smaller. Most corporations set a ceiling of about 6 to 10 percent of salary as a maximum tax-deferred contribution by an employee.

About 77 percent of employers give the plan a boost by matching employees' contributions with a contribution from the company—typically 50 cents for every $1 contributed by the employee. It's like getting an immediate 50 percent return on your investment! In addition, many plans allow employees to make additional nondeductible, after-tax contributions that will continue to grow along with the other money in the account.

Most companies offer a choice of three or four different investment options, which will include the company's stock, a stock mutual fund, a guaranteed fixed-income fund, and perhaps a money market fund. Employees are usually allowed to switch between the funds three or four times a year. Some plans allow switching only at the beginning of each quarter of the year; others allow employees a fixed number of switches that can be made at any time.

That gives the employee the ultimate responsibility for the performance of his or her 401(k) retirement fund. And it can be quite a responsibility, as some found during the October 1987 stock market crash. Again, the debate arises as to whether these funds invested over the long term do better in guaranteed income accounts or in stock market investments. And again, the answer depends on your personal tolerance for risk.

When you invest in a 401(k) plan you can put away more money than you can in an IRA, although you have slightly less freedom to choose your investments. And you may have the bonus of an employer-matched contribution to help your money grow. Unlike an IRA, you cannot do this on your own; the company has to have a sponsored plan, even if it does not contribute on your behalf. If you work for a company that does not have a 401(k) plan, speak to the human resources person or the president about creating one.

Like an IRA, the money must be left inside the 401(k) plan to grow tax-deferred. If it is taken out before age 59$^{1}/_{2}$ there is that 10 percent penalty to pay, in addition to regular income taxes. But one of the greatest advantages of a 401(k) plan is that it has slightly more flexibility—allowing withdrawal of funds in certain hardship conditions where an employee can demonstrate "immediate and heavy financial need." Those circumstances may include purchase of a house, medical expenses, or college tuition for a family member. Even if you take money out of your 401(k) plan under the hardship withdrawal provisions, if you are under age 59$^{1}/_{2}$ you will still have to pay the 10 percent early withdrawal penalty.

You may have access to your 401(k) money through a loan from your plan, if your employer has set it up in advance. In this case the withdrawal of a certain amount will not have tax consequences. You will have to set up a repayment schedule that includes provisions for interest. The interest you pay on the loan should be credited to your plan account. Be sure to check with your own company about its withdrawal conditions.

KEOGH PLANS

If you are self-employed and not incorporated, you can set up your own retirement plan, called a Keogh plan, which is named after the sponsor of the bill that created it back in the early 1960s.

Any individual who is self-employed may establish a Keogh account with money earned through self-employment. If you are self-employed part-time, only the money you earn from self-employment can be counted in calculating what percentage can be put into your Keogh account.

There are two types of Keogh plans—defined contribution and defined benefit plans. Most frequently used are the defined contribution plans, which set the percentage amount that may be contributed in any one year, based on compensation. The annual maximum is $30,000 or 25 percent of compensation, whichever is less. That gives you the flexibility to make minimal or no contributions in a year in which you do not have net income.

If a defined benefit plan is chosen, then the annual contribution is at least the amount needed to fund an actuarially determined annual benefit, or 100 percent of the employee's average salary for three years. This may commit the company to making a contribution no matter what the profit picture.

If the boss makes a *percentage* contribution for himself or herself, then there is an obligation to make a similar *percentage* contribution for all full-time employees who meet certain nondiscriminatory employment requirements. The minimum age requirement to participate cannot be more than 21, and the employee must be included if he or she has worked for the company at least two years.

In order to be tax deductible, a Keogh account must be opened by December 31 of that tax year. Contributions can be made up until

April 15 of the following year or until the regular date for filing taxes, including extensions.

Both employer and employees can make voluntary, nondeductible contributions of up to 10 percent of net earned income. However, the combination of the nondeductible voluntary contributions and tax-deductible contributions cannot exceed 25 percent of earned income or the $30,000 maximum annual contribution limit.

A Keogh plan can be invested much like an IRA. You will need an official plan document, which will not cost any legal fees if you use a standardized form offered by most mutual funds, banks, and other financial institutions. The institution becomes the custodian and you invest the money through it. It may charge you a small annual fee for this service.

You can invest your Keogh account in certificates of deposit, money market accounts, mutual funds, or stocks, depending on the custodian you use. You can establish several different custodians for different types of investments. Again, as with an IRA, the money contributed to a Keogh plan must be clearly segregated and cannot be used for everyday purposes, nor pledged against a loan.

A Keogh plan was designed to allow a small, unincorporated business or sole proprietorship to create a pension plan that would compete with those offered by corporations. It allows a business to set aside money that would otherwise be paid out in salary or retained as earnings (on which taxes would be owed). A properly designed Keogh plan allows flexibility of contributions in good years and bad and puts small businesses on an equal footing with big companies in offering employee benefits.

COMPANY RETIREMENT PLANS

When you are thinking about accepting a job or changing jobs, benefits like the company pension and savings plans should be an important consideration. It may not be worth changing jobs if you give up some previously earned retirement benefits with your old employer. It may not be worth accepting a job—even at a higher pay scale—if there are limited retirement benefits offered by the new employer.

Not all employers provide retirement benefits for their employees. In the mid-1980s, only about 43 percent of workers were covered by a company retirement plan. These benefits, along with Social Security, are expensive to the company—costing roughly one-third of an employee's salary. So while a company may have a retirement plan, it may be limited to certain employees, as long as it meets certain nondiscrimination rules.

In recent years, the government has stepped in to regulate the behavior of company retirement plans. The ERISA laws passed in 1974 (Employee Retirement Income Security Act) provide most of the rules by which retirement plans must be guided.

Some of the key provisions of the ERISA law state that if you work full time, are over 21, and have worked for your employer more than one year, you must be included in any *qualified* plan. A qualified plan is one that is officially set up by the company and for which the company takes tax deductions when it makes a contribution. Once those contributions are made, the employer cannot dip into the plan's assets for any reason except to pay benefits to plan participants.

Once you are part of a retirement plan, any amounts contributed on your behalf by your employer become yours—once they are *vested*. Full vesting may occur all at once—after a specific number of years. This is called *cliff vesting*. As a result of the latest reforms in retirement benefit law reforms, once you have participated in the plan for at least five consecutive years you must be 100 percent vested. Companies are allowed to use an alternative vesting system that can stretch out the time period to seven years, but only if 20 percent vests after three years, with another 20 percent each year thereafter, making the employee fully vested after seven years. If your employer has a plan that allows you to make voluntary contributions, you are always considered 100 percent vested in the amount you have directly contributed to the plan.

If you leave the company before you are fully vested in your retirement plan, you must leave behind the portion of your benefits that is not fully vested. It must remain in the fund and may be used to lower the amount the employer must contribute to the fund next year on behalf of the remaining employees. Frequent job changes can result in loss of unvested benefits and lower pension benefits at retirement.

When you leave a company, you might have to let your retirement account remain with the company, even if it is fully vested. The account will continue to grow tax-deferred, although the company you left will no longer make contributions on your behalf.

Since defined benefit pension benefits may be based on your final salary with the company, if you switch to another job and leave your vested interest in the company pension behind, when you ultimately retire and ask for your benefits to be paid out, your check will be lower than someone who continued to work for that company.

A break in your service with the company may affect your vesting. Also, the number of years credited for vesting purposes is not necessarily the number of years used when considering credits for benefits. Earned pension benefits may also be based on the number of hours worked each year. Check your company's pension plan to make sure you will receive full benefits if you take another job and then return to work there.

Defined Contribution and Defined Benefit Plans

There are two ways a retirement plan can be set up by a company. In one type—the *defined contribution plan*—the amount the company puts in each year for each employee may be a set percentage of the organization's profits, a fixed match of employee contributions, or a discretionary amount determined each year by the company. If the contribution is either discretionary or based on profits, the company is not obligated to contribute each year.

In a defined contribution plan every employee has a separate account. Many plans allow employees to contribute additional amounts to their account through payroll deductions. The value of this retirement account grows in two ways: from the amount of the annual contributions, and from the performance of the investments in the fund.

At retirement, the overall size of the employee's account will determine the size of the employee's benefit. As we'll see later, there are several ways this account balance can be distributed, but the important thing to note is that with a defined contribution plan there is no guarantee of the size of that ultimate retirement benefit.

Some companies set up *defined benefit,* or pension plans. This means that the employer (perhaps in negotiation with a union) decides in advance what the employee's benefit will be at retirement. Then the company hires mathematicians called actuaries to calculate how much must be invested in the plan each year, based on projected growth of the investments, to meet the guaranteed retirement benefit that has been promised to each employee.

Using certain assumptions about years of service and pay, employees can estimate how much they will be getting in their pension check each month at retirement; they simply do not know how much their pension dollar will buy in the future.

Pension Terminations

In recent years, many company defined benefit pension plans have built up a wealth of assets—even more than the actuaries certify as necessary to pay out the promised benefits. These plans are deemed *overfunded.* This may happen because of excellent investment performance by those managing the fund or because a number of employees leave before they are fully vested, increasing the assets that can be allotted to other plan participants.

When the company plan is overfunded, the employer may not have to make a contribution for that year. It also may be considered a "plum" ripe for picking by anyone seeking to acquire the company. As we noted earlier, the company may not dip into the assets of the plan for ordinary working capital, but under certain regulations it may terminate the plan or convert it into another plan.

If the company terminates its pension plan, even if it replaces it with another, the amount that is overfunded can return to the corporation—which may use it to buy back stock and fend off a raider. Or the raider may acquire the company and use the excess in the pension plan to pay off borrowings used to make the acquisition.

What happens to the plan and its assets? The employer can use some of the assets to buy annuities to fund the promised retirement benefits. The excess can be taken back into the corporate general funds. Or the fund can be terminated and the assets belonging to planholders can be distributed directly to them, with any excess left in the corporation.

Pension Distributions

A qualified plan must start paying out to the beneficiary by April 1 of the year on which the employee reaches age 70$^{1}/_{2}$, regardless of the date of retirement. The minimum annual distribution must be based on the life expectancy of the retiree and, if designated, a survivor.

When you retire, you may have to make some choices about how you will take your retirement benefits. One option may be to take a lump sum, with the tax consequences previously discussed. The employer is *not* required to offer the lump sum payment option.

The employer may offer a choice of annuities as a way to receive pension benefits. The annuity pays out a regular check every month to the retiree. The amount may be determined by the provisions of the annuity, which can be structured to pay out only over the retiree's lifetime or to pay benefits to a surviving spouse when the retiree dies.

Pension Guarantees

It is comforting to know that the federal government has created some insurance guarantees for the assets of company defined benefits pension funds. These plans are insured by the Pension Benefit Guaranty Corporation (PBGC), into which employers pay regular premiums. When a defined benefit plan (one that promises fixed benefits to retirees) terminates, or when the company fails, the PBGC supervises the distribution of the assets of the plan. If there is not enough money to provide the promised benefits to retirees, then the PBGC will pay the balance up to a maximum set by law.

Like other federal insurance funds, the PBGC has itself been running low and may require a bailout from Congress in order to keep performing its function. The PBGC has already been forced to assume the obligations of a number of underfunded plans—including the giant LTV Steel Corporation. This has resulted in higher premium demands on companies with well-funded pension plans. Their resistance to contribute more to the plans of failing companies is understandable. Starting in 1988, higher premiums were charged to riskier, underfunded plans—an extra burden that can only make them less sound.

Pension Benefits and Retirement

Every year you should request a statement of accrued benefits from your company pension fund. It will give you the size of your accrued benefits. It may provide other information such as projected retirement income based on your age and expected salary over the next years. If your company does not automatically distribute such a statement, consult the employee benefits or human relations person. You are entitled by law to receive at least one benefits statement each year.

Some company plans are *integrated* with Social Security, which means that the benefit formula recognizes the income you will receive from Social Security, since employers pay into the Social Security system during your working years. An integrated defined *contribution* plan can reduce contributions based on the amount of Social Security tax the company pays. An integrated defined *benefit* plan can reduce the pension benefits given to retirees by a certain limited percentage of their Social Security benefits.

An integrated plan can have a real impact on the amount of benefits a low-income worker will ultimately receive. It will have less impact on a highly paid executive, because reducing benefits by a portion of Social Security tax paid or benefit received will reduce the executive's payment by a far smaller percentage. It's worthwhile to take a close look at your company's retirement plan and all its provisions. Someone in the human relations department should be able to answer your questions and give you an estimate of projected retirement benefits.

When you take a look at the projected retirement benefits of your company plan and add them to your projected benefits from Social Security, you will have to make a third projection: What will those dollars buy when you are ready to retire? That's the hardest estimate of all. Inflation could make those fixed benefits far less attractive. So perhaps you should look into additional retirement savings—an IRA or purchase of tax-deferred annuities.

RETIREMENT DISTRIBUTIONS

If you are about to receive a large lump sum distribution from an employer's retirement plan, you should consult with your tax advisor before deciding whether to take the money or roll it over. Depending on your age, you may be eligible for certain income tax averaging provisions that could lower the tax burden if you choose to take the money out.

If you are over age 59½, you are eligible to use a special five-year income averaging formula if you have participated in a retirement plan for five or more years. Under this formula you calculate the taxes on your lump sum as if you were receiving it in equal installments over a five-year period. But you pay the tax only once—when you receive the one-time distribution.

The rates for this five-year averaging treatment are fixed rates and are not related to your regular personal income tax bracket. The tax is calculated on the amount of the distribution and is not affected by any other income you receive that year.

People who were born before January 1, 1936, also have the option to use a ten-year averaging formula that is based on the 1986 tax rate tables. If you qualify for this provision, it is best to consult a professional who will calculate the tax based on both formulas and give you an opinion about which is best for your situation.

There are restrictions on all of these situations. You must have been a participant in the plan for at least five years, and you must receive the entire account balance from the plan in one year.

If you were under age 50 as of January 1, 1986, you will not be eligible for special tax treatment on your lump sum distribution. You will be taxed on the money at your ordinary income rate in the year you receive the distribution. And if you take the distribution before age 59½, you must pay the 10 percent penalty for an early distribution.

Another consideration for those taking lump sum distributions is the new 15 percent excise tax that must be paid on very large distributions. This is in addition to any special averaging tax you might be eligible to use.

Because you are dealing with the IRS, you should carefully check the tax rules with a qualified professional.

CONCLUSION

Now that you have studied the language of money—from CDs to stock options, from IRAs to insurance—how will you put that knowledge to good use improving your life? I hope you have gained not only knowledge, but confidence that you can make decisions to improve your financial position. Now it's time to take action.

One of the most successful motivational recordings in history is entitled *The Strangest Secret* by Earl Nightingale. It's worth listening to in its entirety, but let me give away the secret right here: *You become what you think about.* If you think you are going to be happy, successful, or famous and admired, then that is the first step on the path to achieving your goals. If you think that you are destined to be unhappy, poor, or unsuccessful, then you have created your own limitations. By reading this book you have shown that you are willing to take charge of your own financial future. As we said at the beginning, knowledge is power. The corollary is: "It's easy if you know it!"

I'm often asked for the one best investment a person could make. Surprisingly, the answer is both simple and universal. The best investment you can make is in *yourself*. If you make the investment in your own education—whether about things financial or about a profession or creating a talent that can leave your mark on the world—then you have made the most potentially profitable investment I could ever recommend.

If you have the faith in yourself to make this personal investment, your future success is unlimited. You can start a business, become a teacher, lead others. The rewards are not simply measured in dollars—they are measured in self-satisfaction.

We live in an age and a country of unprecedented opportunity. There is no doubt that we have economic problems. The savings and loan crisis will not go away quietly. Debt—personal, corporate, and international—weighs heavily upon our financial system. But the free-market, free-enterprise system is being recognized around the world as the way to prosperity. Not only are people from other lands crowding to our shores to make their fortunes and their futures. Countries once diametrically opposed to our political and economic system—the Soviet Union, Poland, even China—are starting to follow the United States' economic model.

The emerging economic freedom of the rest of the world, combined with the plans to unify Europe, opens a great new market and creates new trading partners for the United States. That means there will be new and potentially unlimited economic opportunities for individuals who are willing to take the risks. And for those less able to accept personal risk, the changing world offers the potential of economic growth that can benefit all members of our society.

Money talks. And it can talk loudly and successfully in your future if you make the investment in yourself.

INDEX